Praise for *The NeuroGeneration*

"We're on the cusp of some of the most significant advancements in brain science—and in brain enhancement—in all of human history, and Tan Le has her finger on the pulse of these developments. Her book *The NeuroGeneration* is a smart, compelling, must-read that will take you on a tour through the most exciting neurotechnologies that will reshape humanity. You won't be able to put this book down, and you won't be able to stop talking about it afterward."

—*Klaus Schwab, founder and chairman,*
World Economic Forum

"Tan Le has reinvented her reality—as an immigrant, an entrepreneur, and a visionary—and now she's reinventing ours. Her own breakthroughs in neuroscience are literally unlocking the power of our minds, creating a platform for the world to create a better future. This book is an extension of her efforts to further our understanding of how the brain works and deepen our appreciation for the limitless possibilities ahead. And like everything Tan does, it's both exciting and inspiring."

—*Zenia Mucha, chief communications*
officer, The Walt Disney Company

"This book should not be missed by anyone with a brain, or by anyone who is curious about the healing power of the brain! *The NeuroGeneration* offers inspiration and hope for a more powerful mind and sheds light on possibilities that seem like sci-fi but are actually in the works."

—*Roger Craig, three-time superbowl*
champion (XIX, XXIII, XXIV)

"Our species' future is already scattered in labs and companies around the globe, and Tan Le—an amazing writer, thinker, and entrepreneur—shores up the pieces to reveal a new architecture. This book is a page-turning, electrifying ride into the technology that surrounds us, and how it interfaces with the three-pound organ inside us."

—*David Eagleman, neuroscientist at Stanford University,* New York Times *bestselling author*

"Most books about innovation are written by people who stand on the balcony and observe it. *The NeuroGeneration* is different. Tan Le is one of the great innovators of this generation. She is creating the future and taking us along for the ride. I don't know which is more extraordinary, the story of how Tan Le's company EMOTIV is changing what is possible or the story of her life. *The NeuroGeneration* is a must-read for those of us who believe that innovation actually is about mind over matter."

—*Jeff DeGraff, "The Dean of Innovation," professor, Ross School of Business, University of Michigan*

"As scientists continue to unlock the mysteries of the brain, innovators are developing cutting-edge neurotechnologies that have the potential to reshape humanity. Yet these advances also create serious new challenges our society has never faced before. Tan Le unpacks both sides of this watershed era in the *The NeuroGeneration*—an exciting book that couldn't be more timely . . . or important."

—*Michael McCullough, M.D., M.Sc., founder and president, BrainMind*

THE NEURO GENERATION

The New Era in Brain Enhancement That Is Revolutionizing the Way We Think, Work, and Heal

TAN LE

BenBella Books, Inc.
Dallas, TX

BenBella

BenBella Books, Inc.
10440 N. Central Expressway, Suite 800
Dallas, TX 75231
www.benbellabooks.com
Send feedback to feedback@benbellabooks.com

Printed in the United States of America
10 9 8 7 6 5 4 3 2 1

Library of Congress Cataloging-in-Publication Data:
Names: Le, Tan, 1977- author.
Title: The Neurogeneration : the new era in brain enhancement that is
    revolutionizing the way we think, work, and heal / Tan Le.
Description: Dallas, TX: BenBella Books, Inc., [2020] | Includes
    bibliographical references and index.
Identifiers: LCCN 2019034505 (print) | LCCN 2019034506 (ebook) | ISBN
    9781948836487 (hardcover) | ISBN 9781948836739 (ebook)
Subjects: LCSH: Neurotechnology (Bioengineering) |
    Neurosciences--Technological innovations.
Classification: LCC TA167.5 .L48 2020 (print) | LCC TA167.5 (ebook) | DDC
    681/.761—dc23

LC record available at https://lccn.loc.gov/2019034505
LC ebook record available at https://lccn.loc.gov/2019034506

Editing by Alexa Stevenson and Laurel Leigh
Copyediting by James Fraleigh
Proofreading by Kimberly Broderick and Michael Fedison
Indexing by WordCo Indexing Services, Inc.
Text design by Publishers' Design and Production Services, Inc.
Text composition by Aaron Edmiston
Cover design by Pete Garceau
Printed by Lake Book Manufacturing

Distributed to the trade by Two Rivers Distribution, an Ingram brand
www.tworiversdistribution.com

Special discounts for bulk sales are available.
Please contact bulkorders@benbellabooks.com.

To my newborn daughter,
Ai Le Hatala, who will grow up in the
NeuroGeneration, and to my mother,
Mai Ho, whom I hope will benefit
from the advances we are pioneering
in the field of neurotechnology so
that she will stay cognitively fit and
healthy for decades to come.

CONTENTS

INTRODUCTION

O N A CRYSTAL-CLEAR DAY on a speedway in Brazil in 2017, Rodrigo Hübner Mendes took a deep breath and revved the engine of a bright blue Formula 1 race car. The engine's throaty growl suffused his senses as he sat in the driver's seat waiting for the "go" sign. A mix of excitement, fear, and curiosity welled up inside him, and his heart thumped so hard in his chest, it felt like it might explode. The CEO of a Brazilian nonprofit, Mendes had spent weeks training for this moment, a feat that was the brainchild of Brazil's largest broadcast network, TV Globo.

When he got the okay, he accelerated, roaring down the track. As he came upon the first tight curve, a thought flashed through his mind: *This is it, the moment of truth*. Could he maintain control of the car? It wasn't smooth, but he managed to bank around the hairpin turn without crashing. Exhilarated, he continued around the course, completing three laps before passing the finish line as a checkered flag waved him in.

This would have been an exciting experience for anyone who has ever dreamed of driving a race car, but for Mendes it was something far more special. In fact, he had just accomplished a feat no one else ever had.

He'd driven a race car using only his thoughts.

Mendes, then age forty-five, is a quadriplegic who lost the use of his arms and legs after being shot during a carjacking when he was just eighteen years old. The customized car he drove had no pedals and no steering wheel. Instead, it was equipped with an onboard computer that translated mental instructions into mechanical action. Mendes directed it thanks to a one-of-a-kind helmet outfitted with EEG-powered technology to capture his brainwaves. When Mendes wanted to speed up, his brainwaves told the car's computer to do so, and it propelled the vehicle forward. When he wanted to turn right or left, the computer interpreted his thoughts and angled the massive tires in that direction.

Mendes's incredible feat quickly became a viral sensation. It signaled thrilling new possibilities for people with disabilities, and it offered a captivating glimpse into the future of the human brain.

Fast-forward several months to Buenos Aires, Argentina, where a veritable brain trust of the world's most promising young scientists, CEOs, government leaders, intellectuals, and media gathered for the Young Global Leaders Summit. As a female inventor, tech entrepreneur, and CEO myself, I was attending as a member of the YGL community, which includes over eight hundred innovative, enterprising, socially minded emerging leaders from all walks of life. At dinner, I noticed a gregarious man in a wheelchair on the opposite side of our large, round table. After he left, the woman seated next to me leaned over to ask if I knew him. When I shook my head, she told me his name and said he had recently made headline news when he drove a race car with his mind. He had accomplished this, she told me, thanks to some type of special technology that read his brainwaves.

I said goodbye to my dinner companions and hurried out to see if I could find him. There he was at the valet station, waiting for a special vehicle to pick him up. I ran up to him and told him I was curious about the mind-control helmet he'd worn. He took one look at my name tag and shouted my name with an exuberant grin.

At that moment, we knew we shared a special connection.

The device Mendes had worn to drive his race car in Brazil used cutting-edge, EEG-based brainwear—developed by my company, EMOTIV, which is headquartered in San Francisco but whose development team extends to Sydney, Australia, Hanoi, and Ho Chi Minh City, Vietnam. Helping people like Mendes use their minds to overcome physical limitations was just one of our motivations behind creating the technology. We also designed the platform to aid worldwide neuroscience research, and to take that research one step further toward enabling people everywhere to supercharge their mental capacities.

I've been fascinated by the brain, technology, and the promise of the future ever since seeing *Star Wars* as a child. I can vividly remember watching the scene in which Jedi-in-training Luke Skywalker practices defending himself with a lightsaber against the unpredictable blasts from a humming, hovering training ball. He's terrible at it. His mentor, Obi-Wan Kenobi, reminds Luke that "a Jedi can feel the Force flowing through him," and has Luke put on a helmet before he tries again, telling him to "let go your conscious self and act on instinct." Luke protests that he can't see with the helmet's blast shield down. "Your eyes can deceive you," says Obi-Wan, instructing the young Jedi. "Stretch out with your *feelings*!" Only when Luke lets his mind take over does he successfully anticipate the moves of the ball.

Later, in *The Empire Strikes Back*, Luke's X-wing starfighter crashes and sinks to the bottom of a swamp, leaving him stranded, along with astro droid R2-D2 and legendary Jedi Master Yoda. To Luke, the situation seems hopeless, until the small but powerful Yoda raises a hand, points his gnarled fingers toward the muck, and lifts the spacecraft from the murky swamp with his mind. "I don't believe it," says Luke, and Yoda responds, "That is why you fail." This is when it finally dawns on Luke that the only way he will ever be able to access the full power of the Force is if he truly believes in the power of his mind.

It was scenes like these that opened my own mind to the idea of a future world in which seemingly impossible things—like using thoughts to control objects—might not always seem so impossible. Translating that big-screen fantasy into reality became an obsession of mine; I dreamed of transforming people's lives for the better by helping them achieve more than they had believed possible.

I already knew that lives could be transformed in this way. I'd seen it in my own family.

From Refugee to Neurotechnology CEO

My earliest memories are of a boat—the rhythmic thrum of the engine, the bow dipping bravely into the rough waters, the vast and empty horizon. Disguised as a fishing vessel, a 21-meter tugboat nosed its way off the coast of Vietnam and out into the South China Sea under a pitch-black sky at three o'clock in the morning. It was 1981, six years after the fall of Saigon had marked the end of the Vietnam War; I was four years old. I huddled with my mother, grandmother, and little sister in that boat, crouching to stay out of sight—as did the other 150-plus people crammed on board.

All the adults knew the risks of the voyage: capture and a lifetime of misery in a Vietnamese prison camp; a failed engine and a lingering demise at sea; storms and drowning; and, perhaps worst of all, pirates, which for the women and girls on board would mean rape, and for all a violent death. Like most of the grown-ups on our journey, my mother had tucked away a small vial of poison. She and my grandmother had made a pact: if we were captured by pirates, my sister and I would drink from the vial first, then they would swallow the last drops.

My father had stayed behind so he could care for us in the event that we were captured, returned to Vietnam, and imprisoned. He planned to follow on a separate boat in the following weeks when the chance of us being returned to Vietnam was no longer a possibility. Unbeknownst to us, before he could make the voyage, he was captured by Vietnamese officials for organizing and attempting escapes out of the country. I did not reconnect with my father and learn of his story until I was twenty-one years old, visiting Vietnam as a Goodwill Ambassador for Australia. That's when I discovered he had spent ten years in jail isolated from the outside world, attempted suicide, and was eventually released, a sick and broken man, to piece together another life.

I don't remember seeing any pirates on our voyage, though my mother tells me they circled us many times but were wary of the steel-hulled tugboat. I don't recall the engine dying or the rising panic as it failed to start back up time and time again for six long hours. But I do remember running out of food and water after five days at sea. And I'll never forget gazing out into the endless blackness and then, all of a sudden, seeing stars everywhere—not above but right in front of us. They were the bright lights of a British oil tanker, and the tanker's crew gave us two options: they could help us navigate to Malaysia, or we could intentionally sink our boat and send an SOS signal so they could legally take us on board.

The choice fell to my mother. After all, the boat belonged to my family. We had put up everything we owned to organize the escape, including recruiting the navigator, ship captain, and crew, as well as bribing officials.

It took only a second for my mother to decide. With the tugboat disappearing below the water, we were hoisted onto the tanker's deck. We were saved! But not everyone made it off the boat alive. One young man collapsed and died as we were being transported to the tanker, the treacherous journey too much for him. I'll never forget the apple the men on the oil tanker gave me. I was so hot, hungry, and thirsty, the flavor seemed to explode onto my taste buds. No apple since has ever tasted as sweet.

After three months in a Malaysian refugee camp, we were given political refugee status and offered the opportunity to settle in a country of asylum. My family voted and chose to go to Australia based on the words of my grandfather before he died: "Australia is a young country with lots of land." (He thought we could start a new life as farmers there.) We started our new life in Footscray, an inner-western working-class suburb of Melbourne teeming with layer upon layer of immigrants. We were four women across three generations living in the same house, with three of us—my mother, my sister, and I—sharing one bed. My mother arrived with nothing: no money, no English, no qualifications, no husband. But she was safe, and determined to give me and my sister more than she'd had, something better. For the first time, her world wasn't dominated by terrifying risks, but rather seemed filled with endless possibilities.

The possibilities were harder for me to see at first, as I endured the humiliations so familiar to many migrant kids—the teasing about the "smelly" homemade Asian lunches I brought while other kids ate Vegemite sandwiches, the rare but searing chants of "slit eye," and the occasional graffiti demanding, "Asians, go home." *Go home to where?* I thought. I never fit in, or developed a strong sense of belonging. It was extremely painful at the time, but my lack of a comfort zone also pushed me to embrace uncertainty and, later, would give me the courage to venture into unknown territory.

In those early days, my mother held a series of punishing jobs, leaving home before dawn and putting in double shifts six days a week to make ends meet. And although we were poor, she always managed to find the money to cover the costs of extra instruction in English, mathematics, and music for my sister and me. But that meant other expenses didn't make the cut. Our clothes were secondhand: two pairs of stockings for school, layered to hide the holes in each, and a school uniform that fell to the ankles instead of the knees because it had to last for six years. Despite my failure to fit in, I loved school, especially the science and math classes where my inner nerd could shine. I had a real thing for cars and robots and still dreamed about moving objects with my mind. The classroom was my laboratory.

Within a decade, my mother had opened a nonprofit center to help other refugees find their footing in their new home. As a teenager, I volunteered at the resource center, offering translation services, helping immigrants find vocational training and work, and, after I'd started law school, guiding them in navigating the Australian legal system.

In my last year of law school, I was recognized for these community service efforts and named the 1998 Young Australian of the Year, a prestigious national award that thrust me into the limelight. To say I was shocked is an understatement. *Why me?* I wondered. I wasn't an Olympic athlete, an entrepreneur, or an award-winning musician like so many of the recipients before me. I was just a poor immigrant kid from Footscray helping other refugees like myself. For me, this honor was like being thrown into the deep end of the pool when you don't know how to swim.

After winning the award, I existed in parallel worlds. In one, I was an ordinary student living daily life as part of a working-class family—my mother, sister, and I were still sleeping in the same bed!—while in the other, I was being lauded at events full of incredibly successful people and being invited to speak in venues I had never even heard of. In the first world, I was myself; in the second, I felt like a fraud, an imposter. At these posh events I simply smiled and agreed with anything anyone said, because I was terrified. I didn't know the protocols. I didn't even know how to use cutlery. But when I told my mother I couldn't do it anymore, she reminded me that I was the same age she had been when we boarded that boat and set off on the South China Sea, risking our lives and launching ourselves into the unknown. "I can't" had never been an option for her. "Just do it," she told me, "and don't be what you're not."

So, I kept accepting invitations, but I stopped smiling and agreeing, and I started speaking out: on youth unemployment, double standards in education, and the neglect of the marginalized and disenfranchised. And the more candidly I spoke, the more I was asked to speak—at high-level gatherings and think tanks, and at schools and service clubs. As a result, I had the chance to meet an incredible variety of people, from professional athletes and musicians to high-flying executives and brilliant scientists. Those that stuck with me were the ones who'd found success doing something they loved, living on the frontiers of possibility. My mother had always told me success meant one of two things: being a doctor or a lawyer. Both careers would allow me to help others and make a positive contribution to society. It was implied but never directly spoken that they could also provide financial rewards. Of the two, I had chosen lawyer (despite my love of science) because I got queasy at the sight of blood. I graduated law school and started my career, but I could tell the law was the wrong fit for me, and those I'd encountered as my world expanded had opened my eyes to a new view of success.

I thought of the amazing individuals I had met who were making their mark in unconventional ways, and after a few years I listened to my intuition, followed their lead, and quit my job. It was one of those "now or never" opportunities to hit the restart button, before I had a mortgage or other responsibilities that would lock me into a career I didn't want. I remember the moment I mustered the courage to tell my mum about my decision. I was on a trip as a Special Visitor to the U.K. as a guest of the British High Commission and Foreign Commonwealth Office in

2000, and she was with me. I spilled the news, and then held my breath. Her response took me by surprise. She said I was able to make choices for myself and that, no matter what, I would always have her support.

With that green light, I forged ahead, assembling a team of people I had met through my travels and speaking engagements—people like me for whom the words "it can't be done" were an irresistible challenge. I rented a town house, where some of us lived together, and we got to work.

For a year, we were penniless. I borrowed $5,000 from a mentor to avoid eviction. Each night I made a huge pot of soup that we all shared. It was the height of the tech boom, and we were brainstorming ways to make some small contribution to our new Information Age. We pushed and probed and explored well into each night. Most of our ideas were crazy, but a few were brilliant.

In 2001, we broke through with a successful tech business—the first to introduce SMS voting on TV. That opened the door to deals to expand the service throughout Australia and in Southeast Asia. We ended up selling this business in 2003, and I found myself once again at a crossroads. I was in the privileged position of having options. I could try to repeat the success of my first venture and build another piece of information technology at the application level, or I could return to the law and my earlier goal of becoming an advocate for those in need.

But when I considered what was truly important to me, neither of these routes felt really satisfying. My main motivation had always been—and still is—to make my life meaningful, to make a positive impact by creating something that didn't exist before, that would improve the state of the world. Fundamentally, I wanted a project that was worthy of the great sacrifices my family had made to give me the opportunities I'd had in my life.

One night during a dinner with friends, we began talking about the brain, its central place in the human experience and its incredible capabilities. Research into neuroplasticity was revealing the extent of the brain's potential for change; tapping into that potential could give us the ability to reshape ourselves and our thought processes, to improve our health and extend our lives, and to enhance and augment the ways we interact with the world and others around us. That conversation ran on late into the night.

Over the next few weeks I found myself returning to the subject again and again, captivated by the possibilities and challenges of enhancing the most powerful and mysterious object in the universe. It became clear to me that I had found the fuel for my fire. I wanted to be a part of the future of the human brain, and as Alan Kay once said, "The best way to predict the future is to invent it."

So, I started inventing.

Welcome to the NeuroGeneration

Since the night that discussion with friends flared into inspiration, I have devoted my life to advancing the understanding, enhancement, and augmentation of the human brain. In the past fifteen years, I've become an award-winning inventor with multiple patents in the field of neurotechnology; my company's brainwear, which has been cited in over 4,000 publications and distributed in more than 120 countries, is tapping into the power of the human brain to push the boundaries of our cognitive powers. It's what helped Rodrigo drive that race car with his thoughts, and it's being used in worldwide neuroscience research to further our understanding of the brain and our ability to treat its disorders.

I'm one of a growing cadre of neurotechnologists, neuroscientists, and other innovators who are harnessing advances in research and technology to usher in a new era I call "the

NeuroGeneration." Don't mistake this moniker for a reference to our youngest population, the kids who are seamlessly growing up with new technology. The NeuroGeneration is an all-encompassing age of unprecedented change in the way we use and understand the brain that may forever alter what it means to be human. It will touch all of our lives, whether we actively participate in it or not.

With the transformation of the human brain coming at such a blistering pace, we find ourselves at a major inflection point in human history, on the precipice of massive disruption not only in the way we think and learn as individuals, but also in the way we do business and lead as societies. Professor Klaus Schwab, the founder and executive chairman of the World Economic Forum (WEF), coined the term "the Fourth Industrial Revolution" to define this emerging era, characterized by the increasing integration of the physical, digital, and biological realms. Although we can't envision all of the ways this integration will impact our world, we're already seeing dramatic changes in healthcare, education, transportation, finance, security, entertainment, and media, to name just a few. For instance, the medical community is already embracing artificial intelligence (AI) and machine learning to help detect cancerous tumors, and self-driving cars are already hitting the United States' highways.

As an inventor and entrepreneur in this field, I understand that our creations hold great promise but also pose risks—physical, psychological, and ethical. The promise of a superhuman brain is also linked to a potential for peril; there is always the possibility that some of these futuristic technologies could be misused. Governments need to jointly develop unified policies about how to foster and regulate AI and other brain-augmentation technologies to ensure they serve the greater good. Nations will have to rethink education systems, healthcare systems, labor laws, and more to address the vast implications of these technologies. I'm honored to serve as a member of WEF's Global Future Council on Neuro-technologies, a group of neuroscientists, neurologists, technologists, and biopharmaceutical and corporate leaders that explores the effects of developments in neurotechnology on individuals as well as industry, government, and society as a whole. Together, we attempt to design innovative governance models to ensure we can maximize the benefits of these developments while minimizing their risks.

These days, when I'm not ushering the sci-fi world I love into reality, I'm traveling the world talking about it. When *National Geographic* or the Discovery Channel wants someone relatable to discuss the future of the brain without all the "science speak," it is an honor that they turn to me, and I'm thrilled to have the opportunity to deliver keynotes at conferences around the world, introducing renowned CEOs, CIOs, entrepreneurs, tech innovators, and government leaders to the NeuroGeneration's incredible advances in brain enhancement.

But although I routinely meet with influencers on the world stage, I never forget my roots as a refugee, an immigrant growing up in a poor neighborhood. There has never been a more important time for those of us in the neurotechnology industry to champion not only the promise of tomorrow, but also the democratization of its advances. As the latest tools for brain enhancement and augmentation revolutionize our world, it could lead to greater disparity and a "neuro-elite" class that has an unfair competitive advantage in business and life. Or, it could act as a great equalizer, letting all of us make the most of the supercomputer inside our skull. I feel a sense of responsibility to make sure that my inventions are working for the betterment of the human brain and society at large. There are many avenues I could have pursued in my quest to contribute to the future of the brain. I chose to create a more portable, less costly way to collect, analyze, and use the data from EEG—electroencephalogram, a means of recording brainwaves. My hope is that by taking this technology out of the lab and putting it in the hands of consumers, entrepreneurs, and others, we will accelerate the pace of innovation while ensuring more equal access to it, so more of us can contribute to and shape the future of our world.

I am keenly aware that many people can't afford expensive technology, and I have made it my mission to change that. I also understand that most people never get the chance to attend international conferences to hear from the world's greatest neuroscientists, technologists, and innovators. In an effort to share what I've learned about the advances that will affect us all, I am introducing you to the future of your brain with this book.

Humankind's Quest to Master the Brain

Some people may be uneasy with the idea of "brain enhancement," but the quest to boost our brainpower is nothing new; it's an essential part of human nature. Ever since *Homo sapiens* emerged nearly 200,000 years ago, we have been searching for ways to upgrade the wetware in our heads, and we've been creating and using tools to help us do it—physical and cognitive tools that help us solve problems and complete tasks more efficiently, tools that extend our natural abilities and allow us to do things that weren't possible before. Language, numbers, science, education—these are all tools we've developed to improve our mental capacities. They have provided us with a massive advantage in shaping and surviving our environment.

Our most powerful tool for navigating the ever-changing world, however, is the brain itself. It took billions of years for modern humans to arrive on Earth, and although we continue to evolve genetically, this process occurs at a painstakingly slow pace. Our brain is nature's way of allowing us to adapt more quickly than we evolve. It's the cognitive machinery that lets us create and cope with the modern world.

This most vital asset is also the seat of the self and the center of our personal universe. Everything we see, hear, and smell is a product of our brain, which filters the data gathered by our senses and converts it into the model of reality we experience. And yet we still know surprisingly little about the organ that is responsible for our human condition. Courtesy of recent advances in imaging tools, however, we've begun to unlock some of the secrets of the human brain. And of everything we have learned so far, the thing I find most amazing is that it is built to change. Our brains are three pounds of pure potential.

For centuries, most doctors and scientists believed that the brain was a fixed entity. Long-held theories claimed that once you reached adulthood, the neurons, synapses, gray matter, and white matter in your skull could not be changed. Correction—it could change, but only in one way: for the worse. Injury could damage your brain, and recovery was thought to be impossible. Old age could lead to the death of neurons, which could never be replaced. If you had a mental health condition, you were stuck with it for the rest of your life. According to these beliefs, our fixed brains controlled us, and a faulty one could hold us hostage. What a grim view.

Fortunately, the revolutionary science of neuroplasticity[1] has debunked these notions. The medical and scientific communities now understand that the brain is in a constant state of change, a dynamic entity that has the ability to rewire, reprogram, and heal itself. The brain's neurons, like trees in a rain forest, can sprout limbs that connect to other neurons in new ways to alter the neural networks inside our heads. Not only do our brains change in response to the world around us; they are also constantly rewiring in response to how we use them. Activities that we frequently repeat are reinforced by the formation of additional neural pathways to support them. Neural pathways that we use often are strengthened, but if a neuron isn't "fired and wired"—used within the network—it can weaken or even die off. This means that, far from our brains controlling us, we can control our brains. The transformative discovery that our thoughts, actions, and environment can impact how our brains are wired is what opened the possibility of using emerging technologies to intentionally shape them.

Despite all the knowledge that we have gleaned about the universe so far, the greatest mystery remains the one that lies within our skull—the workings of our brain's 100 billion neurons and the trillions of synapses connecting them. Several things limit what we know about the enigma between our ears:

Dead brains don't talk. Much of what we have learned about the brain comes from dissecting those of deceased people. Jacopo Annese, an expert neuroanatomist at University of California, San Diego, has been dissecting and slicing brains since 1994. In 2009, about 400,000 people around the globe tuned in to watch Annese make 2,401 slices in the brain of famed amnesia patient "H.M."[2] Although the slices provided a new look at neuronal architecture, it was still dead tissue. It's like looking at a flat map of a city: it depicts where the roads lead and where the buildings are located, but it doesn't reveal what the people are doing inside those buildings, how they communicate and work with each other, or why they do what they do. That is the great mystery we are still trying to solve.

Pictures don't tell the whole story. As humans, we are inherently attracted to images. About 30 percent of the brain's neurons are dedicated to vision, compared to just 8 percent for touch and a mere 3 percent for hearing.[3] This helps explain why, in our quest to understand the brain, we have looked to pictures to tell the story. Perhaps the first brain imaging tool, the microscope was invented in the 1590s, offering a way to view brain tissue at high magnification. Since then, brain imaging has come a long way with MRI, PET, CT, and SPECT. Modern-day imaging tools that attempt to map brain activity, such as functional MRI (fMRI), now provide clues as to *where* things happen and *when* they happen. Unfortunately, they don't necessarily tell us *why* they happen. Without the *why*, we can't decode the dynamics of the brain's behavior. And with a system like the brain, which is constantly evolving, it's the dynamics that hold the answers to many of our questions.

Mice and men. Researchers have relied heavily on studying the brains of mice and fruit flies to uncover the specific regions and neurons behind behavior. One group of scientists recently used artificial intelligence to watch and analyze 20,000 videos of 400,000 fruit flies doing what fruit flies do—fly, walk, and groom themselves.[4] Riveting. But fruit fly brains have only 100,000 neurons compared to the 100 billion in human brains. Extrapolating the seeds of human behavior from their tiny brains has some obvious problems.

When neuroscientists aren't peering into the brains of fruit flies, they're typically studying the brains of mice or rats. Take the brilliant Sebastian Seung, for example. The Princeton neuroscientist is currently leading a team undertaking a herculean task—trying to map the human brain's 100 trillion neural connections, which he calls the connectome.[5] In his book, *Connectome: How the Brain's Wiring Makes Us Who We Are*, Seung contends that we *are* our connectome, that this vastly complex neural network holds all our memories, talents, and personality and is the essence of who we are. He calls his quest to map it one of the greatest challenges of all time, and anticipates it will take generations to achieve. In the meantime, he's aiming for a more modest goal: mapping the neural connections in tiny chunks of mouse brain. Researchers like Seung say rodents make good stand-ins for humans because the structure and connectivity of their brains resembles our own.

Even so, they're still relying on some major assumptions. Consider that a rat's brain weighs less than one ounce and its cerebral cortex makes up just 31 percent of brain volume, compared with 77 percent in humans.[6] Rats have about 200 million neurons, while mice have only about 75 million—not even close to our 100 billion. And a huge portion of rodent brains is dedicated to their whisker system. Since humans don't have whiskers—and no, mustaches don't count—it's hard to see the similarities.

No two brains are alike. The folds of the human cerebral cortex are as individual as a fingerprint. This means that with 7.5 billion people on Earth, there are 7.5 billion unique brains. The vast majority of brain research to date, however, has focused on educated males from the Western world. Females remain underrepresented in both human and animal trials. A 2017 review in *eNeuro* revealed that brain trials using only male animals were 6.7 times as common as female-only studies.[7] Existing neuroscience research has also virtually ignored people in areas such as Africa, South America, and Asia. The few studies that have emerged from those regions reveal that their brains can be vastly different from those of Westerners. In order for their findings to be valid, universal, and useful, the research community needs to study a much broader swath of the population.

While the drive toward cognitive enhancement is nothing new, what has changed over time is the scope and scale of the enhancements available to us, at a pace that has been accelerating since at least the Middle Ages. In the twentieth century, our capacity to enhance the human organism surged in a historically unprecedented manner. This period saw incredible advances in medical enhancements, such as the move from crude wooden prosthetics to sophisticated mechanical models. It saw the development of electronic calculating machines that quickly outgrew their original functions and gave humans the ability to perform tasks previously inconceivable. And in the less tangible realm, all sorts of new approaches to cognitive enhancement also came to the fore, such as the creation of various schools of psychotherapy and analysis as well as culture-wide exercises in implementing new educational approaches. Cognitive enhancement has come to define our modern era.

As dramatic as the developments of the last century have been, what is to come in this century—even in just the next few decades—will be still more astounding. Our understanding of our limitations will be shattered as we explore the possibilities that arise when we bring minds, machines, and the material world together. While this integration will take many forms, what is most exciting to me is the way in which it allows us to expand the vast potential of the human brain. Thanks to more powerful tools, we are on the brink of unraveling the brain's secrets—and using them to our advantage.

In the NeuroGeneration, we will have a much more intimate relationship with our neurons and synapses, understanding how they work and intentionally directing their activity to improve attention, creativity, productivity, and more. Enhancing and augmenting our brainpower in these ways will revolutionize the way we learn, do business, and heal disease.

This Book—Your Guide to *The NeuroGeneration*

In this book, I'll take you along with me as I crisscross the globe to meet the daring innovators and forward-thinking neuroscientists on the frontiers of brain enhancement and augmentation, and I'll introduce you to some of the individuals whose lives are already being transformed by their creations. You'll see how brilliant minds in labs around the world are using technology to take neuroplasticity to unprecedented levels, and discover the dizzying array of emerging technologies that promise to alter our mental landscape forever: mental health apps that work like medicine, an artificial hippocampus that restores lost memories, cranial stimulation that turns you into a math whiz, neural stimulation and bionic exoskeletons that allow paralyzed people to walk, even a brain–machine interface that can digitize the knowledge stored within your 100 billion neurons. It sounds like the stuff of science fiction, but it is quickly becoming "science faction," as I like to call it. This book doesn't attempt to explore every emerging brain-related technology, but rather focuses on those that are already available or imminent and those that will have the most transformative impact. The neurotechnologies I showcase represent the breadth of innovations underway—from noninvasive tools to those that require surgical procedures, tools that let us peer into the brain and others that allow us to change it, tools developed for the healthcare industry and others geared to consumers. *The NeuroGeneration* also examines the potential risks and ethical issues that come with these advances—from questions of accessibility and privacy to who owns the rights to your neural data and more.

Part I includes seven chapters, each offering an eye-opening look at the latest advancements in a specific area of brain-science innovation to show how what used to be impossible is now in the realm of reality. It will paint a panoramic picture of the human brain of tomorrow. **Chapter one** examines humankind's search for chemical shortcuts to improve our cognitive capabilities and looks at the latest neuropharmaceuticals that modulate the brain's neurotransmitters for better performance. It also introduces you to the concept of the "neuropharmacy" that goes beyond pills to include emerging technologies that could replace or reduce the need for pharmaceutical medications. **Chapter two** reveals how breakthrough EEG-fused brainwear is opening the door to *Star Wars*–style mind control to transform the lives of people with physical limitations and to unlock seemingly impossible abilities. **Chapter three** focuses on how innovators are zapping the brain with electrical pulses in an effort to unleash the genius within and to boost brain function. **Chapter four** looks at the revolutionary advances in motion that are blending biological beings with robotic prosthetics to make humans who have lost a limb whole again. **Chapter five** delves deep inside the brain where devices are paving the way to transform us into cyborgs with beyond-human sensory perceptions—think night vision or a sense of smell as keen as a dog's—and the ability to download and link our brains to our laptops. **Chapter six** unveils the devastating effects of brain disease and highlights the amazing advances in progress to repair damaged brains at the cellular level. **Chapter seven** explores the connections between artificial intelligence and the human brain and why I believe AI is likely to become a part of an enhanced human organism rather than an "us vs. them" scenario.

Part II will wrap it up with two chapters that focus on the broader ethical and socioeconomic implications of brain enhancement as well as the nuts-and-bolts strategies business leaders, tech innovators, and individuals can use now to ensure success in the NeuroGeneration. **Chapter eight** includes an urgent call for "neuroequality" and urges brain-enhancement innovators and inventors to democratize access to their technologies to ensure we don't create greater disparity in our world. **Chapter nine** outlines the steps we can take to lay the foundation for a seamless transition into the NeuroGeneration and asks the tough questions we need to address now. For example, will brain enhancement eventually tip the scales to a point where we are more machine than human? How do we prevent this? How do we ensure that artificial intelligence and machine learning take human values into account? If we're downloading our brains to computers, how do we safeguard our privacy, and who owns our thoughts?

The innovations explored over the next nine chapters will transform how we treat disease, do business, and think, learn, and interact, transforming our lives and our world in wondrous and unexpected ways. Ultimately, this book offers an invitation to people from all walks of life—whether you're a CEO, government leader, healthcare professional, creative type, stay-at-home parent, or student—to embrace the NeuroGeneration and become an active participant in it; to help shape the future of the human brain.

PART I

MIND-ALTERING TOOLS
TO EXPAND OUR
HUMAN POTENTIAL

CHAPTER 1

THE NEUROPHARMACY IS OPEN FOR BUSINESS

Nootropics, Tools, and Games for Better Cognitive and Mental Health

GEOFFREY WOO STOOD IN HIS LAB—a.k.a. his kitchen—carefully measuring out tiny quantities of white powder from various plastic bags and combining them with the care of a chemist. When he'd achieved what he deemed the ideal mixture, he popped it under his tongue and waited for the magic to happen. A computer scientist with a degree from Stanford University, he'd sold a mobile app company in 2013 and was now exploring his next venture by using himself as a human guinea pig.

While his brainiest friends from college were focusing their enormous talents on making algorithms better, computers faster, and robots smarter, Geoffrey had set his sights on improving what he calls "the human platform," looking for ways to engineer and enhance the one thing that separates us from all other species on the planet: our cognitive abilities. That sent him down the rabbit hole into the world of nootropics. A *nootropic* is simply any drug or substance that improves cognitive function; the term comes from the Greek words *nous* or "mind" and *trepein*, which means "to bend or turn." Nootropics are popular with biohackers, those who attempt to take a DIY approach to improving their own biology, but while many biohackers rely on fuzzy, intuitive, and subjective claims about cognitive enhancers, this zeros-and-ones guy intended to quantify his brain gains. Woo put himself through a rigorous battery of brain-training, psychometric, and other tests to measure the differences in his reaction time, working-memory capacity, memory, and focus. He was hoping the potions he was cooking up in his kitchen would upgrade human brainpower, and he wanted the data to prove it. And sure enough, the numbers showed his homemade nootropics were working. It was like his brain was on steroids.

I first linked up with this whip-smart, out-of-the-box thinker as he was launching a project called the Year of Biohacking. By then he'd started a company, originally called Nootrobox but now called HVMN (and no, it isn't pronounced "human," it's just H-V-M-N), to produce and sell his novel nootropics. He wanted to recommend portable EEG devices like the one I'd created as a way for biohackers to quantify the results they achieved using HVMN's products—"kind of an input and output side of human performance," as he put it.

With a Millennial swagger you don't expect from most computer scientists, Geoffrey filled me in on his efforts to enhance the human platform and invited everyone in my office to test-drive one of his first creations. He placed a small chewable cube in front of me. Feeling a little bit like Neo from *The Matrix* when he took that red pill, I wasn't sure what to expect as I popped the cube in my mouth. The caffeine-laden treat was also laced with l-theanine, an amino acid found in green tea, as well as vitamins B6 and B12. As I started chewing, the caffeine made a bee-line to my brain, where it suppressed the action of adenosine, a neurochemical that slows nerve activity in the brain and makes us drowsy. At the same time, it ramped up production of the feel-good neurotransmitter dopamine for a surge of energy and a quick mood boost. Tempering the caffeine's stimulating effects, the l-theanine triggered the release of the calming, anti-anxiety neurotransmitter GABA. And those B vitamins? They activated neural networks involved with mood enhancement, memory performance, and cognitive function. This combo of neurochemical action left me more alert and laser-focused on my work. As someone who typically doesn't consume caffeine, though, this seemed like a mega-dose and gave me a case of the jitters. But the mind-altering cube did make me feel almost superhuman, at least for a few hours.

Geoffrey is one of a new breed of neuropharmacists attempting to develop chemical shortcuts to unleash our cognitive potential, alter our neurotransmitters, modulate our moods, and heighten our productivity. As sci-fi as it sounds to pop a pill to supercharge your brain, this search isn't new—cognitive enhancers and mind-altering substances can be traced back at least 50,000 years. And there is scientific research backing up many of their claims:

▸ **Ephedra:** In the late 1950s and early 1960s, American archaeologist and Columbia University faculty member Ralph Solecki led a team that uncovered the graves—dating back 60,000 to 90,000 years—of nine Neanderthals in the Shanidar Cave in northern Iraq.[1] One was found buried with several plants with medicinal properties, including ephedra, a stimulant, which studies show increases alertness and energy. Although ephedrine, an extract of the plant, has been banned by the U.S. Food and Drug Administration (FDA), its applications include use as a mental concentration aid.

▸ **Caffeine:** Caffeine, which can be found in more than sixty plants and has been used by humans for thousands of years, is the most popular drug on planet Earth. Tea and coffee, which contain caffeine, are the world's most popular beverages after water, with humans consuming about 2.2 billion cups of tea[2] and 1.6 billion cups of joe every day.[3] Although the scientific community continues to debate the details of its effects and the ideal dosage for various cognitive benefits, billions of consumers swear by its mind-altering abilities to improve mental focus, quicken reaction times, boost moods, and enhance alertness.

▸ ***Bacopa monnieri:*** An herb native to India, *Bacopa monnieri* has been used for over one thousand years as a cognitive enhancer. Traditional lore claims scholars used the herb to help them memorize ancient religious texts. A 2012 review in the *Journal of Alternative and Complementary Medicine* looked at six studies on the herb and found that it improved performance in nine of seventeen tests in the domain of memory recall.[4] A 2013 study in the *British Journal of Clinical Pharmacology* examined the effects of *Bacopa monnieri* and ginseng in comparison to modafinil, a drug used for attention-deficit/hyperactivity disorder (ADHD), and found that the two nutraceuticals could each produce cognitive-enhancing effects similar to those of the pharmaceutical.[5]

▸ **Ginseng:** Ginseng has been used in traditional Chinese medicine for thousands of years to enhance cognitive function and shore up memory. In addition to the findings of the aforementioned *British Journal of Clinical Pharmacology* study, a growing body of research shows that Panax ginseng—also known as red ginseng—positively affects cognitive performance. For example, studies have found it reduces mental fatigue during cognitive processing tasks[6] and promotes neurogenesis in the hippocampus, one of the brain's memory centers.[7] Researchers have also noted enhancement in working memory in healthy young adults[8] and middle-aged people[9] when using American ginseng, also known as *Panax quinquefolius*.

▸ **Gingko biloba:** People seeking a mental boost have also turned to gingko biloba, and with good reason. Several studies point to an improvement in cognitive performance and memory when taking the herb and have found it especially advantageous in combating the mental decline that comes with age.[10]

▸ **Green tea:** Green tea has long been hailed as a cognitive enhancer. A 2017 review of twenty-one studies in *Phytomedicine* found evidence that green tea influences the brain in a number of beneficial ways, including reducing anxiety, increasing attention, and improving memory—particularly working memory.[11]

▸ **Vitamins:** Even ordinary vitamins have been found to alter cognitive function, moods, and mental health. For example, studies show that B vitamins improve moods, stress, and executive function, which includes higher-level thought processing.[12] A wealth of studies have found that vitamin D supplementation may help alleviate symptoms of depression,[13] while low levels of the "sunshine vitamin" have been linked to an increased risk for memory loss.[14] And dozens of studies on omega-3 fatty acids reveal their mood-enhancing properties.

Today's neuropharmacists often incorporate long-standing brain boosters like these into their chemical cocktails, but they also rely on a newer crop of synthetic nootropics, including piracetam, oxiracetam, and Noopept. Although the scientific research on these lab-derived substances remains relatively sparse, some studies suggest they may improve brainpower in a variety of ways. Piracetam, a derivative of the neurotransmitter GABA, ramps up neuroplasticity, according to a 2005 study in *CNS Drug Reviews*.[15] Studies have found that oxiracetam improves memory in seniors[16] as well as mice and rats,[17] and it enhances long-term potentiation, a process that strengthens the synaptic connections between neurons and is key to learning. In animal studies, Noopept shows neuroprotective properties,[18] restores spatial memory,[19] and increases the production of brain-derived neurotrophic factor, a compound that promotes brain cell generation.[20] And in one of the few human studies on Noopept, patients with mild cognitive impairment showed improved cognitive function with the compound.[21]

Many biohackers, including Geoffrey, have reported sensory enhancements when taking Noopept. Geoffrey recounted his first experience taking the Russian nootropic, which is an unscheduled drug in the U.S., but not illegal. "It was spring or summer and I remember walking to my office and there were these dandelions, and the yellow of these flowers seemed so vibrant. And I thought, 'Whoa, there is definitely something happening here.'"[22] It was that subjective $N = 1$ experiment, which he admits was very unscientific, that inspired Geoffrey to delve further into the underlying biology and science of these substances and develop metrics to quantify his biohacked brain.

Geoffrey has come a long way since his days as a kitchen neuropharmacist, and he has his diet to thank for leading him to his latest discovery. In the human performance arena, biohackers have turned to intermittent fasting—cycling between periods of eating and fasting—and virtually no-carb diets, not only for rapid weight loss, better blood sugar control, and improved physical performance, but also for enhanced cognitive function. The key to many of these benefits is these diets' production of ketones, substances created from stored fat to be used as fuel when the body is low on carbohydrates. After becoming interested in intermittent fasting, Geoffrey launched the Facebook group WeFast, now one of the largest fasting communities online, with over 12,000 members.

A true "quant" guy, Geoffrey wanted to see what intermittent fasting was doing to his biological makeup, so he tracked his blood metrics using finger sticks to check his glucose and ketone levels. He could see the effects on his biochemistry, but what about his brain? Using productivity software, he monitored how he was spending his time on his computer—whether he was completing projects in Excel or Word with focused attention or being distracted by the siren call of social media. Over time, it became clear that the days he engaged in fasting were some of his most productive. Finally! It was the mental performance boost he had been looking for.

Science backs up what he had noticed. A 2013 study in *Plos One* found that mice following an intermittent fasting diet for eleven months performed better on tests of learning and memory and also showed positive changes in brain structures related to memory compared to mice that had free access to regular chow.[23] In a 2016 trial, twenty researchers from top labs in the United Kingdom and the U.S.—at the University of Oxford, the University of Cambridge, and the National Institutes of Health (NIH)— teamed up to explore the effects a ketogenic diet would have on rats.[24] They fed the rodents a novel diet with a ketone ester, a bioavailable form of ingestible ketones, for five days and then let them loose in a maze that would test their working memory—the brain's ability to temporarily store information required to carry out complex tasks. The ketone-fed rats completed the maze 38 percent faster than rats on other diets and made more correct decisions before making a mistake. Basically, the diet made the rats smarter. It makes humans smarter, too, according to a growing body of research. In a 2012 trial involving older adults with mild cognitive impairment, those eating a low-carb diet that resulted in higher ketone levels performed better on memory tests than participants eating a higher-carb diet with lower resulting ketone levels.[25]

Today, Geoffrey has teamed up with the University of Oxford and the NIH to research ways to accelerate the elevation of ketones in the body without the agony of fasting or the ridiculous amount of discipline it takes to follow a ketogenic diet that's low in fruits and vegetables, devoid of doughnuts and bread, and high in ghee and coconut oil. After years of research, they've introduced a drinkable ketone ester. The innovation originated as a way to enhance mental and physical performance during military missions, courtesy of a collaboration with the Defense Advanced Research Projects Association (DARPA), the U.S. Department of Defense agency charged with developing advanced technologies for military use. Now the supplement is available to consumers. It's particularly popular with athletes looking for physical advantages like increased endurance, but I can't wait to see the published research on the cognitive benefits from taking a swig of the stuff.

Geoffrey is equal parts researcher, entrepreneur, and proselytizer. When he isn't in the lab (which is no longer in his kitchen) or developing products, he's hitting the conference circuit spreading the word about human enhancement as well as helping people see the value in monitoring the human platform. The last time I saw Geoffrey give a talk, he was sporting a Fitbit and Apple Watch, in addition to a heart rate variability sensor, a sleep-tracking device called the Oura ring, and a continuous glucose monitor to track how his blood sugar levels respond to his eating protocols and other nutritional interventions.

Noting that our brain and our body are the most important pieces of equipment we will ever possess, he says it's a travesty that people generally don't check under the hood unless something goes wrong. "Most don't ever get their blood drawn until they're sick," he laments. "That seems very archaic to me . . . in the future I think we'll have real-time streams of data of all our different biomarkers and performance markers related to brain performance and health. And we'll be able to shift and optimize our days and our diets and our exercise to optimize what the data is actually telling us." A nootropic-fueled human with a tech-assisted biofeedback loop, Geoffrey stands at the forefront of the unfolding revolution that will allow us to monitor and enhance our brain in real time.

Getting all of these tools into the hands of people who want or need them—whether it's a Silicon Valley entrepreneur looking to get an edge in the cutthroat tech industry, a college student hoping to supercharge focus and memory before finals, or a shift worker trying to stay alert in the middle of the night—presents a big challenge. Like most of us in the field, Geoffrey fervently believes that the biohacker community, industry, government regulators, and academics will have to work together to ensure equal access. But he is optimistic, pointing to technology's long history of rapid democratization.

"Look at mobile phones," he says. "They used to be so expensive, only Wall Street elites and Hollywood superagents could afford them." By 2016, nearly 63 percent of the world population owned a mobile phone, and the number of cell phone users is expected to reach 2.87 billion by 2020.[26] Similarly, the global brain-health supplement market is growing at warp speed and is projected to jump from $2.3 billion in 2015 to $11.6 billion by 2024.[27] Leading the market is the memory enhancement segment, with other key supplements including depression and anxiety relievers, attention and focus boosters, longevity and anti-aging agents, and sleep aids.

Those eager to dose their way to the top need to be aware of the potential downsides of emerging neuropharmaceuticals. They may allow our brains to make extraordinary synaptic connections, but this ability fades as the drug wears off. Will smart pills, liquid superfuels, and other nootropics become a must-have in the workplace? And if our heightened cognitive abilities allow us to get more done in less time, will they simply lead to an expectation to do more?

"I think people are inherently ambitious and like to be better at what they do," says Geoffrey. "I think we should empower people to be the best possible version of themselves, as long as it isn't deleterious to health in the long run. In the end, we're all $N = 1$ animals running around figuring out how to best live our own lives."

In the NeuroGeneration, we'll be using substances not just to reclaim our health, but to enhance our brains and bodies. But the promise of the next-gen neuropharmacy extends beyond new drugs; it also means applying fresh insight into how they work. Prescription medications for mental health disorders will be increasingly tailored to our individual brain chemistry to produce better results. Precision medicine, which involves assessing a patient's DNA and unique biomarkers in bloodwork along with more traditional evaluations, has already gained traction in cancer treatment, targeting tumors and interventions based on genetic and immune-system variations. Now it's entering the mental health arena, where advanced brain imaging and DNA testing are being used along with other data to help pinpoint the specific drugs that will be most effective for specific patients. Many mental health practitioners already offer some of this testing. And at Stanford University, a precision medicine center for mental health is enlisting psychiatrists, data scientists, geneticists, and others to investigate physical and psychological profiles of depression in the hopes of identifying subtypes of the condition that could help them target antidepressant treatment more effectively.[28]

The neuropharmacy will also be more than just a pill-dispensing outlet; it will also dole out brain-enhancing neurotechnologies. Some of these emerging tools are subject to regulation and approval by the FDA, which means they are actually considered "drugs" or treatments that healthcare professionals can prescribe. In the NeuroGeneration, virtual reality will help veterans cope with posttraumatic stress disorder (PTSD), chatbots will act as therapists, and our smartphones may guide us in balancing our neurotransmitters and strengthening positive synaptic pathways to help ward off conditions like depression, anxiety, and bipolar disorder. In the rest of this chapter, you'll meet the innovators behind some of the most promising new "techno-drugs."

Siri, Can You Check My Mental Health?

Imagine grabbing your smartphone and firing off a text message, posting a few comments on Facebook, playing a quick round of Words with Friends, and scrolling through your contacts list. Now, imagine that while you were engaging in these routine habits, an app on your phone was hard at work in the background analyzing all that activity—gauging how quickly you skimmed your contacts list, noting how often you hit the delete key, and more. What if, by tracking your phone use in this way, the app could give you a warning that you were about to slip into a depressive state, that your antidepressant meds weren't working well enough, or even detect that you were teetering on the verge of becoming suicidal? If Tom Insel has his way, that's only the beginning of the future of neuropsychiatry.

The World Health Organization (WHO) estimates that, globally, over 300 million people suffer from depression and more than 260 million from anxiety disorders.[29] According to the National Institute of Mental Health (NIMH), the world's largest mental health research institution, nearly one in five American adults live with mental illness.[30] Sadly, 56 percent of them don't receive treatment.[31] That's bad news, considering the impact these conditions can have on a person's relationships, career, and general health. They also take a heavy toll on the economy. A WHO study estimates that depression and anxiety disorders cost the global economy a staggering $1 trillion each year in lost productivity.[32] Broadening access to treatment could have a huge benefit. A 2016 study in the journal *Lancet Psychiatry* estimated that scaling up treatment for just depression and anxiety disorders in thirty-six countries from 2016 to 2030 would cost $147 billion but would yield a far more massive return.[33] In addition to 43 million extra years of healthy life, valued at some $310 billion, the economic productivity gains would net nearly $400 billion. Investors are seeing the potential; they poured a record-breaking $6 billion into digital health startups in 2017.[34]

I met Tom Insel in 2017 at a scientist-led conference on breakthroughs in brain and body health at the MIT Media Lab in Cambridge, Massachusetts. I was immediately drawn to his calm, reassuring demeanor and impressed by his lifelong dedication to finding better solutions for mental health patients. A year later, I was thrilled to have the chance to connect and chat more deeply when we served on the same panel at the Organization for Economic Cooperation and Development (OECD)'s Workshop on Minding Neurotechnology in Shanghai, an incredible event that attracted some of the best minds from around the world to delve into the unique ethical, legal, and policy challenges associated with cutting-edge neurotechnology.[35]

After thirteen years as the director of the National Institute for Mental Health, guiding some of the most groundbreaking research into mental illness, Insel grew weary of seeing all that magnificent research fail to result in practical applications for those in the healthcare trenches. Now, Tom is one of the NeuroGeneration pioneers working to devise next-gen mental health treatment modalities and find smarter ways to provide access to treatment.

When we spoke, Tom zeroed in on five things holding back progress in mental health care:

- lack of access to treatment
- delayed treatment
- issues with quality of care
- problems getting a diagnosis
- lack of objective measurements

That last one is a glaring flaw that virtually no other medical specialty faces. "We don't measure what we do," Tom says. Forget the usual blood tests, blood pressure monitors, CT scans, X-rays, MRI tests, and biopsies used to diagnose everything from cancer to thyroid dysfunction to heart disease. People with neuropsychiatric disorders are diagnosed based solely on their symptoms, and these symptoms are generally self-reported, which presents an obvious problem. The evaluations of providers are similarly subjective and can reflect personal or societal biases—biases that are sometimes evident in the diagnostic criteria themselves, which rely on behavioral norms that may not be equally valid for people of different genders or cultural backgrounds. And because diagnosis isn't linked to any underlying biology or brain function, there is just as little precision in the way we treat these disorders. "We don't know whether we're giving the right dose or whether we're giving the right treatment," Tom says.

Then there's the gap between the number of people who need care and those who actually receive it. Ask Tom what lies behind this gap, and he'll give you a laundry list of factors. First, there's the stigma attached to mental health issues. Some people can't find a mental health professional, or face a months-long wait for an appointment. Others can't afford it—many providers, especially psychiatrists, won't bill insurance or don't accept it, especially Medicaid. But the problem isn't just stigma or lack of access. "It's also the fact that when you're depressed, you're hopeless," Tom explains. "When you're psychotic, you don't think you're sick. And when you're manic, you can't slow down long enough to make an appointment."

When Tom stepped into the role of director at NIMH, he thought it would take about a decade for the emerging research to translate into the kind of practical treatments and increased access that would make a significant dent in the numbers of people suffering from mental health issues. But over a decade later, prohibitive costs, late detection, and ineffective treatments continued to dominate the landscape. So when the folks at Google called him, Tom started musing about whether technology might be the answer to scaling up mental healthcare. He left his government gig and dipped a toe into the churn-and-burn private sector with a brief stint at Google Life Sciences, which quickly morphed into Verily. A few years later, he joined forces with a handful of others to launch Mindstrong, a tech firm he's hoping will remake the way we diagnose neuropsychiatric disorders, access care, and measure treatment effectiveness. And it aims to put those functions right in your own hands—with your smartphone. Smartphones are used by over two billion people globally, and as noted earlier, that number is expected to be closing in on three billion by 2020. These ubiquitous devices could help eliminate all five of the stumbling blocks Tom identified.

One of his founding partners in Mindstrong, Paul Dagum, is a cardiovascular surgeon who also holds a PhD in computer science, and who ditched his surgical career to become a serial entrepreneur focusing mainly on cybersecurity. You might not think there would be a connection between cybersecurity and mental health, but Dagum helped develop "user-entity behavioral analytics," which identifies and tracks individual hackers based on the way they type—a sort of digital fingerprint that has become a crucial forensic tool in the cybersecurity industry. Dagum, along with Tom and third co-founder Rick Klausner, wondered if they could apply this digital fingerprinting to the mental health industry. Could they use the technology to track and develop profiles of how people with dementia, depression, or anxiety use their smartphones? And if so, could machine learning identify those at risk or in the early stages of those conditions so they could benefit from early intervention?

"We wanted to create a source of data from which we could learn from the way people are typing—not *what* they type, but *how* they type," Tom tells me. "We wanted to learn the signals that would tell us, 'This is a pattern that suggests someone is about to relapse, someone is about to become suicidal, someone is about to develop PTSD, or someone is about to become psychotic.' For the first time, it would provide the field of neuropsychiatry with this interesting insight based on objective, continuous measurements that could be completely passive." No more subjectively filling out self-evaluation forms.

Tom's team at Mindstrong is still in an intense research phase, investigating forty-three keyboarding activities at last count—everything from swiping to how you use the space bar—and mapping them out over more than twenty time series. (That's a type of statistical data analysis over particular periods of time or intervals.) Altogether, this comes to over one thousand potential biomarkers. The initial results are promising, according to a study by Dagum that was published in a 2018 issue of *npj Digital Medicine*.[36] For the study, human–computer interaction from seven days of smartphone use in twenty-seven people was analyzed using the quant app in an attempt to identify digital biomarkers associated with cognitive functions. After the week-long period, the app pinpointed a cluster of digital biomarkers that accurately correlated to cognitive functioning in areas including working memory, memory, executive function, language, and intelligence.

Finding less-subjective measures for neuropsychiatric disorders would improve more than diagnosis. These machine-learning tools could detect whether interventions are working—even before the patient feels their effect. Take antidepressants, for example. Most take four to six weeks to produce noticeable results. "What's really fascinating is that although the recovery is slow, it is perceptible to almost everybody except the patient," Tom explains. "Depressed people are the last ones to realize that they're getting better." Objective measures could reassure depressed patients by letting them see their levels of functioning improving—positive reinforcement that might encourage people to stick with a medication until they start feeling better. And having this stream of data available to both patients and their caregivers could make waiting a week or a month for that next appointment in order to change a medication or dosage a thing of the past, with treatment delivered or adjusted much more quickly.

Tom is quick to insist that this doesn't mean machine learning tools will be replacing healthcare professionals any time soon. Instead, it's about creating tech-enabled care. The idea is to make healthcare more efficient, accessible, and precise, helping healthcare providers make better decisions, and patients and families experience better outcomes. "It's not going to be as simple as just replacing a primary care doc with a chatbot," he says. "We think chatbots are going to be conversational tools that will be really important for care in the future, but they will be part of the solution, not the whole solution. We still need this combination of both high-tech and high-touch."

The promise of a smartphone app that continuously monitors mental health status based on specific biomarkers comes with some big Big Brother–type risks. Could it turn into a surveillance tool that employers use to spy on how their employees are functioning? This possibility isn't lost on Tom, and the team at Mindstrong is taking the lead in addressing the ethical questions that come with the emergence of digital mental healthcare technologies, collaborating with the Stanford Center for Biomedical Ethics and the Stanford Medical School to create a set of guidelines to ensure privacy and transparency. "We want to make sure that the information is being used to help people function better and not to discriminate against them," Tom says. He is also one of the intellectual heavyweights on the board of the International Neuroethics Society, which brings together scientists, ethicists, clinicians, lawyers, educators, and other professionals to explore the implications of advances in neuroscience. "With every new technology, you've got to balance out the benefits and the risks. We have to ask ourselves, where's the value? What are the risks? How do we navigate this and find the right balance?"

In the Neuropharmacy, It's Game On!

Video games get a bad rap. Turn on the nightly news, flip through the pages of a magazine, or scroll through an online parenting article, and you'll find a litany of warnings that video games are ruining your health and turning your kids into problem children. In the years since *Pong* became the golden child of video arcades in the 1970s, a rash of studies have linked gaming to obesity, muscle stiffness, aggressive behavior, poor grades, addiction, sleep deprivation, and attention problems. But not everyone agrees that video games, even violent ones, are harbingers of evil. The authors of *Moral Combat*, psychologists Patrick M. Markey and Christopher J. Ferguson, expertly contribute to the video game debate, debunking the myth of a link between virtual game-play violence and an individual's propensity to commit real violence: "Despite the widespread notion that violent video games are related to increases in violent crime, the exact opposite seems to be true. Countries that consume more video games have lower levels of violent crime than those devoid of this media."[37] In fact, Markey and Ferguson explore how playing video games may positively affect components of our social dynamic, including possibly making us more morally sensitive and offering an outlet for stress.[38] And the games themselves are undergoing a seismic shift thanks to some future-thinking neuroscientists. In fact, in the NeuroGeneration, a doctor very well might prescribe a video game as therapy—or "VGTx" for short—for ADHD, PTSD, depression, traumatic brain injury (TBI), early Alzheimer's disease, or a host of other conditions.[39] Don't believe me? Just ask Adam Gazzaley.

If ever there was a rock star neuroscientist, it's Adam. With his camera-ready appearance and a natural gift for making audiences hang on his every word, he exudes star power. He even hangs out with Mickey Hart, the former drummer of the Grateful Dead (more on this later).

Adam grew up playing video games in the Atari generation. These days, in what is arguably one of the coolest neuroscience labs in the nation, he's creating cutting-edge games that aim to do far more than lure players into spending hours and hours trying to get to the next level. I visited Adam at the Neuroscape lab at the University of California, San Francisco, and my jaw dropped. Talk about a brain researcher's dream, Neuroscape has it all—an fMRI machine, sixty-four-channel EEG equipment, spaces dedicated to immersive virtual reality and augmented reality experiences, video monitors lining the walls, and more. And so far, what's coming out of this lab is just as stunning. Adam is developing video games that target neural circuits intended to give cognitive function a sustainable boost. His work is opening the door to a whole new generation of diagnostics and therapeutics that may replace or reduce the need for traditional psychoactive medications—some of which come with daunting side effects. If you've ever seen a TV commercial for an antidepressant, you've heard the warnings about possible nausea, weight gain, weight loss, constipation, diarrhea, fainting, sexual dysfunction, abnormal heart rhythm, fatigue, insomnia, and on and on. According to Adam, it's time for a change. "In my mind, we've been stuck in a completely silent system for sixty years where our incumbent is so dominant that everything else is labeled 'alternative,' and that's not really the healthy way of going about this," he says.[40]

I first connected with Adam about a decade ago when he was toiling away in a much more modest lab—nothing like the impressive digs he has now. He'd been studying attention and working memory in older adults, but the rebel inside him didn't want to take the classic approach of medicating people with pharmaceuticals; he wanted to build an interactive experience that would harness the brain's plasticity to improve function. He reached out to me because he was looking for ways to measure the participants' cognitive performance and was considering using EMOTIV's EEG technology.

Adam admits the concept is actually an ancient one, relying on the same processes by which meditation can affect brain function. "The twist was to use modern technology," he says. "It was a short leap to building a video game because we wanted this interactive experience to be immersive and engaging, and it seemed like the best way to do that was to bring in the art, the music, the story, and the reward cycles that go into video game play." He reached out to friends at LucasArts to help design a game people would want to play for fun, not just because it was part of a research study. The result was *NeuroRacer*, a driving game that tested seniors' ability to multitask.

Sadly, the human brain isn't very good at multitasking. According to a 2008 study in *Brain Research*, for example, just listening to something while driving decreases activity in the parietal lobe, the region tasked with spatial navigation, by 37 percent.[41] That's bad news for a modern society in which we're often juggling multiple text message conversations while simultaneously scrolling through our social media feeds and binge-watching Netflix. A team of researchers at Stanford University found that those who are heavy media multitaskers pay a big price for all that high-tech screen-hopping. Their 2009 study in *Proceedings of the National Academies of Science* (*PNAS*) showed that these people are poor at paying attention, controlling their memory, and switching from one task to another, likely because of a reduced ability to filter out distractions caused by irrelevant information.[42] And as the brain ages, we become even more easily distracted.[43] Adam's own research in a 2011 issue of *PNAS* confirmed that, compared to younger subjects, older adults have a harder time multitasking and more difficulty switching between tasks.[44] It's a problem with what neuroscientists refer to as cognitive control, which involves the ability to prioritize.

Once his *NeuroRacer* game was ready, Adam set out to see whether he could reverse this deficit. Joystick in hand, the seniors were tasked with maneuvering a virtual car on a winding road that twisted and turned as it went up and down. The goal was to keep the car in the center of the road while reacting to or ignoring specific signs that popped up on screen. As subjects improved, the game adapted to become more challenging, something neuroscientists call an adaptive staircase algorithm. A closed-loop system monitored player performance and, every three minutes, updated the software to continually challenge and reward the user.

Study participants played the game for an hour three days a week over the course of one month, for a total of twelve hours. After their month of training, they showed dramatic improvements in multitasking as well as in other areas of cognitive control, including attention and working memory. In fact, these sixty- to eighty-five-year-olds outperformed twenty-year-old controls. More surprising was that when the seniors returned to the lab for a follow-up after six months of no game play, Adam's team found that their multitasking abilities on the game had not diminished significantly. Any researcher would be thrilled with these results, but the reason this study made such a splash—and what landed it on the cover of the journal *Nature* in 2013—was what's known as the transfer effect.[45] The older adults who played the game not only showed significant improvement in game play; they also performed better on unrelated memory and attention tasks. That's the holy grail of therapy—targeting one task for improvement and achieving brain enhancement that carries over to other tasks as well.

Since that study put Adam and his team firmly on the map, their work has advanced at a lightning pace. Today, the closed-loop system they designed to scale game difficulty based on performance metrics updates in real time rather than every three minutes, and they're working to incorporate neural data, heart rate data, and a variety of other types of biosensing into that feedback loop. Using real-time brain data would allow the game to adapt not just to how well you play, but also to the specifics of how your brain is processing the game's information. For example, if the system saw a deficit in your visual processing stream, it could reward you for engaging visually to encourage you to use—and strengthen—that pathway. Another person might be challenged in different ways based on how their own brain operates. Unlike drugs, which are static and developed for broad populations, digital therapy that uses brain data could be highly individualized.

The engine behind the original *NeuroRacer* game has since been licensed by tech medicine firm Akili Interactive, where Adam sits on the board of directors and acts as chief science advisor. Akili has raced ahead with a version of the game called *Project: EVO*, in which players must navigate an avatar down a rushing stream by angling an iPad up and down while simultaneously reacting to certain monsters but not others. During a demonstration at a *Fortune* Brainstorm Health conference in 2016, Adam invited host Sanjay Gupta to give it a go in front of a live audience.[46] Not surprisingly, the neurosurgeon excelled at the game. As he tilted the tablet from side to side while tapping furiously at the monsters, the game adapted to his skill level, speeding up and adding new obstacles to keep it consistently challenging.

As I was writing this book, *Project: EVO* was undergoing a clinical trial and in the final phases of the regulatory process in an effort to receive FDA approval as the first video game able to be prescribed as a therapeutic tool for children with ADHD.[47] It's hard to imagine that something parents have been trying to get their kids to stop doing could actually be beneficial for them, but results from a preliminary trial published in 2018 in *Plos One* indeed showed that this novel video game treatment increased attention, inhibition, and working memory in children with ADHD.[48] And according to Adam, the levels of improvement were comparable to those seen in many ADHD drug trials. It's the high-level validation and pending FDA approval that takes Akili's game out of the arena of consumer-driven brain-training games—those popular games that came under fire in 2014 when an international group of scientists released a scathing joint statement on the lack of scientific grounds for their claims of enhanced cognitive function—and into the realm of legitimate medical treatment.[49] Akili has a number of other VGTx programs in the pipeline, including games geared to treat symptoms of depression, TBI, autism, and Parkinson's disease.

The promise of digital therapy that sidesteps the bothersome and sometimes dangerous side effects associated with drugs could be life-changing for the millions of people affected by these conditions. And digital treatments like VGTx could cut through some of the barriers to access that Mindstrong's Tom Insel described. But as with any new therapy, VGTx presents a host of new challenges. Adam rattles off some of the questions he and his team are grappling with: What's the minimum viable dose? What's the optimal length of treatment? How can we predict beforehand who it's going to work best for? Will people need "boosters," and if so, when? How will it interact with other ongoing medical therapy? Investigations into these fundamental issues are all part of the process of bringing a new treatment to market.

Adam's vision for the future of the human brain goes far beyond treating neural deficits. At the epic Neuroscape incubator, his team is also crafting technologies intended to augment cognitive function in healthy people, possibly elevating us to that elusive superhuman status. One of the coolest projects on the Neuroscape slate is called Rhythmicity. This is where his collaboration with Grateful Dead drummer Mickey Hart comes in. The mobile cognitive-training platform is designed to teach rhythm to see what benefits it might have on other cognitive abilities. "We know that anticipation and timing, which are key components of rhythm, are also key components of how our brain works in pretty much every way, including attention and memory," Adam says. "We think that if rhythm can make you better at anticipating events and responding precisely in time, then we may have a sort of fine-tuning of the brain's information processing abilities and we'll see better attention and memory when tested in the lab."

I won't deny that our love affair with technology has taken a toll on our cognitive abilities in some respects, but with people like Adam in the driver's seat, it's easy to envision a future in which we are able to flip the script and see digital therapy and devices enhancing and augmenting our cognitive function instead. Along with being excited about the possibilities, I'm equally heartened that innovators like Adam and Tom are fully aware of the ways such advances could be misused, and that they are working diligently to address those risks before these new technologies make their way into our hands—and our brains.

CHAPTER 2

MIND CONTROL

Brainwave Technology, Neurofeedback, and Brain-Controlled Interfaces

W ITH LIVELY BROWN EYES and a thousand-watt smile, Cora Lovio had a magnetic personality that made her the life of every party. The heart and soul of her social circle, Cora craved human connection above all else. Although the vibrant teen had an artistic bent and enjoyed drawing, writing, and listening to music, her favorite pastime by far was simply hanging out with her friends in her hometown of Mount Shasta, California. She was one of those rare individuals who lived in the moment, fully engaged in the here and now. Who wanted to think about the future when today was the best day ever? The New Millennium had just dawned, and life was good.

Seventeen-year-old Cora hadn't even begun to dream about what she would do with the rest of that life when a devastating car accident brought those blissful days to a screeching halt. Just a few minutes of oxygen deprivation left her brain permanently damaged, and she lost control of her body and her world. She couldn't walk, couldn't talk, couldn't feed herself, couldn't hold her head up, couldn't even control the movements of those big brown eyes. Gone was that dazzling smile. Gone was that sparkling personality.

Reliant upon a wheelchair and unable to communicate, Cora led an increasingly isolated existence. A decade after the accident, she hadn't made any progress—in fact, she seemed to have regressed. With her head hung low and her wide eyes wandering aimlessly, she had disengaged from everything and everyone. The teen who had once thrived on socializing with her many friends was now a young woman cut off from the people and the world around her. Her situation seemed hopeless.

That changed in 2010, when a neighbor named Roslyn McCoy showed up with a video game system that used an EEG headset to turn inner thoughts into on-screen actions.[1] With a degree in psychology, Roslyn worked with people with disabilities. After taking a class on biofeedback, she wondered if this technologically advanced system might allow her young neighbor to reconnect with the world. With Cora's mother's permission, Roslyn placed the brainwear device on the young woman's head, carefully positioning fourteen small electrodes on her scalp. Then Roslyn pressed "play."

In the video game, the player must complete a series of challenges for a virtual sensei. But there's no joystick or controller involved. Instead, the controller is the player's mind. Cora would have to harness her inner Jedi to navigate the game. The first challenge required her to concentrate to make a group of rocks float in the air. Could Cora do it? Completely dependent on others to care for her, she hadn't been able to do much of anything for herself since that fateful day ten years before. As Cora tried and failed, Roslyn kept up a stream of enthusiastic encouragement, until—*WHOOSH!* Cora had visualized the rocks levitating and, eventually, up they went. Like a Jedi knight, she had used mind control to move a virtual object. The Force was with her.

Cora broke into a broad smile, a rare occurrence in those days. For the first time in years, she had made something happen. *And she was excited!* Maybe this game and a renewed sense of control could help bring some of that personality back to life. Roslyn began working with Cora on a regular basis, videotaping their adventures with the headset and posting them on YouTube.[2] In subsequent games, Cora tapped into her brainpower to rotate, raise, and pull a virtual cube. She relied on her thoughts to bend trees. She used mind control to make her avatar fly—soaring high over forests and canyons.

And Cora made progress not just in the virtual world, but in the real one as well. She regained the ability to hold her head up by herself. She developed better control of her eyes and was able to maintain a consistent gaze. More important than these physical improvements was what she chose to do with them: she started interacting with people again, turning her head to look at them when they spoke, something she hadn't done in years. She was reemerging into the world. After accomplishing one particular feat in the game, Cora threw her head back and laughed out loud.

"Her dad said it was the first time in ten years he'd heard her laugh," Roslyn told me.

Cora's experience wasn't just a major breakthrough in her own life; it also provided a glimpse into the technology's future promise. Video game applications—controlling virtual objects in a digital landscape—are only the beginning. Someone like Cora could use mind control to send texts or emails; adjust the thermostat; direct a wheelchair; and turn on the lights, faucet, and TV. "Wouldn't that be incredible?" says Roslyn, musing about the possibilities. These powerful steps toward personal autonomy would be transformative not only for people like Cora who require full-time care, but also for the more than 38 million adult Americans who, according to the U.S. Centers for Disease Control and

Prevention (CDC), have some form of difficulty with physical functioning.[3]

Cora doesn't know it, but she inspires me every day. When I watched her YouTube videos, tears filled my eyes. It is still hard for me to describe what I felt when I saw her smiling and laughing as an EEG headset from my company—the device that, over a decade ago, was just scribbles on a piece of paper—allowed her to exert control over bits of her world again. I felt a rush of emotion and validation I'd never experienced before. It proved to me that the brainwear we created is more than a cool futuristic toy—alongside its future promise, it holds real value today, changing the lives of ordinary people in extraordinary ways.

Brainwave Technology and What It Teaches Us About the Brain

To comprehend how an EEG headset enabled Cora to navigate a video game, we have to get inside our own heads. Since I began exploring EEG technology over a decade ago, I've watched thousands of brains at work—none more than my own. Like many inventors, I'm constantly experimenting on myself, testing our equipment and attempting to enhance my own mental hardware. I wear an EEG headset almost every day, and have played the same video game Cora played over a thousand times. As I play, when I think "rotate," "yes," or "no," some of the 100 billion neurons in my brain fire off electrochemical signals at speeds of up to 268 miles per hour to communicate with other neurons. They do this thanks to the wire-like tails called axons that trail off their ends. The electrical impulses travel down the axons of the neurons sending the signals and jump over to other neurons' dendrites, which are branch-like nerve endings that receive these transmissions. Think of axons like microphones and dendrites like your ears. The same way sound travels across the space between the microphone and your ears, the electrical signals in your brain zip across gaps—called synapses—between axons and dendrites.

Neurons, by nature, are not solitary creatures. They work in large collectives—picture how a school of fish swirls in a wave-like motion through the ocean—coordinating within and between various regions of the brain to process visual input and sounds, give rise to thoughts, retrieve memories, and more. The complex neural network that makes up the information highway inside the human brain is more powerful than any computer network, and far more elaborate. In fact, if you laid this network of nerve fibers out end to end, they'd stretch about 100,000 miles, enough to wrap around the earth's equator four times.

All of this brain activity produces enough electricity to power a light bulb. (Maybe that's why we say a "light bulb came on" when we have a bright idea.) The electricity takes the form of waves that oscillate at different frequencies depending upon the patterns of coordinated neuron firing they reflect. There are five major frequencies of brainwaves—gamma, beta, alpha, theta, and delta—each associated with various brain states and functions, from active thought to deep sleep.[4]

EEG allows us to capture and interpret these brainwaves, thanks to a German psychiatrist named Hans Berger who pioneered the technology nearly a century ago. According to neurologist David Millett's account in *Perspectives in Biology and Medicine*, the brooding, introverted Berger spent years attempting—and failing—to record the electrical activity of the brain.[5] He finally succeeded in making the first EEG recording on July 6, 1924, from a seventeen-year-old college student, a brain tumor patient named Zedel. The resulting scratches on graph paper were decidedly unimpressive and bore little resemblance to the clear spikes and waves we see on modern-day EEGs. Berger's accomplishment was viewed as less than electrifying by his colleagues, who remained skeptical of his quest to chart the brain's electrical activity altogether, unconvinced that this activity could reflect mental functions. "Nobody, least of all Berger's associates, expected him to make a great scientific discovery," wrote Raphael Ginzburg, a young doctor who acted as one of Berger's EEG research subjects.

Perhaps stemming from the distinct lack of enthusiasm from his fellow scientists, Berger waited until 1929 to publish the first paper—"On the Human Electroencephalogram"—about his findings. By then he had developed the world's first electroencephalograph and had already performed hundreds of EEGs, including more than fifty on his own brain.

EEG is like a "read-only" PDF file; it shows the activity taking place within your skull but doesn't alter it in any way. The discovery of a noninvasive way to eavesdrop on brain function upended our understanding and treatment of brain ailments, and physicians now use the technology Berger developed to detect conditions like epilepsy, sleep disorders, and brain trauma. But identifying different patterns of brainwaves by frequency was only a jumping-off point for EEG. Current technology lets us pinpoint the brain regions where activity is taking place, and maps the way this activity syncs and de-syncs throughout the cortex. Sophisticated machine learning detects the tiniest fluctuations—far tinier than we could see looking at an EEG tracing with the naked eye—to extract meaningful data. All of this activity is analyzed by mathematical models and algorithms to derive patterns that correlate to thoughts and commands, allowing us to assess auditory processing, language recognition, and a host of emotions—excitement, interest, stress, engagement/boredom, attention, and relaxation—along with cognitive and performance metrics. Far from looking at waves on graph paper, this is more like a 3-D visualization of the brain. And it's all done in real time.

Despite today's upgraded technology, EEG still has limitations. Even when millions of neurons fire together in the brain, from the outside the electrical activity they produce registers as only a tiny blip. First, the impulses have to penetrate the meninges, three layers of thick tissue that protect the brain. From there they have to pass through your skull, your scalp, and finally your hair before arriving at the electrodes. This is why EEG performs best when there are tsunami-like waves of neuronal activity in the brain. Imagine you're a drone hovering hundreds of feet in the air over a football arena. You can easily make out the mass exodus from the stadium after the game is over. But it's much harder to detect a lone fan heading to the concession stand at the end of the third quarter. EEG picks up major, not granular, activity in the brain.

Rodrigo discovered this when he began training for his Formula 1 race car endeavor. He quickly realized the computer wasn't reliably differentiating between his thoughts of "turn right" or "turn left." He had to find a way to create big waves in his head; little ripples wouldn't do the trick. So he ramped up his inner wave machine by adding thoughts aimed at activating his senses—vision, taste, and touch—to his commands. As he thought about accelerating the race car, he also envisioned celebrating a soccer goal. As he thought about turning right, he imagined eating something delicious. To the command "turn left," he added the remembered feeling of holding the handlebars of a bicycle. It worked. The computer picked up the rising swell of these combined thoughts and translated them into action.

The faintness of the electrical emissions isn't the only thing that makes it difficult for EEG technology to capture our brain's signals—there's also all the other noise in our heads. The human brain is far from a peaceful place. While our thoughts are creating beautiful brainwaves that ripple through our cortex, a host of other things are creating electrical activity as well. Every time you smile, frown, or raise your eyebrows, for example, this muscle movement launches a cascade of electrical activity that can interfere with our ability to listen in on those brainwaves. Just think of how hard it is to hear your spouse asking you a question when you're in the bathroom with the door shut—and blow-drying your hair, using an electric razor, or taking a shower. Your ears have to pick up the sound waves carrying your spouse's voice through the door . . . while tuning out the whir of the dryer, the buzz of the razor, or the drops of water echoing around you.

Creating a system that could distinguish mental commands from all the other noise in the brain—what EEG experts call "artifacts"—was one of the biggest challenges we faced when designing the EMOTIV headset. To separate the signals from the noise, we built algorithms to detect smiles, grimaces, eye movements, and more. And rather than just filtering that data out, we put it to work, tracking those expressions and using them to activate responses, such as in the game Cora played. Raise your eyebrows, and your avatar soars into the sky. Clench your teeth, and the menacing look causes a group of fairies to vanish from the game screen. Wink, and a character breaks out of the background to acknowledge your presence and wink back at you. It makes the interaction in the game seem more lifelike. Together, these capabilities open the door to unprecedented mind control that goes far beyond video games. The result of all these technical and design advances is the capability of the brainwear to understand not only the mental commands you're giving, but also to register facial cues and associated emotions to get a more complete picture of cognitive performance.

The data these EEG headsets gather can be used in two broadly related ways. On the one hand, we can take the signals received from the brain and use them as *commands* to control electronic devices. The ability to convert brainwaves into digital signals lets us communicate with anything that speaks in ones and zeros. It can be used to create a brain–computer interface (BCI) that allows seamless integration of our analog brains with our increasingly digital world. People are already using the headsets to exert

Star Wars–style mind control over real objects—making a drone hover in the sky, entering text into a computer without touching a keyboard, or, like Rodrigo Mendes, driving a custom-built race car with his mind.

On the other hand, we can use these headsets to *monitor* our brains with the aim of collecting data about the way they behave. This data can then be analyzed to better understand our brain's functioning—and help us work toward improving it. Being able to see our mental states in action gives us priceless insight, and researchers are already using portable brainwave technology to observe our neurons at work in real-world environments.

Taking Neuroscience Research Out of the Lab and into the World

Imagine if primatologist Jane Goodall had hunkered down in a lab to study caged chimpanzees instead of venturing to Tanzania to observe them in the wild. Our knowledge of these amazing social creatures would be severely stunted.

In the neuroscience field, the vast majority of research to date has come from the sterile lab setting. And although these studies have produced some amazing discoveries, they barely scratch the surface of the human experience. This is partly because of the physical limitations of brain imaging technology—big, bulky, expensive machines that can only look at one brain at a time. Costing tens of thousands of dollars each, and requiring shielded environments to avoid electromagnetic distortion of their signals, EEG systems have long been virtually unattainable outside the research and medical worlds. The time-consuming process of placing dozens of electrodes on the scalp, recording their position, and wiring them to the variety of equipment required to capture and analyze the data made the technology even clunkier.

What has taken EEG out of the lab and ushered it into the NeuroGeneration is a complete retooling of the technology and a reimagination of its design. Today's sleek, wireless EEG devices connect to any computer, tablet, or phone, take only a few minutes to set up, and can be worn on the go. And they can be ordered online for the price of an Xbox console. With their arrival, a new breed of neuroscientists is getting the chance to explore the human brain in its natural environment.

At New York University, Suzanne Dikker is one of these next-gen field researchers. When Suzanne, who combines cognitive neuroscience and BCI art, told me she wanted to head out into the wild—the schools, museums, and theaters of New York City—to crowd-source her experiments, I helped her get set up with our portable EEG headsets. Her goal was to study the social brain, and in particular brain-to-brain synchrony, which refers to the state of literally "being on the same wavelength" with others through brainwave synchronization. Neuroscientists have a lab model to study this kind of human connection, but it generally involves looking at one individual's brain at a time and analyzing how it responds to social or emotional cues, such as by showing the subject pictures of happy and sad faces. Suzanne wanted to explore the way the brain acts in social situations by observing it *in actual social situations*—something that sounds obvious, but hadn't been practical before the arrival of mobile EEG technology.

I checked in with Suzanne to talk about some of her latest research.[6] In one study, she and her colleagues equipped high school students with our EEG headsets and recorded their brainwaves over the course of a semester. She wanted to determine to what extent their brain activity was synced with one another and the teacher. The results? In classes during which students were most engaged with each other, their EEG readouts were most likely to follow similar patterns. Basically, students who were more social with other classmates synchronized more with each other, and students synchronized more with their teacher if they liked her better. These findings might seem obvious, but they reflected the fact that things like social dynamics matter for synchrony, which could be detected even in less structured class situations when there were more fluid social interactions among the students. And brainwave synchronization isn't just a cool EEG phenomenon—it affects how well we process information and sort stimuli when interacting with others.

One particular aspect of the experiment offered an eye-opening insight. "The students were assigned random seats, and before the class started, we told them to turn to the student next to them and engage in eye contact for a brief time," Suzanne explains. "They're high school students, so that was kind of tough at first, as you can imagine," she added with a laugh. Yet just this small amount of eye contact had a big impact: when students looked at each other beforehand, they experienced higher levels of synchrony during class. This was true whether they were involved in a group-learning task or something that didn't involve direct interaction. "Doing something together, even for a few seconds, creates more of a connection," Suzanne tells me.

This simple revelation could have a number of real-world ramifications. Think about a theater performance, movie premiere, or art exhibit, for instance. Could a momentary eye-lock or some other shared moment with another audience member enhance the entire experience? Would this translate into better word-of-mouth reviews—and bigger box-office returns? In the business world, could having employees look each other in the eye for a few seconds before a meeting, brainstorming session, or training activity help ensure that everyone is on the same wavelength? Preliminary results from Suzanne and her colleagues also suggest that team success is indeed reflected in brain-to-brain synchrony, predicting team performance better than teams' own judgments of how well they did. Taking this concept further, could EEG data someday help managers create higher-performing teams based on brain-to-brain synchrony? What if companies used the devices to weed out individuals based on something they noted in their neural data?

There are still plenty of unknowns, and questions for scientists—and ethicists—to explore. But there is no doubt that the new technology that allows Suzanne and others like her to experiment on brains in the real world opens the door to previously unimaginable possibilities—including, for the first time, the ability to scale the collection of brain data.

Getting into Consumers' Heads

Millions of dollars are spent on market research every day. Traditionally, this research has taken the form of focus groups, customer surveys, and other self-reporting methods. But not only are these methods time consuming and costly, they are largely ineffective. The picture they provide is at best incomplete, and at worst inaccurate. That's because market research conducted this way makes two big assumptions:

1. **People are telling the truth, the whole truth, and nothing but the truth.** People actually may provide less than complete and truthful responses for a variety of reasons: their memory is faulty, they are giving answers they think are more socially acceptable, or they want to be seen a certain way.

2. **People know why they do the things they do.** In reality, we don't always know why we do what we do or why we buy what we buy. Asking customers what drove them to make a certain purchase—say, choosing a white car over a red one—is often met with frustrating statements like, "I don't know," or "I don't like red." And there's a huge gap between what we say we want and the

actions we take. Most of us simply aren't aware of the thought processes behind many of our decisions.

Newer strategies like data mining avoid the problems of self-report, but while they can provide information on the who, what, when, where, and how of customer purchasing, they still miss the all-important *why* behind the thought processes that result in a sale.

Since the 1990s, corporations have been exploring "neuro-marketing" as a way to bypass the guesswork and go straight to the source—the brain—to see what's driving consumer choices. This followed a watershed moment in the history of imaging—the arrival of fMRI scanning, which offered an unprecedented view of the functioning brain. It was the beginning of a revolution in the understanding of consumer behavior, according to Professor Olivier Oullier, a neuroscientist I met through the World Economic Forum's Young Global Leaders community, and who now works with me. Considered one of the world's leading experts in consumer neuroscience and neuromarketing, Olivier quickly saw the limitations of fMRI: it's prohibitively expensive and very restricted in terms of scale. You simply can't scan millions of brains. And recording the brains of only a handful of consumers who are lying in a scanner isolated from the purchasing environment doesn't give those trying to understand and market to large segments of the population much to go on. Enter affordable, portable EEG technology, and scalability finally promises to disrupt the marketing world. "The next frontier isn't the brain," as Olivier likes to say, "it's brains, plural."[7]

The ability to tap into the brains of thousands or millions of consumers will reveal patterns unlike anything ever seen before. With a suite of algorithms that detect cognitive functions, marketers and PR agencies can decode the instinctive feelings that compel customers to buy—feelings they may not be aware of themselves. Wondering which of two advertising campaigns will resonate with your audience? Need to decide which product prototype to manufacture? Not sure if you should go with the azure or the cerulean blue for your packaging? EEG can measure consumers' neural responses to stimuli—ads, products, packaging—to reveal a clear winner.

In the late 2000s, a consortium of anti-tobacco associations in the United Kingdom added neuromarketing to their traditional mix of market research methods to determine which of three PSA campaigns (A, B, or C) was most effective. When the marketers asked people via survey which campaign they thought would be most effective, the overwhelming majority chose campaign A. When they looked at the brain responses from these same people, however, campaign B was associated with the biggest increase in activity in their brain's reward system, hinting that they preferred it to A or C. In fact, campaign A produced the smallest reaction and turned out to be the least effective.

In another study, three campaigns were tested, and each campaign included a call to action with a phone number. The phone number that received the most calls? Not the one from the campaign that a surveyed sample declared to be the most effective. Instead, it was from the campaign their brains revealed to be the most engaging.

"Who do you believe, the mouth or the brain?" asks Olivier.

Understanding the gap between what people say and what their brains say—between their stated intentions and their actions—is the key to marketing and PR. After years at the forefront of this fast-evolving field, Olivier has developed a proprietary method to measure that gap thanks to mobile neurotechnology pioneered at EMOTIV. The method first proved itself in a study on sustainable consumption conducted in several countries, including China, India, and the U.K., for the World Economic Forum and some of its strategic partners (Coca-Cola,

Unilever, Marks & Spencer, Accenture, and British Telecom). By combining EMOTIV's brainwear with eye-tracking technology, the multi-country in-store research revealed that, when packaging or advertising are environment-friendly, sustainability lingo ("eco-friendly") was much less effective than action description ("these jeans were manufactured with 50 percent less water than usual")—despite customers declaring otherwise when asked. Presented publicly at the 2014 World Economic Forum meeting in Davos, Switzerland, these findings have since served as a benchmark for the use of mobile neurotechnology at scale to better assess consumer behavior in various segments of consumers, including Millennials.

EEG technology also allows marketers to engage in seamless usability testing known as human-in-the-loop (HITL) to find out how consumers are actually using products. No more relying on customer satisfaction surveys, which research shows can be hopelessly flawed. A 2016 study by Interaction Metrics concluded that about one-third of all questions retailers asked in customer surveys were worded in such a way as to lead customers to give the answers retailers wanted to hear.[8] How is that helping a business? Finding out how customers are actually interacting with products provides useful information that can help you stay one step ahead of the competition. If customers are experiencing high levels of boredom or frustration with a product, you can immediately start a redesign to address those issues. You can also combine brain insights with other biometric sensors, such as eye tracking and heart-rate measurements, to gain a fuller picture of consumer choices. Wondering which products, displays, and signs catch the customer's eye? It's now possible to get quantifiable metrics in real time as a customer is walking through your store, showroom, or venue. Rather than waiting for customers to respond to surveys, which average only a 10 to 30 percent response rate—and, of course, are skewed toward the kinds of people who have the time or desire to respond to surveys—you can potentially receive instant feedback from a much wider group. "Potentially," of course, because there is the question of how consumers will react to what might seem like invasive peering into their brains. And how can businesses assure customers that their neural data will only be used in certain ways—and that it won't be sold to the highest bidder? These are ethical questions that I will explore more fully in an upcoming chapter.

Using Brainwave Technologies to Intentionally Reshape Our Brains

Neuroplasticity, the brain's ability to rewire itself to support neural pathways we use often—and prune those we don't—has both upsides and downsides. Think about how hard it is to forget negative experiences, even if they occurred decades ago. Every time you recall them, the memories are reinforced. Bad habits are hard to eradicate for the same reason. And epilepsy is another example: once a person has a first seizure, the brain lays down new neural pathways to reproduce that event in response to the electrical misfiring.

Enter William "Bill" Bosl. A neuroscientist at the University of San Francisco whom I've known for almost a decade, Bill has been investigating ways to detect brain changes that precede a first seizure.[9] According to the CDC, 1.2 percent of the U.S. population has epilepsy.[10] That's 3.4 million people nationwide, with a total indirect and direct annual cost of $15.5 billion.[11] There are treatments and medicines for epilepsy, but they often have serious side effects, and those who live with this chronic condition face a lifetime of struggles to manage it.

Epileptic seizures are a result of brain wiring that goes awry. Bill thinks if we can identify people at high risk—such as those who have experienced a TBI or a concussion—and monitor them using EEG, we could detect the changes in brain wiring that lead to seizures. With this early warning, we might be able to suppress a first seizure, allowing the brain to heal while preventing the creation of neural pathways to automate the seizure response. This means future seizures might be avoided.

The positive flipside of the neuroplasticity coin, of course, is that you can change your brain for the better by identifying valuable patterns and training your brain to lay down strong pathways to support them by seeking to repeat them. In the NeuroGeneration, EEG-based technology is on track to upend the field of health and wellness. The FDA has approved EEG-based diagnostics for ADHD, and mental health practitioners are already using EEG-based neurofeedback as a therapy for anxiety, PTSD, concussion and TBI, and stroke recovery. Neurofeedback treatments involve using EEG to identify abnormal brainwave patterns, and then training the brain to change these patterns. For instance, we can give the brain an audio or electronic signal it recognizes as "positive" when the new, desired pattern is achieved, or have people perform tasks—such as through games like *NeuroRacer*, as discussed in the last chapter—that support more functional brain states. Providers can also use what they learn about how a patient's brain responds to certain stimuli to treat brain-activity patterns associated with mental problems; music is already being used in this way as a therapy for depression. And there is an opportunity to use software tools with biosensing to create more targeted, individualized therapies and interventions.

The potential for improvements with closed-loop neurofeedback systems is very high, but certain challenges have held back progress. Many mental health professionals get little or no training in neurofeedback, and because of the cost of EEG neurofeedback systems, many practitioners are stuck using antiquated equipment. The science and technology are changing so rapidly in the EEG arena that it can be difficult for providers to keep up. Adopting evolving talk-therapy protocols is one thing, but upgrading equipment and re-skilling with each new neurofeedback technology iteration is a much bigger investment in terms of money and time.

Affordable EEG headsets are not only a huge step in making this kind of treatment more widely available in the offices of mental health practitioners; they are also putting the ability to change our brains directly in our own hands.

The key to avoiding destructive patterns and replacing them with positive mental states is being able to identify them when they occur—better yet, when they are about to—so that we can change our behavior and edit the way we think. This is the basis for cognitive behavioral therapy, a practical and effective form of psychotherapy. But how many of us are so tuned in to our thought patterns and emotions that we are aware of when we are starting down that slippery slope, about to tumble into a morass of negative thinking? Beyond offering us a window into our brain, portable EEG technology presents a dynamic way for us to monitor what is happening and make changes based on what we see. The same way we wear a smartwatch to monitor our heart rate, log our steps, and count our calories to track our physical fitness, we can now wear an EEG headset to graph our brainwaves, monitor our moods, assess our attention, and chart our mental performance.

A single set of principles can be applied to enhancing how our brain performs all sorts of tasks. For instance, we can train ourselves to focus effectively by identifying the factors that contribute to maintaining and increasing attention. Using an EEG headset, it is possible to identify the brain activity that corresponds with a high level of focus and then objectively test which variables affect this. We can add different types of music to our environment and see what impact each has. We can determine the best time of day to work, the optimal lighting levels, the effect of coffee breaks, and the degree to which different distractions detract from our concentration. With all this data in hand we can create and edit environments that are objectively suited to the tasks we want to perform. This is already happening now. The automotive industry is tapping into this technology to develop ways to gauge the attention level of drivers and sound an alert or stop a car if they begin to nod off. Air traffic controllers are turning to brainwear to help them maintain laser focus in the face of high-stress situations.

In the very near future, EEG headsets will go even further, by offering seamless integration between the analog (your brain) and the digital (any technology) to control your environment for you. Your relationship with your digital assistants—think smartphone, Siri, or Alexa—will be far more symbiotic. Say it's 6 PM and a potential major client asks you to storyboard an advertising campaign for a meeting the following day. To hit the deadline, you'll need to get "in the zone" and stay there. If your headset already knows the environmental settings that put you into that magic "flow" state, it can read your brainwaves, detect changes indicating your attention is straying, and optimize your surroundings to help you maintain that flow. Your focus is waning? Need an energy boost? Your headset will sense this, brighten the lights in your office, and automatically hit "play" on the music that drives you. You won't have to think, "Hey, I should turn up the lights," or "Maybe I should listen to some music." The brainwear will do it for you.

Just as your headset will be able to detect if your attention is waning, it will also be able to focus on signs of stress and either adapt your environment or alert you to change your attitude. In our modern society, we've conquered many of the physical epidemics that used to plague us, such as malaria and smallpox, but we've replaced them with something just as insidious—stress, which the World Health Organization has called the twenty-first-century epidemic. Our fast-paced, always-on world has unleashed a barrage of mental health and cognitive disorders that threaten our existence. The global economic burden of mental illness reached a price tag of $2.5 trillion in 2010 and could skyrocket to $6 trillion by 2030.[12] Factors such as loss of income due to unemployment and a reduction in global output may contribute to the costs associated with mental illness. It adds up to more than the anticipated costs of cancer, diabetes, and respiratory conditions combined. Stress is at the core of much of this, and is also increasingly recognized as a leading cause of physical illness.

The problem with stress is that it's hard to recognize the signs until you are suffering the ill effects. You can't step on a scale and see that your stress levels are on the way up. The toll stress takes, however, can be devastating on personal, professional, economic, and societal levels. People miss work. Productivity takes a hit. Corporations pay the price in healthcare benefits. National economies feel the drag of a sick populace.

If your brainwaves show that you're becoming stressed, your headset can communicate seamlessly to your digital devices to temporarily stop the buzzing, chirping, and pinging from notifications. It can dim the lights, switch to a more soothing playlist, launch a five-minute mini-meditation program, or prompt you to go for a ten-minute walk outside. No more guesswork on your part.

This technology will be a game changer in terms of achieving sustainable high-level performance. Just imagine how much more you could accomplish if your environment automatically adapted to your needs. Of course, the potential won't be lost on corporate leaders, either. Could there be a day when employers require workers to have brainwear? How would employees react to that? Would they see it as a bonus geared to their well-being, or would they view it as an invasion of their privacy?

The Brainwaves of Monks

For decades, people have been trying to decode the secrets of peak performers. What is it that makes these people able to reach the highest echelons while others struggle to get by? People who want to get ahead study superperformers' habits and routines, listen to their words of wisdom, and adopt their advice. But if it were as simple as incorporating a few new everyday habits into our lives, everybody would be at the top of their game. Something is still missing. The truth is, even superperformers may not be aware of the brain processes behind their actions—and their success. What if we could tap into the brains of the most successful CEOs, the most innovative inventors, the most creative artists, the greatest scientific geniuses, and replicate their thought processes for our own gain?

At Plum Village, Europe's largest Buddhist monastery, located near Bordeaux in southwest France, some two hundred monks and nuns weave mindfulness into all their daily activities—walking, eating, gardening, and working—and enjoy periods of silence and meditation several times a day. Thousands of novice meditation practitioners from across the globe visit the monastery every year to experience the joy and peacefulness of a mindful life.

In 2015, several of the monks and nuns traveled to San Francisco, where their teacher, Thich Nhat Hanh, was seeking treatment after suffering a stroke. One of these monks, Phap Linh, whom some, including me, call Brother Spirit (in Vietnamese, "Linh" means "spirit"), was investigating alternative therapies for their teacher and had heard about EEG neurofeedback. He contacted me to find out more about our equipment and came to my office for a demonstration. I was honored to meet him and excited to demonstrate our brainwear. Wearing his brown monk's robe, Brother Spirit sat quietly in my office as I adjusted the headset. It was easy to place the electrodes on his scalp because, like the other monks at Plum Village, his head was shaved. Dealing with hair is usually one of the trickiest parts of getting a good connection.

I flipped on the system and the EEG measurements popped up on my laptop. I did a double-take. Something was wrong. Really wrong. I look at a lot of brains—I've seen several thousand of them by now—and I had never seen anything like this.

Brother Spirit's brain . . . did not look normal. With our EEG device, "normal" usually means starbursts of colors—fiery red, bright turquoise, sunny yellow, and calming deep blue—flashing throughout the brain. It's like an ever-changing, pulsing light show, something you might see at a rave or electronic dance music festival. But Brother Spirit's whole brain was showing only deep blue delta waves, the slow waves typically seen during sleep. And yet he most certainly was *not* asleep.

I told him there must be a glitch with the equipment, so I just kept talking to him as I tried to figure out what was wrong and fix it. No luck. Everything seemed to be in place and in working order. Then, as I ran a few quick diagnostic checks, Brother Spirit started talking to me, and his brain moved swiftly into the beta frequency associated with active thinking—what I had expected to see in the first place.

"Oh, it's fine now," I told him. But then he stopped talking, and his brain shifted back to delta waves again. This happened a few more times before it finally dawned on me: there wasn't anything wrong with the equipment.

"Are you doing that on purpose?" I asked.

"Doing what?" Brother Spirit responded.

"Whenever you stop talking, the screen goes dark," I said, explaining that this indicated his whole brain was lowering its activity and frequencies. I asked him to do it again, to stop talking, and the same thing happened. "What are you doing when you aren't talking?" I asked.

"I'm doing what Thay [my teacher] taught me to do whenever I'm not talking—bringing my mind back to my breath and my body, to the sensation of sitting in this chair, to the feeling of my feet on the ground," he said.

"So, when you're feeling your breath and body, you're not thinking?"

"Right."

"And you're doing that all the time you aren't talking?"

"Well, maybe not *all* the time, but our teacher has encouraged us to try to do it as often as possible. That's our training."

Brother Spirit's brain was unlike any I had ever seen before because it was perfectly quiet, with none of the typical "noise" usually visible on an EEG. With most people, getting them to empty their mind of thoughts is a challenge. There's so much incessant chatter in between our ears. I've seen people who are capable of lowering their brainwave frequencies for a few seconds, but none were able to sustain it like this. Brother Spirit's years of meditation and mindfulness had vastly transformed the way his brain functioned.

I was blown away. As I showed him how the equipment works, he seamlessly slipped in and out of thinking and non-thinking states. His masterful command of his brain and thought processes shocked me. He got a kick out of seeing his brain activity, too.

"It had a funny effect on me," he said. "Thay always said this is a powerful practice, that it can quiet the mind . . . That inner voice is often comparing, judging, self-criticizing, and has an anxious tone to it, and it can stress you out. There's a general belief that you can't do anything about it, that you have to live with that voice. What our teacher taught us is that it isn't that hard to quiet that voice. Seeing the objective measures of it on the screen was really interesting for me."

Brother Spirit wasn't raised in a monastery. As a child growing up in England, his brain was formed in the modern world. He was accepted to Cambridge University at age seventeen, immersing himself in science, music, math, and philosophy. But his scholarly path took an abrupt turn the following year, when his mother died unexpectedly from an aneurysm. "Everything changed. I couldn't study. I couldn't focus. I really fell apart," he said during an interview for this book.[13] Feeling lost and adrift, he stopped going to classes and failed his year-end exams. When a classmate invited him to come along on a summer holiday to Plum Village, he thought, "Why not?"

The visit proved to be a transformative experience for the scientific-minded student, who had long believed that humans are just "atoms and particles bouncing off each other meaninglessly." By the third week, his entire belief system had been upended by the teachings of Thay, and mindfulness and meditation became the most important things in his life. About eight years later, in 2008, he was ordained as a monk. Brother Spirit's story shows that his ability to calm his brain wasn't something he was born with; he cultivated the skill through his practice.

Brother Spirit assured me his brain wasn't that special and that any of the Plum Village brothers or sisters would be able to empty their minds the way he did. He invited me to see for myself, and so I paid a visit to the house in San Francisco where they were staying. It was the San Francisco residence of Marc Benioff, founder and CEO of Salesforce, who is a big believer in the power of meditation. Each of the monks and nuns tried on the headset and, just as Brother Spirit had predicted, all were able to control their brain activity just as he had. The monks quickly decided to have some fun with the technology and began challenging each other to test their control even further. While one of the monks was wearing the headset, the others tickled, teased, and jumped up and down in front of him in an effort to be as distracting as possible. But they couldn't sidetrack him from his focus on his breath and body. It was a sight I'll never forget.

Brother Spirit traveled back to Plum Village with the headset so he could give a demonstration to his fellow monks and nuns. In the monastery, standing in front of them, he put the brainwear on his head and wondered if he'd be able to pull off what he'd done in my office. "I wasn't sure if I could do it with thirty-five people looking at me," he told me later. But he could, and he proceeded to control and showcase various parts of his brain. Just by thinking about it, Brother Spirit was able to intentionally activate or calm brain activity in specific regions. After working in the EEG brain enhancement arena for over a decade, I have to say that what he was doing is physically impossible. Impossible! This wasn't just pushing or pulling a virtual cube. This wasn't making an avatar fly in a video game. This wasn't making a drone hover. This went beyond driving a race car with your mind. He was willfully controlling the fluctuations of electricity within different areas of his brain. This awe-inspiring demo proved just how much untapped power we hold. We really can learn to control our brains, and we are only at the tip of the iceberg in terms of what we can do with them.

Of course, most of us don't have the time or inclination to spend hours a day in mindful contemplation. Some 18 million adult Americans practiced meditation in 2012, according to the National Health Interview Survey,[14] but are they getting the results they seek? There is no shortage of scientific research on the mind-enhancing benefits of meditation—stress relief, heightened attention, improved planning, reduced anxiety and depression, neuroprotection from cognitive decline—but how much time do you need to devote to it to see changes in brain activity? To gauge its effectiveness on you as an individual, however, you mostly have to go by your gut feelings. Do you feel like you can focus better? Do you feel like you can filter out distractions better? Do you feel less stressed? Unfortunately, feelings don't tell the whole story. But just as Brother Spirit was intrigued by the objective measurements seen on his EEG readout, you can use this technology to quantify your own practice. With portable EEG monitoring, you can get rigorous feedback that lets you gauge your progress. This same concept can be applied to any mental state you want to achieve or cognitive function you want to improve.

EEG, AR/VR, Analog Astronauts, and the Leap to Humanistic Intelligence

In recent years, tech prognosticators and the media have been hyping the coming arrival of the "Next Big Thing"—augmented reality/virtual reality (AR/VR). Global revenues for the AR/VR market are expected to jump from $11.4 billion in 2017 to nearly $215 billion in 2021, according to the latest update from the International Data Corporation.[15] But what most have yet to grasp is that mobile EEG brainwear has the potential to make this market even bigger and more powerful in terms of experience. The neurofeedback that EEG provides dovetails with AR/VR, which creative industries are already using to offer mind-bending, immersive experiences in video games. With EEG bridging our analog brain to the Internet of Things, the possibilities are staggering and go far beyond entertainment and video sectors.

In the near future, EEG-fueled AR/VR apps and software will open up new potential in the health and wellness sector as well. Just think, for someone like Cora, a doctor could one day prescribe an AR/VR computer game to enhance her physical and cognitive rehabilitation. Healthcare professionals may also recommend an app to treat depression or prescribe music for epileptic seizures. And as we all become more comfortable with tech wearables—AR/VR glasses, headphones, headsets, and caps, for example—EEG technology can be integrated into these environments. If someone is already seeing things through an AR/VR lens that has wireless communication, it's very simple to add a few EEG sensors that would bring brainwave activity into this cloud of data. Your augmented, virtual world will become even more mind-blowing.

Blending EEG sensors into AR and VR settings turns out to be the necessary step for taking full advantage of these technologies. Right now, you have to press a button, make a certain gesture, or say a word for the information that appears in your smart glasses or VR headset to unfold, disappear, or otherwise react. Seamless integration of AR/VR will require, at the very least, that a Yes/No mental command be available. This way, without saying a word or moving a muscle, you will be able to choose among the options being offered simply by thinking.

The future power of EEG combined with VR is already unfolding. Just ask Dr. Susan Ip-Jewell, a space physician/scientist, visioneer, innovator, and "Astropreneur." The president of Mars Academy USA and AvatarMEDIC, she integrates exponential technologies in experiential learning by forming and deploying crews to analogous environments—that is, locations on Earth that have features similar to situations in space. "Analog astronauts" like Susan are conducting immersive, real-time missions in some of the most inhospitable geographic areas across the globe—from the frozen terrain in Antarctica to the blistering, sunbaked deserts in California and Utah—to simulate life on Mars. The missions to these austere, extreme environments are part of Mars Academy's multi-year NEAMAE Project (Nepal, Everest, Antarctica, Arctic, Africa, Americas Mars Analog Astronaut Exploration Expeditions). She and the analog astronaut crews live in isolation in these Mars-like environments for weeks, months, or even a year at a time. Their missions involve conducting scientific exploration as well as testing human behaviors and cognitive performance. That's where our EEG headsets come in.

I checked in with Susan in 2017 to find out exactly how they're using the technology.[16] On some of these analog missions, she has integrated the EEG brainwear with a VR training system designed to teach non-medical crew members—engineers, scientists, and artists—how to perform telesurgery and tele-anesthesia. On a real mission to Mars or in a futuristic human settlement there, teaching individuals with little or no medical training to handle health emergencies could mean the difference between life and death. To simulate this scenario, Susan's team uses a software program that creates a virtual operating room with a virtual patient they endearingly call "AstroMan." AstroMan's blood pressure, heart rate, and other bodily functions are constantly monitored, and if his levels go beyond certain parameters, alerts start beeping the same way they do in an OR on Earth.

For this experiment, the analog astronauts don their VR/EEG headsets, watch a telesurgery protocol, and then have to memorize it. If AstroMan has a medical emergency, they have to administer tele-anesthesia and perform telesurgery under stressful time constraints. The EEG portion of the headset tracks their brainwaves to assess their cognitive performance as they perform the exercise. The goal is to determine if multiple practice sessions in this virtual scenario enhance cognitive performance and memory retention under pressure. Susan expects the data, which is still being collected, will offer clues to enhance VR training for Mars missions. These findings will also have implications for more earthly training endeavors.

Brainwear may turn out to be a must for life on Mars, but here on Earth the idea of wearing an EEG headset is just beginning to catch on in the zeitgeist. Brainwear is starting to pop up on TV—*Two and a Half Men*, the *Bachelor* franchise—and as a fashion statement on the runways during Paris Fashion Week. As EEG wearables continue to evolve, they will eventually become as commonplace as wearing a smartwatch. When this happens, the technology will become embedded into the daily fabric of our lives, and wearable computers will become an integral part of the human brain, a concept known as humanistic intelligence. This signals one small step toward brain enhancement, one giant leap into the NeuroGeneration, when people like Cora will be able to use their mind to navigate the world around them, and when we just might be able to hack into the minds of experts—with their permission, of course—and follow their neural pathways to success.

CHAPTER 3

GETTING WIRED

Changing the Brain with Electromagnetic Interventions and Sound Waves

I N A SMALL APARTMENT IN BERLIN, a young musician took a seat on a piano bench and locked his eyes on the sheet music before him, a prelude by Bach. Originally from Spain, twenty-three-year-old classical music student Mario Marzo started taking music lessons at age six. He's spent thousands of hours practicing everything from Mozart to Rachmaninoff, but he had never played this particular prelude before.

Ready to begin, he slipped a pair of headphones over his spiky brown hair, switched them on, and let his fingers fly across the keys. As he played, electrodes in the band of the headphones sent low-level electrical currents into his brain's motor cortex. A video camera in the corner of the room captured the scene as it unfolded—all part of a homemade experiment to see if neuro-stimulation could help Mario speed up his learning process.

A few months earlier, Mario had been surfing a Spanish news-paper's website when he came across an intriguing article about headphones that zapped the brain with transcranial direct current stimulation (tDCS) to enable athletes to perform better—run faster, exert greater force, master complex movements more quickly, drive a golf ball farther, and so on. The article focused on the benefits for sporting types, but Mario couldn't help but think about all the physical work he did as a pianist—attacking the keys with his upper body, maneuvering the pedals with his lower extremities, and improving his dexterity to increase the speed at which his fingers danced through the notes. The amount of coordination it all requires is astounding. "At some point, musicians are athletes, too," Mario told me over Skype one day in 2018, from the apartment where he'd conducted his experiment.[1] "We train every day as athletes. We need physical precision, endurance, and accuracy, just like athletes do."

After reading that article, Mario wondered if the device could help him, so on a whim, he reached out to Halo, the San Francisco–based company that had created it. They were thrilled to assist Mario with his experiment. "When I decided to do the trial, I wasn't skeptical or a fan [of the technology]. I was just interested," he says.

To make the test as accurate as possible, Mario wanted to figure out a way to establish a baseline so that he could judge the difference in learning *au naturel* versus with the headphones. He headed to the local music library, where he selected two Bach preludes that were comparable in complexity, in the same key—and, most importantly, new to him. For six days, twenty minutes a day, he would plan to practice one of the preludes without the headphones; the next week he would tackle the other prelude with the device. Learning a piece of music by heart takes time, but once you've committed it to memory, Mario explains, you no longer have to think about the notes. In fact, he says, if you did try to pull all the notes from your mental iPod as you performed, you wouldn't be able to play it. The key to mastering a piece is motor control and muscle memory. "The fingers just know where to go because I've been practicing," Mario says.

After the fifth day of working on the first prelude without the headphones, his results were on par with what he'd expected. He'd memorized the piece, but didn't feel comfortable with it. He wasn't *feeling* it yet. He'd planned to do a sixth day, but the headphones had arrived, and the lure of the FedEx box proved too tempting for him.

Mario switched to the second prelude while wearing the device. In the first twenty-minute practice session, he noticed a difference—not in accuracy or speed, but in that it felt like he had more time, almost as if everything had slowed down, making it easier. The biggest change came on the second day. On the video he produced of his experiment, he explains, "When I sat down to play, I felt that I already knew the piece. The fingers went where they had to go. It was precise. I had most of it by heart. It was impossible. It's impossible that I know the piece in only twenty minutes."[2] Ultimately, he tapped into the fluidity he wanted in just three days—much faster than normal.

Inside Mario's head, his neurons were being primed by the mild electrical pulses that tDCS was producing, making them more likely to fire. As neuroscientists like to say when explaining neuroplasticity, neurons that fire together wire together. Making neurons more likely to fire in synchrony as he learned a new piece and created new neural pathways meant those connections were reinforced. Priming neurons with tDCS creates a sort of hyperplasticity, which when paired with high-quality training can deliver results faster.

Since that first remarkable challenge, Mario has taken his experiment to the next level by enlisting other musicians to complete similar trials with the device. And he's launched a podcast where they can share their insights, sensations, and experiences. So far, he says the results range from a 20 percent improvement in twenty minutes to a 300 percent total improvement. What he's finding is that not only is each brain different, but the learning curve also depends on the instrument. "Some see the learning process go faster," he explains. "Some gain accuracy. With violinists, there's just one melody, so it's better technique they get. Piano is harder to learn, so they gain different things."

Mario can hardly contain his excitement at having a new tool to accelerate learning and performance. "Athletes get new improvements all the time—shoes, balls, shirts to help them sweat less or sweat more," he says. "Our last improvement was about twenty years ago when we got a new chair with oil so it's smoother. For us, this is a very big deal." But for some of the musicians he's talked to, the notion that an external device is giving them a leg up in their performance rattles their confidence. Mario calls it an ego thing. "It means they have to admit there was something they weren't great on. It was the headset that helped. They didn't do it alone."

When I ask him if he thinks using the device is cheating, he lets me know I'm far from the first person to pose this question, and it's obvious he's given it a lot of thought. "Is it cheating if both my parents are musicians?" he asks. "Is it cheating if I come from a rich family and have a better piano? . . . In a completely pure world, yes, the device gives me more facilities. And yes, there are some great musicians whose parents weren't musicians and they had a bad piano. But really, it's no more cheating than having a Steinway."

He has a point. When you consider the extreme biohacking that goes into making an elite athlete—exacting diets and fine-tuned supplements, VR training platforms, smart uniforms that relay real-time performance data to coaches, heart rate variability trackers, and a litany of other devices and technologies—neurohacking doesn't seem that different. In fact, it seems like the logical next step. Mario believes this neurotechnology has the potential to transform the way millions of students learn to play an instrument. Could tDCS and other electrical stimulation methods emerge as the next must-have training tools for performers? In Mario's opinion, "This is the future of classical music." And it could be the future of much more.

The Halo Effect

One of the brilliant minds behind those headphones is Brett Wingeier, the chief technology officer and co-founder of Halo Neuroscience in San Francisco. He and I connected years ago when I was hoping to harness the power of his EEG knowledge, and we've remained friends ever since. With a PhD in biomedical engineering and years of postgraduate research in brain physics and EEG, Brett has a long history in the neurotech space. At a company called NeuroPace, he helped navigate the labyrinthine FDA process for a neural implant to prevent epileptic seizures. That journey began in 2001 and took more than a dozen grueling years before approval was granted in 2013.

Following NeuroPace's FDA success, Brett shifted gears and joined the cadre of neurotech entrepreneurs by co-founding Halo Neuroscience. He had been following the intriguing findings about the effects of tDCS and found himself drawn to this emerging field. "There was all this really amazing research being conducted," he says when I ask what inspired him to set off in his new direction.[3] He was fascinated by the way tDCS seemed to improve learning. Who wouldn't want that, he thought. "But all of it was being conducted with devices that were basically wires and sponges and beige boxes that sit on your lab bench with big blue knobs, and eight seven-segment LED readouts and things like that." He kept thinking that with such a noninvasive technology, there was an opportunity to create a consumer-friendly product that went beyond the beige box.

While some tech innovators may have raced forward full speed to release a product, Brett and Halo co-founder Daniel Chao, the former head of business development at NeuroPace, took a step back and approached it first as a research project. "We're conservative medical guys here," Brett says. "Nothing is ever real until you see the results for yourself." Step one—creating their own beige box with wires and sponges and attempting to duplicate some of the amazing research that was coming out of scientific labs. They succeeded, reproducing the results achieved by multiple labs showing that tDCS can improve neuroplasticity and increase the rate of motor learning.

"It soon became apparent that movement really was the best first application," Brett says. "It's very quantifiable, the mechanism was relatively well understood, and there are existing markets in sports and music." Another reason that targeting motor learning made sense is that the brain's motor cortex lies directly beneath the area covered by the band of a pair of headphones. That was it! They could toss the beige box, forget about creating some complicated apparatus, and create a pair of brain-changing headphones. "It's something people could wear to the gym," Brett says.

That's when the research stage gave way to a hard-charging race to production, and the team at Halo began racking up sleep debt. They had to come up with proprietary electrodes—what they called "Primers"—that would work with all types of hair. Without those, they'd be back in the dull world of beige boxes, sponges, and straps. But by the end of 2015, the relentless team had a prototype, and was shipping it to elite athletes for trials.

In a four-week study with the U.S. Ski and Snowboard Association, ski jumpers wearing the Halo Sport headset achieved a 13 percent boost in propulsion as well as an 11 percent gain in smoothness compared with a control group.[4] In a five-week trial at Michael Johnson Performance, a training organization founded by the four-time Olympic gold medal sprinter of the same name, a group of twenty elite college athletes performed a series of squats and jumps to measure lower-body explosiveness. Half of the athletes used the Halo while the other half did not. Those using the Halo achieved a 12 percent gain in lower-body explosiveness over baseline compared with a 2 percent gain in the control group.[5]

With these results under their belt, Brett and his team rocketed out of stealth mode and began shipping the world's first mass-market, consumer, noninvasive neurostimulator. Since then, the San Francisco Giants, the USA Cycling team, and the U.S. Naval Special Warfare Command (a.k.a. Navy SEALs) have all begun using Halo's tDCS headphones to ramp up performance. And since Mario uploaded the video of his experiment with that Bach prelude, plenty of professional musicians have taken the dive.

But if you think all it takes is slipping on a pair of tDCS headphones, camping out on the couch, and having new talents downloaded into your brain, think again. "You don't put on the headset and—*bam!*—you know a Beethoven piece," Brett cautions. "If you use it while sitting on the couch, you're probably just going to get better at sitting on the couch. And if you pair it with bad training, that's probably going to be counterproductive." His team makes it very clear that results come from a two-part process: neurostimulation combined with high-quality training. There's no way to get out of practicing. You still have to put in the work, although you may be able to do that work faster and get better results.

You also can't expect to dial in a consumer tDCS product to improve precision in your non-dominant hand or increase explosiveness in just one of your legs. That kind of specific targeting is the next frontier. For now, any noninvasive neurostimulation has to pass through the skull, which diffuses the currents. And devices are one-size-fits-all. Brett is hoping to change that and is actively researching the use of bio-signals and performance data to produce more individualized results. With Brett's background in the medical device field, he can't help but see the enormous clinical potential for usable tDCS devices as a way to accelerate stroke rehabilitation or physical therapy. "So much of any kind of rehab is relearning patterns, and your brain learning to work around the injury," he says. Scientific research already shows tDCS can be beneficial for regaining language and motor control following a stroke,[6] but right now it is used for this only in health-care settings. Making these benefits available via something a patient can take home could be revolutionary. Eliminating the need to go to a facility would not only make it easier to accelerate the pace of therapy with more frequent sessions; it would open up treatment options for those who can't access traditional therapy because of disability, cost, or living in a part of the world with few physical therapists. In some cases, a physical therapist might remotely supervise patients.

The benefits for motor learning and physical performance are only the beginning. tDCS affects electrical activity in two ways depending on the kind of current applied: it can make neurons more likely to fire or inhibit them from firing. As technology improves, the ability to promote some activities and tamp down others could lead to more focused applications. On the horizon is tDCS aimed at improving cognitive control by stimulating the prefrontal cortex, the region associated with attention, focus, and multitasking. "The science there has just been evolving through all this, and we are really looking forward to diving into that field," Brett says. Research shows tDCS can improve language learning[7] and math skills[8] and may be useful in the treatment of chronic pain,[9] depression, and other mental disorders.[10,11] According to a 2012 study in *Current Biology*, it may even enhance social skills.[12]

The U.S. military has been keenly aware of this technology's potential for years. With funding from those sci-fi fans at DARPA, researchers affixed tDCS devices to about one hundred participants to see if it could improve their ability to detect concealed objects.[13] The volunteers immersed themselves in a virtual reality environment known as "DARWARS Ambush!" in which they had to detect bombs that were hidden by or disguised as deceased animals, roadside trash, barrels, boxes, cars, and toys, as well as zeroing in on snipers and suicide bombers in concealed locations. Published in *Neuroimage* in 2012, the study found that participants who received low-current tDCS improved their accuracy by over 14 percent, while those receiving the full current boosted their accuracy by more than 26 percent—an 87 percent increase in performance accuracy compared to the low-current pulses. Citing its safety, low cost, and effectiveness for improved learning, the study authors suggest tDCS with neuroimaging could have real-world application.

A subsequent series of experiments at Wright-Patterson Air Force Base in Dayton, Ohio, provided evidence that tDCS has the ability to enhance multitasking capabilities, skills military personnel like drone operators and air crews require in abundance.[14] In a report on the findings, scientists explain how military personnel can experience a slump in performance, saying, "With an increasing demand to process and respond to critical information, the mental and physical demand endured by the human operator can become overwhelming."

Tech Sergeant Brandon Shapiro, one of those who underwent testing with tDCS at Wright-Patterson Air Force Base, admitted that it felt a little weird at first, but reported feeling more focused in the second set of tests, administered after stimulation.[15] "I do feel like a superhuman . . . It's definitely like X-Men," he says, in a video appearing on *AirmanMagazineOnline*. "I'm looking to have some superpowers, maybe wake up in the morning and having some new cognitive abilities."

In the video, Dr. Andy McKinley, the leader of the Non-Invasive Brain Stimulation team at the base—and the U.S.

military's lead in-house tDCS researcher—says one of the goals is to help subjects sustain attention for long periods of time. So far, the tests show enhancement of attention with tDCS that lasts for about six hours. McKinley explains why this is important: "When you enhance for attention, you can also improve things like learning and memory. The more you can pay attention during training, the more you can encode and retrieve later." In addition to better focus and attention, the test subjects also experienced a boost in energy and minimized fatigue, even if they were sleep deprived.

What if you could slip on a tDCS device to increase your attention span so you could perform better in college or on the job? Given the impressive results of testing so far, this application is bound to make its way from the military into civilian life. Brett's working on it at Halo, and a handful of other neurotechnology firms have entered the field to produce consumer products that use tDCS to enhance brainpower. I can't wait to see how they drive this technology forward, to wire us for success.

Supercharging the Brain with Magnetic Currents

The idea of treating the brain and body with electrical current has its roots in the ancient world. As far back as two thousand years ago, the Greek and Roman physicians Hippocrates, Galen, and Scribonius Largus were plastering torpedo fish, which produce an electrical charge, onto people's scalps to relieve headaches.[16] And ever since scientists like Hans Berger became aware that cognitive functions were the result of electrical impulses, researchers and clinicians have been seeking to alter the brain by affecting its electrical activity. Most of us are familiar with electroconvulsive therapy (ECT), or "shock treatments," which use powerful electrical current to induce seizures and alter the brain's function. ECT is still used in psychiatric settings, generally reserved for people with severe mental health conditions, but it is a blunt tool with serious side effects. Today, new technologies like tDCS and transcranial magnetic stimulation let us affect the delicate electric activity within the brain without sending massive jolts of brain-scrambling electricity into the skull.

Anthony T. Barker, an English physicist at Royal Hallamshire Hospital in Sheffield, reported the first demonstration of transcranial magnetic stimulation (TMS) in 1985.[17] Barker and colleagues connected what looked like two giant ham radios stacked on top of each other to a doughnut-shaped coil, which they placed against a volunteer's scalp. When they flipped the power on, their device sent painless magnetic pulses to the volunteer's motor cortex, firing up electrical activity in their brain and producing twitching in a specific area of their hand. That little twitch paved the way for transformative medical therapies and futuristic potential that is still being explored, and Barker was honored as the recipient of the inaugural International Brain Stimulation Award in 2016 for his pioneering work in TMS.[18]

While most tDCS therapies are still in the research stage, TMS has leapt into the mainstream, having accumulated a mountain of compelling evidence and gaining FDA approval. It turns out those ancient physicians were onto something with those electrically charged torpedo fish. An analysis of nine trials with 183 chronic pain patients showed the use of repetitive TMS (rTMS) reduces pain, and it is now widely prescribed as a treatment by doctors at leading research hospitals, including Johns Hopkins.[19] Zapping the brain with magnetic pulses has also emerged as an alternative for treating depression in people who don't see improvements from conventional drug therapy. The American Psychiatric Association has been recommending FDA-approved courses of TMS as a second-line therapy since 2010.[20] In 2017, the National Network of Depression Centers' rTMS Task Force brought together a group of seventeen expert clinicians and researchers to review 118 studies on rTMS in an effort to create guidelines and share best practices for the technology's use in clinical settings for the treatment of major depressive disorder. Their landmark conclusions were published in a 2018 issue of the *Journal of Clinical Psychiatry*.[21] "These consensus recommendations provide a foundation for integrated healthcare teams to implement evidence-based rTMS antidepressant practice," says one of the paper's authors, Dr. Shawn M. McClintock.[22] If you suffer from depression, and Zoloft, Wellbutrin, or Lexapro isn't doing the job, your psychiatrist might recommend that you get wired up for a series of rTMS sessions.

I've been fortunate enough to get to know some of the most forward-thinking experts in the brain stimulation arena. After I sold my first company, one of the friends I met with to brainstorm ideas about what I wanted to do next with my life was Dr. Allan Snyder, and for good reason. With a mass of unruly silver curls peeking out beneath a sideways baseball cap and round, wire-rimmed glasses, he looks the part of a mad scientist, and he has been pushing the boundaries of brain stimulation for more than two decades. The director of the Centre for the Mind at the University of Sydney & Australian National University, Allan firmly believes that we all possess hidden genius within the folds of our brains—and that neurostimulation is the key to unlocking it.

He points to people who have acquired savant skills later in life as the result of injury to the brain's temporal lobes, frontotemporal dementia, or stroke. Look at Jason Padgett, a former party-loving jock and college dropout who became a mathematical virtuoso after getting kicked in the head during a mugging. In his memoir, *Struck by Genius*, Jason describes how the violent attack left him with an out-of-the-blue ability to comprehend math and physics in addition to altering the way he saw the world.[23] Since the night of his mugging, Jason sees everything—from the leaves of a tree to the water pouring out of a faucet—as complex geometric patterns and repeating fractals. And he's able to draw those intricate geometric images by hand, creating award-winning artwork despite a lack of any artistic talent prior to his brain injury.

It's people like Jason who sparked Allan's quest to tap into that brain potential—*without* the injury. In a paper in *Philosophical Transactions of the Royal Society B*, Allan hypothesizes that "savants have privileged access to lower level, less-processed information, before it is packaged into holistic concepts and meaningful labels . . . Owing to a failure in top-down inhibition, they can tap into information that exists in all of our brains but is normally beyond conscious awareness."[24] For years, he's been performing cutting-edge research using breakthrough technology in an effort to allow ordinary people that same privileged access to the raw data in our brains. Basically, this involves stimulating the brain with electricity in such a way as to turn *off* certain areas that typically inhibit our ability to notice detail in favor of quickly assigning meaning—an important cognitive skill for survival that lets us filter out the unimportant and make lightning-fast judgments, but that also may make it harder for us to see the parts of a whole. When we see a tiger, we register the concept of "tiger" speedily to enable us to make our getaway, but we aren't necessarily seeing the tiger itself in a way that, for example, would allow us to draw it.

I've spent hours with Allan, listening to him talk about his fascination with savants. One day, he told me about finding inspiration in something written by neurologist and bestselling author Oliver Sacks, who was a Foundation Fellow at Allan's Centre for the Mind. In *The Man Who Mistook His Wife for a Hat*, Sacks details the astonishing mathematical abilities of a pair of autistic twins. Although they had IQs of sixty and could barely do basic arithmetic, they possessed an uncanny ability to accurately guess the number of matchsticks that fell on the ground.[25] In

2006, Allan and fellow researchers at the Centre for the Mind decided to see if they could re-create this savant-like numerosity skill in average people. They enlisted twelve participants and applied low-frequency rTMS to inhibit activity in the left anterior temporal lobe, which is believed to be involved in semantic memory—our acquired knowledge about the world, such as words, numbers, the names of famous historical people, and general facts. The research team then showed the participants random collections of elements on a screen and asked them to guess how many there were. Immediately following rTMS, ten of the twelve participants improved their ability to accurately guess the number of items, which ranged from 50 to 150. And as the effects of the magnetic pulses receded, eight of those ten became worse at guessing. According to Allan's study, which appeared in the journal *Perception*, the probability of this happening by chance alone is less than one in a thousand.[26]

Allan acknowledges that brain stimulation, or inhibition in this case, might be more effective in some people than in others. There are any number of factors that might affect this, from the orientation of an individual's brain sulci (grooves) to the amount of myelination they have (myelin is the fatty tissue that surrounds synapses and enhances the speed of connectivity). Plus, the electrical pulses of rTMS have to travel through the hair, skull, cerebrospinal fluid, and meninges before reaching the brain, making it challenging to deliver to an exact location, which is what's often needed to inhibit a specific function while leaving others intact.

Allan's belief in superhuman skills lying dormant within all of us inspired his invention of a "creativity cap" that he hopes will be the answer to unleashing them. For this device, he swapped out rTMS technology for tDCS, which can be miniaturized to fit in the cap and is better for consumer use. With tDCS it's just 1.5 milliamps of electrical current—barely a blip—pulsing through the brain. Allan, who has acted as a guinea pig by testing the cap on himself numerous times, says it feels like a tiny tingle on the scalp. For a 2012 study in *Neuroscience Letters,* he put the cap to the test with twenty-two participants as they attempted to crack a well-known brainteaser known as the nine dots puzzle.[27] The puzzle takes the form of nine dots arranged in a three-by-three square; the challenge is to connect all nine using only four straight lines, without picking up the pen from the paper. According to Allan, fewer than 5 percent of people can solve the puzzle.

For this study, he divided participants in two groups. All wore a creativity cap and were given nine minutes, broken into three-minute segments, to try to solve the puzzle. In one group, the creativity cap was turned on during the second three-minute segment, while in the other group it remained off the entire time. Not a single one of the participants was able to solve the puzzle in the first three minutes. In the second three-minute segment or immediately thereafter, however, five of the eleven participants wearing the activated creativity cap—more than 45 percent of them—managed to figure out the solution. None of the people in the other group did.

These successes have Allan fired up about the potential to upgrade our creativity and problem-solving abilities. "Isn't it fascinating that we're going to enhance creativity not by exciting part of the brain, but by turning part of the brain off?" he asks in a documentary called *Automatic Brain: The Magic of the Unconscious Mind.*[28] Despite his intriguing findings in the lab, a consumer-based creativity cap that unlocks savant-like art, math, and problem-solving abilities has yet to find its way to market. But with all the big thinkers in the neurotechnology space, it may not be long before it does. I think it would be fitting if it looked like one of the baseball caps Allan loves to wear.

The Sound of a Cure: A Medical Thriller

John Grisham calls the short novel he wrote in 2016 "the most important book I have ever written." That's heady stuff coming from the author who has dominated the legal-thriller genre for three decades, with 300 million copies of his forty books in print. He says this slim volume—available for free on Amazon and his website—is more important than *The Firm*, which sent him rocketing to superstardom in 1991 when it spent forty-seven weeks on the *New York Times* bestseller list and was made into a hit movie. More important than *The Pelican Brief* or *The Client*, both of which hit number one on the *NYT* list and were made into movies of their own. And yet, it's probably one you haven't heard of. *The Tumor* isn't a legal thriller—far from it. It's a fictional tale of how a medical technology can cure disease with sound. I took a dive into the story on a flight to Vietnam and marveled at the potential we have to radically transform the way we treat a wide range of diseases.

The Tumor introduces us to a healthy thirty-five-year-old banker named Paul, who is diagnosed with a tumor about the size of an egg in his brain's right frontal lobe.[29] Consistent with today's standard of care, doctors recommend surgery to remove it. Paul undergoes the procedure: the surgeon drills holes into his skull and uses a power saw to remove a portion of the bone before attacking the tumor, sucking out as much of it as possible without damaging any surrounding tissue. Following the surgery, the tumor is analyzed and Paul gets the devastating news that he's one of about 22,000 Americans diagnosed each year with glioblastoma, a deadly variety of brain cancer that—even with treatment—typically results in death within fifteen months.[30] To give him as much time with his young family as possible, Paul undergoes months of debilitating treatment, including chemo, radiation, and repeat surgery, at a cost of hundreds of thousands of dollars. He spends these months mostly in pain and deteriorating health, and his story doesn't end happily ever after.

Then we fast-forward to an alternate future in 2025, in which our hero Paul is diagnosed at the same age with the same deadly tumor. Only this time, instead of surgery, he opts for a futuristic noninvasive treatment called focused ultrasound. This treatment requires no drilling into the skull, no power saws, no suctioning of the tumor, and no hospital stay. The way it works is analogous to using a magnifying glass to focus beams of light on a point to burn a tiny hole in a leaf. With focused ultrasound, multiple intersecting beams of ultrasonic energy are focused noninvasively on a target deep in the brain with extreme precision, sparing adjacent normal tissue. Where each of the individual beams goes through the tissue, it has no effect. But at the focal point where the beams are concentrated, it can destroy cancerous tissue. It can also enable chemo to be delivered via nanoparticles, which encase the drug and prevent it from having an effect until released by the ultrasound beams. Focused ultrasound is used to activate the chemo only in the area of the tumor, where it is needed, eliminating the systemic effects. When the aggressive tumor recurs, Paul undergoes another focused ultrasound treatment to remove it, turning his condition from a near-immediate death sentence into something chronic. Paul not only extends his life without the side effects of brain surgery, chemo, and radiation; he also does it for a fraction of the cost.

Sound like a futuristic fairy tale? It isn't. This technology is available today and has already been used to treat about 200,000 people worldwide for a variety of brain-related conditions as well as other physical diseases. One of them is Kimberly Spletter. Kimberly was forty-four when she began noticing something strange happening to her body. Her left toes began to curl under, and the fingers on her left hand were going numb. Eventually, she was diagnosed with Parkinson's disease, which led to dyskinesia, the uncontrollable tremors most people associate with the condition. Kimberly had been an avid cyclist: "No matter how bad of a day I was having, I could get on my bike and go for a ride and it would bring a big smile to my face and a sense of independence."[31] But the shaking in her legs got so bad that it forced her to give up riding her bicycle and even interfered with walking.

The medication she was prescribed to control her symptoms, levodopa, came with a laundry list of nasty side effects—everything from dry mouth and diarrhea to forgetfulness and confusion.[32] Medications for Parkinson's have even been linked to unwanted psychological behaviors, including pathological gambling, hypersexuality, and compulsive eating and shopping.[33] In one study, two patients with no prior history of gambling suffered losses of more than $60,000.[34] As for Kimberly, the formerly active woman hit a low when she attended a wedding and her dad asked her to dance, but her foot and back were cramping so badly, she couldn't get out of her chair. Even though they weren't her own nuptials, it made her think of the traditional father-daughter wedding dance. "It's every little girl's dream to have that dance with her dad," she says, "and I couldn't do it."

Then her neurologist suggested she consider participating in a study on focused ultrasound. She would be one of the first people in the U.S. to be treated for dyskinesia with the technique, which would use ultrasound beams to make thermal lesions deep in the brain's globus pallidus or subthalamic nucleus to interrupt the circuits involved in the condition. After researching the procedure and comparing it to other treatments available, including more invasive options like deep brain stimulation, she decided to go for it.

On the day of her procedure in 2015, Kimberly was filled with nervous excitement. She had to be off her medications, which meant her symptoms were flaring up so badly she couldn't walk and had to be taken to the hospital in a wheelchair.[35] Her short-cropped hair was shaved and a frame was clamped to her smooth scalp. She could feel the pressure mount as the frame was tightened like a vice and attached to the table to keep her head perfectly positioned. Then she was slid into the tube-like MRI machine for a series of fourteen sonications, or "zaps" as she calls them.

Without anesthesia, Kimberly was awake as the sound waves penetrated her skull and focused on brain cells in the basal ganglia, a region involved in movement. With each zap during the four-hour procedure, she felt intense heat, but no pain. She could also feel her symptoms diminishing. After each zap, she was pulled from the MRI machine for neurological tests.

When Kimberly emerged from the machine after the final treatment, the nurses wheeled in a bed to take her to the recovery area, but the clinical trial director waved them off, telling Kimberly, "No, get up. You can walk." Once the doctors helped her to her feet, she was thrilled to find that she could indeed walk to the recovery room, taking bigger strides than the shuffling steps she'd managed for the past few years. "It was purely a miracle," she says. A few short weeks later, Kimberly was already back to biking and even ran—not walked!—in a 5K to benefit Parkinson's research.

Ten weeks after her focused ultrasound treatment, a revitalized Kimberly jogged confidently onto the stage at a TEDx event in Charlottesville, Virginia, to share her story. Standing with her on that stage were John Grisham and Dr. Neal Kassell, the founder and chairman of the Focused Ultrasound Foundation, an organization dedicated to accelerating the process of bringing focused ultrasound from the research world into the clinical mainstream. Neal, a neurosurgeon, knows all too well just how long and arduous the process of introducing disruptive technology can be, thanks to his experience bringing another medical innovation into the mainstream—Gamma Knife.

Neal discovered the breakthrough technology—think of it as brain surgery without the scalpel—in 1977 on a trip to the Karolinska Institute in Sweden where it was first developed, at the time the home of the only device in existence. Surgeons there could use Gamma Knife to deliver up to 201 beams of precisely focused radiation, killing cancer cells in brain tumors, controlling non-malignant tumors, and treating vascular and functional disorders of the brain.[36] Neal wanted to bring this alternative to conventional brain surgery to the U.S., but the process proved to be painstakingly slow, taking over a decade to make it to the University of Virginia, where he was practicing. Once he saw firsthand how effective this noninvasive technology was at treating brain conditions that had previously required a major operation, he was sure it was a glimpse into the future. But Gamma Knife's potential paled in comparison when he discovered focused ultrasound.

I first heard Neal tell the story of his discovery when I was in Dubai for the annual meeting of the WEF's Global Future Councils in 2017. With white hair, glasses, and a calm demeanor, Neal looks like someone you would trust to operate on your brain. I've sat through so many talks by physicians touting new technologies, and some of them get so wrapped up in the nuts and bolts they lose the human element of their discovery. Not Neal. With a dry sense of humor and a knack for translating technical details into decidedly human terms, he kept me and the rest of the council enthralled.

He traced his inspiration to a day in about 2005, when he was operating on a patient with a ruptured aneurysm. His usual neuro-anesthesiologist wasn't available, so a very talented cardiac anesthesiologist filled in. As they started to talk, the anesthesiologist mentioned that he was using microbubbles and ultrasound to measure blood flow in the heart muscle, and suggested Neal could probably do the same thing to measure blood flow in the brain. Neal followed his advice and began doing it in the lab.

Not long after that, he was driving home from the hospital when the proverbial light bulb flashed on. *I'll bet there's a way to use ultrasound plus or minus microbubbles to treat patients with otherwise untreatable brain tumors*, he thought. For the earnest surgeon who had been conducting neurosurgery research since 1962, it was an "aha!" moment. He thought he had finally landed on an idea worthy of a Nobel Prize. "I raced home . . . jumped on the internet and discovered that it was a Nobel Prize–winning idea. It just wasn't mine." He may not have been the one who originally came up with the concept, but Neal was still revved up about its possibilities.

It felt like déjà vu, reminding him of how excited he had felt when he learned about the Gamma Knife. "The difference is focused ultrasound had at least one, maybe even two, orders of magnitude greater importance than the Gamma Knife. That's when I really got excited," he told me when I checked in with him to find out more about the technology.[37] Neal says it's a game-changer that's highly disruptive to traditional surgery, radiation therapy, and drug therapy. To date, researchers have pinpointed eighteen ways focused ultrasound can be used on tissue—compare that with radiation as used in Gamma Knife, which has just one. Where the ultrasound waves converge, for example, doctors can destroy tissue, stimulate the body's immune response to a tumor, or deliver drugs in high concentrations. Because of this versatility, focused ultrasound has the opportunity to treat a wide variety of medical conditions. Ten years ago, the medical community had identified only three conditions it could treat. Today, there are more than one hundred. In the brain, it has the potential to treat Parkinson's disease as you saw with Kimberly,[38] brain tumors as Grisham recounted in his book *The Tumor*, Alzheimer's disease, epilepsy, and essential tremors as well as mental health conditions like obsessive-compulsive disorder and depression.

Canadian researchers made a groundbreaking finding when they demonstrated that MRI-guided focused ultrasound can be used to temporarily open the blood–brain barrier (BBB) in patients with Alzheimer's disease. Their study, the first peer-reviewed report of its kind, appeared in *Nature Communications* in 2018 and was reported at the Alzheimer's Association International Conference in Chicago.[39] As Neal says, the ability to safely and repetitively open the BBB is "really, really exciting." The capillaries in the brain have unique properties to prevent toxins and infectious agents in the blood from penetrating the brain and damaging its precious neurons and synapses. But the powerful BBB also prevents many potentially disease-fighting drugs from aiding the brain. Being able to temporarily open the BBB could establish the means to safely administer drugs to the brain that it previously blocked. This could mean hope for people with Alzheimer's disease and many other conditions. "Not only can you get drugs into the brain," Neal adds, "but you can also get stem cells into the brain." Alas, injecting stem cells into the brain via focused ultrasound remains in the realm of science fiction for now; Neal reminds me that the technology is in the early stages and that "most of it is aspirational or futuristic."

So far, only five of one hundred applications for focused ultrasound have been FDA-approved—treatments for essential tremor, bone metastases, uterine fibroids, benign prostatic hyperplasia, and prostate cancer. The treatment for essential tremor is now being reimbursed by Medicare, and some commercial insurance providers are starting to pick up the costs as well. Neal says the technology is at an inflection point, where increased awareness and visibility could lead to rapid adoption of focused ultrasound and open the treatment to exponentially more patients.

That's where people like John Grisham come in. "John is a neighbor and a friend," Neal says, explaining how the former small-town lawyer/suspense writer ended up on the foundation's board of directors. Neal's passion and persuasiveness probably had something to do with it, too. "Several years later, we were at a board meeting and he was scribbling away," Neal says. "We thought we had lost his attention, but in fact, what he was doing was outlining *The Tumor*. It was entirely his idea."

Grisham thought he could use his brand and storytelling skills to spread awareness about the potential of focused ultrasound. "I have found nothing so far, no cause, issue, campaign, project, with the potential of touching as many lives as focused ultrasound. Not just touching, but improving and saving," Grisham says. "The technology is revolutionary. The challenge is getting there."

Why does it take so long for these technologies to be adopted? Neal laments the glacial process, citing Gamma Knife, which was invented in 1950 but didn't become mainstream until the mid-1990s. The evolution from lab device to standard of care involves a number of tremendously difficult steps involving what Neal calls a "bewildering array of organizations in the ecosystem, many of which have their own agendas and timelines." Layered upon that are daunting impediments including lack of awareness among physicians and patients, the need for rigorous scientific evidence of a device's efficacy and safety, and the costs associated with implementing new technology. According to Neal, physicians as a group are notoriously slow to adopt new technologies. He points to the vicious turf battles that occur between the different medical specialties because new technology notoriously disrupts referral patterns and fundamentally changes their practice. For neurosurgeons, it's like going from performing surgery to something akin to operating a video game. He admits, "If you're trained as a microsurgeon or an open surgeon like I was, there's nothing as satisfying as operating on the brain." That being said, he adds that new noninvasive technologies provide better results for patients with fewer side effects, which provides a different kind of satisfaction for surgeons. After all, helping patients is why most people go into medicine in the first place. But even once those hurdles to adoption are cleared, there remains the pile of red tape innovators must wade through in the FDA process, and insurance companies that they must convince to reimburse new procedures.

What keeps Neal motivated to push focused ultrasound to the finish line? "Every month we shave off that process translates into a reduction in death and disability and suffering for countless people," he says. "It's one of the few technologies that fulfills the criteria of the holy grail of both improving outcome and decreasing cost."

Neal isn't the only innovator on a quest to find or develop neurotechnology that fits that description. Some of them, as you'll see in the following chapter, are speeding up the search by acting as human guinea pigs.

CHAPTER 4

I, ROBOT

Brain-Controlled Bionics

LESS THAN FOUR YEARS AFTER becoming paralyzed, famed blind endurance racer Mark Pollock traveled to a lab at UCLA, where he geared up in a robotic exoskeleton while electrodes attached to the skin on his back fired electric pulses to excite his spinal cord. He took one step, then another, and then hundreds more. "It felt like my legs were coming alive," he explained to me.[1]

The occasion marked a notable move forward for Mark, and a giant leap into the future of bionic humans. Had Mark temporarily become a version of the *Six Million Dollar Man* from the 1970s TV show? Yes, his physical body was augmented thanks to the machine, but he remained unquestionably human. His remarkable achievement signaled how the once impossible can be made possible in the NeuroGeneration when we create a symbiotic relationship between the biological brain and a machine.

This chapter explores humanity's relentless quest to create technologies that work with the brain to make damaged bodies whole again. A "cure" for paralysis will likely involve a neurotechnology component, and individuals like my friend Mark Pollock as well as government agencies like DARPA are working hard to accelerate the development of bionics that perform like the real thing.

The Road to Robotic Walking

Inspiring doesn't even begin to express how remarkable Mark Pollock's journey has been, but I didn't realize just how extraordinary his story was until I joined him in a brain health and healing arts workshop session for WEF's 2014 Young Global Leaders Summit in Beijing. For this particular summit, we were staying at the Commune by the Great Wall, a collection of contemporary villas designed by twelve renowned Asian architects. Within these exquisite walls, we shared stories, insights, and the wisdom we've gained from our experiences. I was captivated as Mark recounted his astonishing expeditions despite being blind, the heart-stopping fall that left him paralyzed, and his mission to fast-track a cure for paralysis.

When he finished telling his story, everyone listening had been deeply moved. I personally felt a surge of optimism that if anyone can drive progress toward enabling people with spinal cord injuries to walk again, it's Mark. I desperately wanted to catch up with him to find out more about his story and the promise of healing paralysis in the NeuroGeneration.

Mark's path to taking those steps in a bionic suit at UCLA was an arduous one. At the age of three, the rambunctious Irish lad was diagnosed with extreme shortsightedness. A detached retina at age five left him blind in his right eye, but Mark managed deftly with his good left eye. An excellent athlete, he earned a spot as a rower while he was a student at Trinity College Dublin, and was aiming to one day compete for Ireland at the World Championships.

As he neared completion of his Business Studies and Economics degree in 1998, he started noticing some blurring in his good eye—another detached retina. Doctors operated to try to save his vision, but it was too late. At age twenty-two, Mark realized he was unlikely to see again. His life as he knew it stopped short. In complete darkness, he grappled with his identity. If he wasn't the strapping athlete, who was he? In his memoir, *Making It Happen*, he wrote, "The horror of being relegated to the 'disabled' bin was too awful for words; I felt my life was over. Everything that had defined me was gone forever, and I didn't know myself any longer."[2]

Mark strove to find a new identity as he relearned how to walk the streets, use a computer, and read a watch. He returned to school to earn a master's degree and launched a business, but he still craved the endorphin rush and feeling of accomplishment that came from athletics. Up until then, he'd been making excuses why he couldn't get back in the racing shell, as the rowing boats are known on the competition circuit. As he sees it, in life there are primarily two types of people—those who make excuses and those who make it happen. He was going to stop making excuses and start making it happen.

Within a few years, he was back in the racing shell, rowing with a former college teammate as his guide and winning silver and bronze medals at the Commonwealth Games. The intoxicating rush of competition spurred Mark to push past the limitations of blindness. He began training with a friend for the Gobi March, a 155-mile, six-stage ultramarathon in the Gobi Desert in Mongolia. He'd never run a marathon before. Could he possibly do six in one week? He toughed it out on the rocky terrain and made it to the finish line. Then Mark began using his adventures in motivational speeches, finding a voice that resonated with audiences. If he heard of a challenge in which he could compete, it made him more resolved to take it on and find a way to contribute to his team. He raced to the North Pole, enduring −60°F temperatures and stumbling in the deep snow about a dozen times. He became the first blind person to complete the highest and lowest marathons in the world: the Tenzing-Hillary Everest Marathon and the Dead Sea Ultra in Jordan.

On the tenth anniversary of losing his sight, he embarked on what would be his greatest achievement yet—the hazardous Amundsen Omega 3 South Pole Race, inspired by the epic 1911 race between Norwegian adventurer Roald Amundsen and British explorer Robert Falcon Scott to be the first to reach the South Pole. (Amundsen proved victorious, while Scott's journey ended in his tragic death.) Over forty-three days, Mark and his team endured howling winds, temperatures that dipped below −50°F, and extreme exhaustion as they cross-country-skied over six hundred miles while pulling sleds that weighed two hundred pounds. Reaching the Pole and planting his flag at the finish line marked a high point for the adventure racer. Mark was settling into his new identity, and life was looking good.

Then the unthinkable happened. One month before his wedding in 2010, he tumbled out of a third-story window onto the concrete below, fracturing his skull and breaking his back. He remembers only bits and pieces from that night . . . someone telling him not to move . . . someone stapling the back of his head. In the hospital, he got the devastating news: the broken bones of his back had punctured his spinal cord and he was paralyzed from the waist down.

For an athlete who had spent so many hours of his days building his muscles and shaping his body into a fine-tuned machine, he had never thought much about its intricate nervous system. His doctors explained the basics about how the brain and spinal cord work together to form the central nervous system. The snakelike spinal cord is jam-packed with bundles of nerves, cushioned by cerebrospinal fluid, and housed within a protective bony structure—the vertebrae. It acts like a two-way messaging system between the brain and the peripheral nervous system, which comprises all the nerves that branch out to the limbs, skin, and the rest of the body's organs. Sensory neurons take in information from the external environment and fire it up the tube-like spinal cord to the brain for processing. Motor neurons take information from the brain and shuttle it down the spinal cord and out to the body's muscle fibers to initiate movement.

In people with spinal cord injuries, the neuronal information highway between the body and the brain is disrupted. As his doctors explained it to him, Mark had just joined a group no one wants to belong to, one of the quarter- to half-million people worldwide who suffer a spinal cord injury each year.[3] Roughly 1.5 million individuals are living in the U.S. with a spinal cord injury.[4]

"Spinal cord injury strikes at the core of what it means to be human," Mark said in a 2018 TED Talk with his fiancée, Simone George, a human rights lawyer. "It had turned me from my upright, standing, running form into a seated compromise of myself."[5] His doctors sent him to a rehabilitation gym where he logged hours and hours each day learning the basics of getting in and out of a wheelchair and learning to live life in the device. "In the hospital, the agenda is to get you to accept the status quo that you'll live the rest of your life in a wheelchair. I know why they're trying to do that. You have to learn to live life in a wheelchair, get a job, maintain relationships, and accept that it may never change. But I also needed a hope side to the equation."

He found that hope in a book someone gave him to read in the hospital. Norman Doidge's seminal book on neuroplasticity, *The Brain That Changes Itself*, introduced Mark to the groundbreaking concept that the brain could heal and rewire itself. Mark couldn't help but wonder if the science behind this revelatory discovery about the brain could extend to the rest of the nervous system. Could the spinal cord heal itself, rewire itself, and relearn to send messages to and from the brain? With his doctors and therapists, he toed the line and worked on his wheelchair skills. But inside, the hope for a cure told him he needed to get his body as fit as possible. "Even if it didn't cure me, it was surely going to keep me in the mix for any innovations that came down the line," he says.

It didn't take long for the hope side of the equation to come along in one of those innovations. In 2012, Mark flew to San Francisco, the headquarters of Ekso Bionics, to try to walk in one of the firm's robotic exoskeletons. The futuristic bionic contraption looked like it had come straight out of a Hollywood sci-fi movie. A team of trainers strapped his legs and feet into the battery-operated device. Attached at the wearer's waist and chest and secured at the back with a cable linked to an overhead beam, the exoskeleton's motor whirred quietly. With the aid of a walker, Mark hoisted himself up to a standing position. For the first time since his fall, he was back at eye level with others and taller than his dad, who was taking in all the action. "After an accident, you're pretty much either lying down or sitting down. So to rise up, even just to stand there, is scary and exhilarating all at once," Mark recalls.

Then, as instructed, he shifted his weight to one side as the trainer pressed a button, triggering the device to flex at the hip, bring up his knee, lift his foot, and let it fall back to the ground—his first step! Even though the bionic suit was doing 100 percent of the work, Mark couldn't help but feel a bit like Tony Stark in *Iron Man*. It was a small victory that stoked his hope for a cure.

Mark became the first person in the world to own a robotic exoskeleton outside a hospital or research setting, and back home in Ireland he set about training regularly with the device. In what would be the first of many collaborations he and Simone would forge, they connected the San Francisco engineers with Dr. V. Reggie Edgerton, a true visionary at UCLA who was doing groundbreaking work involving neurostimulation to activate the spinal cord in people with paralysis. The director of UCLA's Edgerton Neuromuscular Research Laboratory had conducted a study in which electrodes were implanted in four spinal cord injury patients. When the devices were stimulated, the participants were able to voluntarily move their legs—flexing at the hip, bending their knees, and wiggling their toes.[6] Edgerton wanted to try a noninvasive option, placing electrodes on the skin, a method he calls transcutaneous enabling motor control, combined with a drug that acts as a neuromodulator. Adding an exoskeleton to the mix was the final ingredient. The UCLA team and the San Francisco engineers knew about each other's work, but as so often happens when scientists are deep into their breakthrough research, they hadn't connected. That job fell to Mark and Simone.

After connecting the two teams and creating a collaboration, the couple traveled to UCLA for the study, which would show if neurostimulation and pharmacology could give Mark the sensory ability to voluntarily assist in taking the steps rather than just being a passenger in the exoskeleton. Each day, he had one electrode placed near the middle of his back just below the line where his sensation starts to fade, and another one near the bottom of his spine where he can't even feel his skin. But with the stimulation activated, Mark could feel tiny pulses. "It was like a little hammer hammering on your back," he recalls. Then the researchers got Mark into the bionic suit, switched it from "max assist" to "variable assist," and asked him to hit the hallway. As the exoskeleton helped power him along, Mark could feel the meat of his muscles and a sense of tingling just below the skin. His lower body was handling more of the effort, and the bionic exoskeleton intelligently adjusted the amount of assistance it provided.[7] Mark was voluntarily moving his legs!

Biofeedback confirmed it. Walking in the robotic device without the stimulator, Mark's heartbeat would get up to about 110 beats per minute. With the stimulator turned on, his heartbeat shot up into the 150 to 160 bpm range, and he worked up more of a sweat. But was his brain in on the action? For Mark and the scientists, the connection between the commands in his brain and the muscle contractions remains a mystery. "If I think 'left quad,' we don't know whether in fact I'm contracting my left quad or my right calf," he says. Scientists are still working to discern whether someone like Mark, who is relearning how to walk, should be concentrating really hard on the movements or not be thinking at all. Mark points to athletes who have real-time access to datasets and biofeedback monitors. Runners have heartbeat monitors as well as time and distance trackers. Cyclists have cadence, speed, and diameter tracking readily available. "I need all of that kind of stuff," Mark says. "It just happens that I probably need bio-feedback from the muscle groups in real time to know if when I think 'right quad,' I'm contracting [my] right quad or if I have to retrain my brain to think 'left leg' when I actually need to contract my right. All of that wearable technology—some of the stuff I need doesn't exist yet." Someone needs to invent it. Mark sees a need for real-time neural biofeedback using EEG technology to be built meaningfully into robotic technologies, alongside virtual reality and augmented reality.

Racing for a Cure

Back when Mark was still lying in a hospital bed after his fall, he came to a realization: "There was a very real possibility that with the combination of blindness and paralysis I just wasn't going to be able to work." In light of the potential expenses ahead, a friend launched the Mark Pollock Trust and set off an initial wave of fundraising to defray the ongoing impact of Mark's catastrophic spinal cord injury. With that stability, Mark was able to get back to his motivational speaking gigs fairly quickly.

He was one of the lucky ones. "In Western Europe, seven out of ten people [with paralysis] never work again, and four out of ten work below the poverty line," he says. In the U.S., only 15.5 percent of people with paralysis are employed, compared with 63 percent who are not living with disabilities, according to the Christopher & Dana Reeve Foundation. A 2013 study by the foundation found that nearly 42 percent of people who are paralyzed say they are unable to work, and 28 percent of households with a paralyzed person earn less than $15,000 annually.[8] Meanwhile the estimated lifetime costs for someone with a spinal cord injury can reach close to $5 million.[9] Nationwide, spinal cord injuries cost about $40.5 billion annually.[10] The economic strain compounds the already devastating physical toll.

As these realities sank in, Mark's race for a cure was no longer just a personal one. And as he had to do after he went blind, Mark once again had to create a new identity for himself. He reminded himself of a quote from the philosopher Friedrich Nietzsche: "He who has a why to live can bear almost any how." He had read it in the inspiring book *Man's Search for Meaning* by Viktor Frankl, a psychiatrist who spent years in a Nazi concentration camp but was able to cope with the horrific situation. Mark had found his why: he was still racing, only now he was applying all of the same principles of expedition racing—going to the gym, training, putting a team together, and raising finances—to finding a cure for paralysis.

In this light, Mark's focus shifted to exploring the intersection where humans and technology collide by searching out the most innovative scientists, surgeons, technologists, and foundations. In his efforts to meet with the most brilliant minds in the field, he has linked up with innovators who are experimenting with nerve bridging, in which surgeons use peripheral nerve grafts and scaffolding to bypass the spinal cord injury site in combination with transplanting stem cells to enhance regeneration. The concept is akin to heart bypass surgery that detours around arterial blockages to get a patient's blood flowing more freely again. A 2014 study in the *Journal of Spinal Cord Medicine* involving fourteen patients with paralysis found that nerve bridging (or nerve communication) improved motor power in the hips, legs, ankles, and toes, but it wasn't enough to enable them to stand upright and/or walk unaided.[11] Mark has also connected with innovators investigating optogenetics, a technology created by my friend Ed Boyden at MIT and Stanford University neuroscientist Karl Deisseroth that uses light-sensitive proteins to switch individual neurons or groups of neurons on and off.[12] In 2010, *Science* magazine called optogenetics the "breakthrough of the last decade."[13] The technology is so new, there remains a shortage of research on how it might aid spinal cord injuries. However, early animal studies have found that optogenetics can restore function to muscles after paralysis, according to a 2015 review of the research in *Asian Spine Journal*.[14] Mark's expedition also included seeking out technology innovators and philanthropic organizations, including the Christopher & Dana Reeve Foundation, where he and Simone currently serve on the board of directors.

Mark says this exploratory mission pointed out several glaring factors that are impeding progress toward a cure. For example, scientists may spend less than 20 percent of their time on their core research activities. The bulk of their efforts goes into chasing grant money, tending to administrative duties, teaching, and traveling to conferences. In addition, those scientists, along with inventors and charitable organizations, often toil away in silos. There's no central hub where experts can easily find each other. That's what spurred Mark and his team to become a catalyst for collaboration, like the one that brought UCLA's Edgerton, the tech stars at Ekso Bionics, and himself together. Since then, he's spearheaded an initiative within the World Economic Forum to connect science and technology startups with capital and expertise. Mark has also facilitated the formation of a $5 million venture philanthropy fund with Silicon Valley ties. And he's creating a centralized hub of experts so they can get out of their silos and forge connections across disciplines, geographic borders, and institutions. "We're at this intersection where humans and technology collide," says Mark. "In that intersection, we're going to find bits of biology, bits of pharmacology, bits of medical devices, and bits of robotics. And in that cocktail, we should be able to find a cure. It's only just a matter of time."

I asked Mark if he believed walking in the exoskeleton with the neural stimulation felt like a major step toward a cure and what that moment was like for him, but he didn't give me the jubilant emotional response I expected. For him, it's all about the endpoint. "Any time I have a win," he says, "I'm always thinking, 'Okay, how can we turn that into a bigger win?'" He compared it to his South Pole expedition. "I had frozen tears as we were skidding into the South Pole. But I wasn't doing that when we were trying to raise the $100,000 to go there, and I wasn't doing that at the start line nor halfway through. I was just doing the race. But when I got to the end, when I got to what we were trying to achieve, I did celebrate that."

Bionics in the War Zone

Two years after the 9/11 attacks in the United States, military intensive care physician and neurologist Geoffrey Ling was proud to serve his country by deploying with the 44th Medical Command (Airborne) to Afghanistan. In the busy combat support hospital, the now-retired army colonel tended to far too many service members who had suffered devastating injuries or had lost limbs to traumatic IED (improvised explosive device) blasts. The soldiers weren't the only ones facing this life-altering fate. "There wasn't a day that went by in our ICU that we didn't see some kid who was missing a hand or arm from an IED," says Geoff, a fast-talking straight-shooter I've known for years through the World Economic Forum and Council on the Future of Neurotechnologies and Brain Science. "If you're missing a hand or arm in that environment, your likelihood of survival, let alone a good quality of life, is dismal."[15]

The mutilation he witnessed was seared into his memory. His patients were outfitted with a standard prosthetic—a model with a hook for a hand that Geoff says is "ugly as sin" and not that functional. He says the 1,650 U.S. troops who have lost hands, arms, feet, or legs since 2001 deserve better.[16] When a person loses a hand or arm, they may mourn not only the absence of the limb but the loss of the ability to easily swing a golf club, wash their own hair, or hold their child's hand.

When Geoff returned back to the States from deployment, he was tapped for the remarkable opportunity to help injured individuals regain their physicality. He got an invitation to join the team of "mad scientists" at DARPA. This Pentagon-led agency is behind some of the world's coolest technological advances. The internet? Thank the brilliant minds at DARPA for that one. Siri? Apple's smartphone assistant originated at the agency. Cloud computing? Ditto. GPS, night-vision goggles, drones? You guessed it. DARPA brings together the globe's best and brightest innovators—scientists, engineers, technologists—with the wildest, most extraordinary ideas and then pours money into the most viable ones in an attempt to make them go from concept to capability . . . *fast*!

The money train is only part of the fast-track process. The agency also streamlines creation by offering regulatory assistance to speed through governmental red tape. The position was ideal for Geoff, a go-getter who as a military trauma physician was used to seeing immediate results. He has no patience for the traditional scientific model, where a researcher makes some wonderful finding in mice, but then it's five to ten years before they do the test in humans. "What kind of rubbish is that?" blurts Geoff.

He seized on his DARPA predecessor's push into the brain–computer interface arena and launched a program called Revolutionizing Prosthetics to create a mind-controlled robotic prosthetic arm with a fully functioning hand. To make it happen, Geoff and his team at DARPA had to hit the ground at an all-out sprint. This was no theoretical research project. "Quite frankly, we don't give a damn about science for science's sake," he says in his rapid-fire manner. "We were actually trying to build the capability for wounded soldiers, and if your research aligned with ours, great. If it didn't, I didn't care who was behind that science, it was irrelevant to my problem."

With troops still losing limbs in war zones, there wasn't any time to waste. First, the team had to define what an ideal artificial robotic arm and hand would entail. They narrowed it down to two key elements. One, it needed out-of-this-world sophisticated engineering so it could handle common, day-to-day functions while still looking like a human arm and hand, because "cosmetics really matter," according to Geoff. Two, it needed space-age neuroscience so people could control it with their brain. On the neuroscience end, he rounded up some of the best minds in the country and teamed them up with engineers and technologists. A veritable brain trust, they went to work.

So Easy, Even a Monkey Can Do It

Prosthetics didn't become widely used in the U.S. until after the Civil War, when some 60,000 soldiers had injured limbs amputated.[17] With each subsequent conflict, advances in prosthetics helped troops regain more functionality, but since World War II they've remained relatively unchanged. Geoff and his team didn't want to make simple tweaks to the existing state-of-the-art model—a myoelectric device with a harness and socket interface that depends on electrical signals from residual muscle for movement. In true DARPA fashion, they looked beyond existing technology and let themselves imagine the capabilities they wanted in an artificial limb. They wanted to venture into *Star Wars* territory with something that would rival Luke Skywalker's cybernetic hand—something that looks like an arm, feels like an arm, and lets you throw a ball or play piano with it. Geoff told the engineers they had two years to make it happen, and the neuroscientists that they had four years to lock down the mind-control function. Their cries of "You're crazy!" and "That's impossible!" subsided when Geoff showed them the money. DARPA invested over $100 million in the project.

On the engineering side, Segway creator Dean Kamen took the lead. As fascinating as the robotics are, I am infinitely more interested in the brain control aspect, and I spent about an hour with Geoff one day in 2018 exploring how they made it happen. Before they could start building an arm that would respond to brain cues, they first had to interpret and understand the electrical signals inside the brain. "We had to decode the brain," Geoff says. "Luckily, I was in the military, and the military has tons of codebreakers." He enlisted some of the military's top cryptanalysts and teamed them up with next-level neuroscientists to do the job. One of their first stops was the renowned Nicolelis Lab at Duke University. In the neuroscience and neurotechnology fields, Miguel Nicolelis is viewed as a real powerhouse, having received the 2017 IEEE Daniel E. Noble Award for Emerging Technologies for his "seminal contributions to brain-machine interfaces." This mastermind embraced Geoff's challenge. Inside the lab, monkeys learned to play a computer game with a joystick while the research team measured the electrical signals firing within the primates' brains. The codebreakers pored over those signals every time the monkeys moved their arms up, down, left, or right, looking for patterns. Over time, they detected recurring signals that allowed them to accurately predict which way a monkey would move its arm. "They broke the code!" Geoff says excitedly, recalling the milestone achievement.

Eventually, Nicolelis deactivated the joystick; as the monkeys maneuvered it, the computer read their minds and moved the cursor on-screen so they could still play the game. The researchers then took away the joystick altogether and restrained the monkeys' arms. As the monkeys looked at the screen, they thought about playing the game and—*voilà!*—the cursor started to move. The monkeys were able to play the game without a joystick and without using their arms. They did it using mind control.[18] As the monkeys' performance improved over time, the researchers noted widespread changes in the frontal and parietal cortical regions of their brains, clear signs of neuroplasticity. The monkeys were laying down new neural pathways for mind control.

The DARPA initiative then headed to Andrew Schwartz's Motorlab, a neurophysiology systems lab at the University of Pittsburgh. There they attempted to determine if a monkey could control a prototype of the robotic arm by using thought. By the end of that trial, the monkey was able to direct the artificial limb with its mind to pick up a piece of zucchini and put it in its mouth.[19] By 2011, they were testing the arm on a human.

Tim Hemmes wasn't an amputee, but he'd had no use of his arms or legs since 2004 when he took his motorcycle out for a ride one evening, swerved to avoid hitting a deer, struck a guardrail, and broke his neck. Leading up to his trial in the Motorlab, surgeons implanted a chip on the surface of Tim's motor cortex that would communicate directly with the robotic arm.[20] When it came time to test the chip, Geoff recognized the importance of the moment and asked the researchers to switch on a video camera to capture the action. "Either his head was going to burst on fire, which would make a cool YouTube video, or the thing would work," Geoff joked in a 2018 keynote at the AngelMD Alpha Conference.[21] In fact, Tim was able to move the arm up and down, give one of the researchers a high five, and even hold his girlfriend's hand. It was a deeply emotional moment for everyone in the lab.

It had taken only two years from concept to produce an engineered prototype. After just four years, they had developed closed-loop nervous system integration, full range of motion, and tactile sensors. And only four years after that, they received FDA approval for the Modular Prosthetic Limb (MPL), which boasts twenty-six joints, seventeen of which can be moved independently of one another. *Bam!* Welcome to the amazing here-and-now, where an amputee can use mind control on a robotic arm to eat noodles with chopsticks, pick up a grape, pour water, and perform so many other everyday functions. With a device like this, independence is no longer just a dream; it's a reality.

Just ask Johnny Matheny. The Port Richey, Florida, resident lost his arm to cancer in 2005 and is the first person to use the MPL outside the lab.[22] For four years, he and a few dozen other men and women have been testing versions of the artificial limb at the Johns Hopkins Applied Physics Lab in Laurel, Maryland. In 2017, Johnny was selected to give it a year-long road test to see how well it works in real life. The researchers want him to push the arm to its limits and report back to them. Johnny's goal? To play the piano before the year is up. That's exactly the type of endeavor Geoff envisioned when he started dreaming up what a prosthetic arm should do. I can hear the pride in Geoff's voice when he talks about how this bionic arm can give people a piece of their life back. In this way, bionics is adding to our humanity, not detracting from it.

The High Cost of Neurotech Bionics

What do all these science faction advances in bionics and neurotechnology mean for the everyday person who's paralyzed or an amputee? What will it take for people to access the technology? Who will be able to afford these sophisticated devices? The DARPA arm will undoubtedly come with a hefty price tag. So will technologies to help paralyzed people walk again. The notion of a simple biological-repair cure for paralysis that allows all bodily functions and processes to return to pre-injury form remains a fantasy for now. As Mark Pollock explains, no two spinal cord injuries are alike, and every patient has individual needs. For example, two people who each fall from a ladder and suffer an injury to the T-10 vertebra might have vastly dissimilar results and respond differently to treatment. A cure that works for one of them may not have the same effect on the other. Mark has come to understand that any form of a cure is going to have to be highly individualized. His vision for the future looks something like this: One patient will go into a clinic and get a combo of soft robotics, neural stimulation, and an EEG device for real-time biofeedback. Another will benefit from nerve bridging, a hard exoskeleton, and a training regimen. And even then, their results may not be similar, and they may have to return for recalibration of the neural stimulation levels, robotics assistance, or training programs.

Who is going to have access to this level of treatment? It's an ethical question we need to address. Mark admits he's one of the lucky ones to be able to have an exoskeleton. He also has one for research purposes placed in a university so other people can access it for a nominal fee. But paying for the robotic unit is just the start. Add in the ongoing costs of physiotherapists required to train people how to walk in the devices and it's not feasible for most people, especially when you consider the dire statistics on unemployment and poverty-level incomes among people with paralysis.

On the flip side, getting people back on their feet thanks to a bio-robotic union could improve their employment opportunities and boost their income. It's a classic chicken-or-egg scenario. Insurance companies have to be convinced that reimbursing these costs is critical to accelerating the progress toward a cure, but providers first want proof of the benefits before they'll pay out. The research remains scanty. A 2013 review in *Ortopedia, Traumatologia, Rehabilitacja* pointed to a dearth of research and concluded there is a major gap for a randomized clinical trial to determine how robotics impact rehabilitation in spinal-cord-injury patients.[23] Mark's trust is catalyzing never-been-tried collaborations to try to fill these research gaps. He's hoping it will have a ripple effect on insurance payouts, job opportunities, increased income, and better health outcomes for people living with these injuries.

Bionics: Beyond a Cure

The concept of an exoskeleton that would allow workers to lift superhuman weights or provide added support to reduce injuries has long tantalized leaders in the industrial space. One automaker has already taken the leap into the future. In 2018, Ford Motor Company rolled out an upper-body exoskeleton vest designed to provide support and reduce worker injuries at fifteen factories worldwide.[24] Imagine screwing in a light bulb or putting away dishes in a high cupboard. Not a big deal, right? Now do it 4,600 times a day, or one million times per year. That's approximately how often some Ford assembly line workers lift their arms for overhead tasks.[25] All that overhead work can result in neck, back, and shoulder pain that can lead to time off and rehabilitation that costs much more than the robotic vest. The exoskeleton vest offers adjustable lift assistance from five to fifteen pounds per arm to ease strain and minimize risk of injury. Other automakers, construction companies, and industrial firms are taking notice and testing the vests as well as other robotic devices. The age of bionic humans is upon us.

And there's more. The technology Geoff's team at DARPA created isn't just about building a mind-controlled robot arm for amputees or people with paralysis. It's about using your brain to control the world around you. When we can do that, the possibilities will be endless. "This means in the future our descendants will no longer be confined to the bodies in which they were born," Geoff says. He envisions a day when humans will be able to see beyond the visual spectrum and wear exoskeletons that allow them to control six robotic arms. "They're going to do things you and I can't even imagine right now," he says enthusiastically. And all those neuroscientists who contributed to DARPA's bionic arm project will be hailed as the pioneers of humans' next evolutionary step.

I can't help but wonder if the revolutionary advances already in motion that are blending biological beings with robotics could lead to superhuman bionics that outperform our natural legs, arms, and eyes. Could we reach a day when people actually consider trading in their flesh and blood for bionic body parts to upgrade their capabilities or their job performance? Could this biological–bionic connection eventually tip so we become more machine than human? And at what cost? Imagine feeling pressured to endure major surgical procedures to get the most advanced bionics so you can keep up with other superhumans. What if something went wrong on the operating table? And what would you have to do when upgrades emerged? Head back into the operating room?

Although these scenarios are still far in the future, I think these are important questions to ask. For now, Mark has no doubt that the bionics that allow him to walk are simply tools; they don't detract from his humanity. He can't wait for a future when bionics help other people around the globe feel able-bodied again. And with bionic eyes on the horizon that can restore blind people's vision,[26] he may actually get to see that future.

CHAPTER **5**

CYBORG NATION

Implantable Technology to
Alter or Enhance Our Senses

W HAT IS A CYBORG? In my view, being a cyborg goes beyond the bionics involved in replacing a lost limb. It involves surgical intervention, often with implantable devices, to help people regain a lost sense or ability, or to enhance the human organism with one or more sensory perceptions or capabilities the average person doesn't have. And it involves technology that relies on some sort of feedback.

Many of us would see no problem with artificial devices like retinal or cochlear implants that help people regain their sight or hearing. However, it's worth noting that the hearing devices remain highly controversial within the Deaf community, with some viewing the technology as a form of forced conformity with the hearing world, reflecting a flawed belief that deaf people need to be "fixed." Nevertheless, cyborgism raises weighty questions. Do humans have a right to self-enhance? Is it ethical? Is it possible to make implant technology accessible so everyone can be a cyborg, or will it be available only to people with financial means?

In this chapter, I will explore a variety of invasive, implantable technologies—from devices that can help us regain lost senses or give us superhuman senses, to a neural mesh intended to allow our brain to communicate directly with computers and tech gadgets—that can elevate humans to cyborg status. You may be familiar with invasive procedures such as deep brain stimulation and vagus nerve stimulation that promise to give people, or cyborgs, the ability to calm tremors from conditions like Parkinson's disease or recover faster from a stroke. I will introduce some of the pioneering scientists behind these advances who are bravely—or unwisely, depending on your viewpoint—experimenting on themselves in an effort to fast-track a path to cyborgism. And I will also pull back the curtain on one of the world's most renowned cyborgs—Neil Harbisson.

When Neil gets dressed, he doesn't choose colors that look good together. He selects his garments by the way they sound. If he's in a happy mood, he dresses in C major—bright pinks, yellows, and blues. When he's feeling blue, he opts for B minor—turquoise, purple, and orange. Completely color-blind, Neil hears colors as musical tones thanks to a computer chip implanted in his brain. A flexible antenna extends from the implant in the back of his skull to his forehead where an "eyeborg" transmits colors to his brain, which interprets them as musical tones. Looking at the colorful clothes in his closet can create a virtual symphony in his mind.

With his extrasensory antenna, Neil considers himself a cyborg, a trans-species individual who is part human, part machine. He's on a mission to encourage others to become cyborgs, too. "Design yourself," he proclaims on the website for the Cyborg Foundation he launched to urge people to explore the possibilities of the union between cybernetics and human organisms.[1] Although at face value, Neil's antenna may seem weird or frivolous, he is very serious about the science of cyborgism and the future of implantable devices that can alter or add to our senses.

I ran into Neil with his unmistakable antenna, bowl-cut blond hair, and wildly colorful fashions when we both appeared at the 2016 Human by Design conference in New York City, a first-of-its-kind gathering of technologists, scientists, authors, thought leaders, and one very unforgettable cyborg. As a group we explored deep and fascinating ideas about human enhancement and cyborgism, and I had the opportunity to hear Neil's firsthand account of his life as a trans-species person. He and I both appeared in Mankind Divided's 2016 documentary film *Deus Ex: Human by Design*, which explores technology's role in the future of humanity.[2] I was so intrigued by his life as a cyborg that I took a deep dive into everything I could find about him.

Technology to Hear Color

Apparently, life wasn't always so colorful for Neil. He is one of the estimated one in thirty thousand people born with a rare visual condition called achromatopsia, a type of complete color blindness that produces a grayscale world ranging from white to black.[3] For Neil, who was born in Great Britain and raised in Catalonia, the sky was gray, rainbows were shades of gray, and every movie was in black and white. He knew there was a world of color out there; he just wanted to find an accessible way to interpret it.

Neil observed that many insects have antennae and wondered if he could have one, too.[4] In 2003, he teamed up with cybernetics innovator Adam Montandon, and later with Slovenian computer software developer Peter Kese and Spanish computer engineering student Matias Lazana, to create a device that could translate light waves into sound. The first prototype consisted of an old pair of headphones, a webcam, and a laptop Neil lugged around in a backpack.[5] Although its design was rather crude, it did the job, and Neil could look at a color and hear a frequency through the device.

Many iterations later, the device had morphed into a flexible antenna-like eyeborg that would be positioned in front of Neil's forehead. It would detect color and send the frequency to a chip implanted in the upper occipital bone at the back of his head, where the signal would travel through the skull via bone conduction; then his brain would interpret the vibrations as sounds.

The eyeborg seemed like a great plan, but there was a major stumbling block. Every surgeon Neil contacted refused, citing ethical issues, to do the operation to implant the chip in his head. The antenna would not be regenerating an existing human sense, so they deemed it unnecessary. They thought it could be dangerous. And they were concerned about public opinion. What would people think if Neil walked out of their hospital with an antenna sticking out of his head? It took him nearly two years to find a doctor willing to do the operation.

After emerging with his new antenna, his brain was bombarded with new information. Everywhere he looked, tones popped into his head. He had to consciously think about the sounds he was hearing and memorize which ones corresponded to which colors. At first, he was acutely aware of the constant sounds in his head. Over time, he no longer had to think about them; he simply felt them. It's similar to the way the brain is constantly coping with the onslaught of sensory input from the world around us. At any minute of any day, we're struck with dozens, hundreds, thousands, millions, even trillions of sensory details that our brains ignore using selective filtering. Our brains choose to ignore the vast majority of sensory inputs so we can focus our attention on the things that are most important to us. Just think of the cereal aisle at your local grocery store. Your brain ignores all the brightly colored boxes with their yellows, reds, blues, and greens screaming out for your attention so you can zoom in on the boringly packaged whole-grain oats you want.

When Neil realized his brain had accepted the technological device as an integral part of his body and as an extension of his senses, he started dreaming in colors. This indicated it was no longer the technology producing the sounds; it was his brain. It signaled the moment he became a true cyborg. He defines himself as a cyborg in three ways: biological, neurological, and psychological. Because of the blending of human and machine, Neil's physical body has changed, his sense of self has changed, and his brain has changed. In fact, Neil's brain is a dazzling display of the power of neuroplasticity. A 2015 brain imaging study in *Frontiers in Systems Neuroscience* proves that Neil's brain has undergone significant changes in response to his new body part.[6] The team of Spanish researchers found changes in functional neural patterns, structural connectivity, and cortical topography at the visual and auditory cortex compared with a group of healthy volunteers. The scientists suggest that understanding these changes could have implications for developing sensory substitution devices and creating rehabilitation programs for people with disabilities. They also say that studying Neil's brain could provide a helpful framework for tackling other neural and sensory issues like blindness and deafness. Cyborg technology may help people with sensory disabilities, and it may also address some of the common issues associated with aging. As we get older, our senses, especially our eyesight and hearing, tend to fade. Imagine if we could reverse this process with a computer chip.

Neil's experience goes beyond interpreting the millions of colors the human eye can detect and truly augments his brain to superhuman status. Thanks to some upgrades to his hardware, he can also hear infrared, ultraviolet light, and Bluetooth. Neil says UV light produces the highest frequency, a very high-pitched tone that can be annoying. That's probably a good thing considering how damaging UV light can be to skin. I think the Bluetooth connection promises even more incredible possibilities. Somebody actually called Neil's implanted chip on their cell phone, and Neil could hear the voice penetrate his skull.[7] He can link up to the internet via the chip in his head, and he's connected to five people on different continents around the world who can send him colors. The cyborg can even venture beyond the earthly realm, linking up with satellites and telescopes or connecting to the International Space Station, where he can hear the colors from space. "Our senses no longer need to be where our bodies are," he says. "I believe the next stage of human exploration is to investigate the disconnection between body and sense and to start traveling without our bodies."[8] He envisions a day when we can explore space and other planets from the comfort of our own bed.

He isn't alone. Neil has met a growing number of humans who would like to become cyborgs. "I think we're now entering the age of transition into cyborgs," he says. He thinks that as wearable technology becomes normalized, it will shift to implantation into the human body. "In the late '20s we'll start seeing people with new body parts and new senses. And I believe that in the '40s it will be normal to have technology implanted . . . I'm sure it will be normal to meet someone and ask, 'What are your extra senses and what's your new body part?'"[9]

What are some of the unprecedented senses he'd like to see? How about being able to sense or see if someone is behind you? He notes that our cars are already equipped with back-up cameras and sensors to help us maneuver and park. Why can't we configure our bodies to have 360-degree sensory perception? I think Neil is right that, in the NeuroGeneration, what is human and what is machine will be forever blurred. Even if someone has some form of technology like his that unleashes a new sense to push them beyond the limits of their biology, they're still undeniably human . . . *or are they?*

The World's First Cyborg

I've always been a big fan of James Bond movies and especially all the next-level tech gadgets the creators dream up. I remember being glued to the screen while watching the 2006 installment of the franchise, *Casino Royale*. That's the one where Bond has a device injected with a pneumatic gun into his left arm that allows MI6 to track his location and monitor his vital signs. Even today, it seems pretty cool and futuristic, right? In reality, something similar had already been done—*eight years before the film's release*! Sorry, Neil, but Kevin Warwick has the distinction of being the world's first cyborg.

A British cybernetics professor and researcher who earned the nickname "Captain Cyborg," Kevin decided to take his lab experiments at the University of Reading to the next level by having a surgeon implant a radio frequency identification device (RFID) in his upper left arm on October 24, 1998. Over two decades later, Kevin still recalls the three-week experiment with wonder and his trademark dry humor. When I chat with him about his experience as a cyborg, he remembers it as being "tremendously exciting."[10] How is having an RFID device implanted any different from microchipping your dog? Yes, you may be able to locate your pooch if she goes missing, but your dog isn't actively using the device to enhance her canine abilities. On the human side, Kevin is convinced that, within days of his operation, his brain was already laying down new neural pathways to adapt to his body's new abilities. He quickly got used to having the power to open doors in the university's smart building and turn on the lights without touching a thing. His favorite novelty was walking to the front door and having it greet him with a cheery "Hello, Professor Warwick."

"When someone else was there with me when that happened, they would wonder, 'What is going on?' That was really fun," he recalls fondly. What surprised him was that he didn't feel like it was the technology that was making all these things happen; *he* was making it happen. "Mentally, when you have an implant, your brain thinks of it as *you*. It's very different from a pair of glasses or a watch, which are *not* you. When it's implants, very quickly, the brain thinks it's you," he says. That became crystal clear when the implant was removed three weeks later as planned. Kevin felt like he had lost a part of himself. He missed being a cyborg.

Buoyed by the success of this one-of-a-kind experiment—which had him fielding hundreds of emails every day from journalists worldwide and landed him on the February 2000 cover of *Wired* magazine—Kevin wanted to edge further toward the next frontier of cyborgism. On March 14, 2002, he was wheeled into the operating theatre at the Radcliffe Infirmary in Oxford, where he became the first person to have the BrainGate microelectrode array (it was called the Utah Array back then)—the same technology that went into DARPA's robotic arm, discussed in chapter four—implanted into the median nerve fibers in his wrist.

The procedure was far more intricate than the one for his RFID implant and required several neurosurgeons. The rectangular implant has one hundred tiny electrodes—each about the same size as a single nerve fiber—and looks like a tiny hairbrush. The array was originally designed to help people with severe disabilities, such as spinal cord injuries or the loss of a limb. The goal is to implant the device into the brain, where it can monitor electrical activity and translate a person's thoughts into commands that control assistive devices, such as robotic limbs or computers. Human trials with the array are currently underway, and in 2018, three implant recipients with quadriplegia were able to control a computer tablet to surf the web, and send emails and text messages with nothing but their thoughts.[11]

Human trials were still years away when Kevin took the plunge. With his first cyborg procedure, the main concerns centered around ways to sterilize the implant and the possibility it might migrate in his body or break. In this second procedure, Kevin faced greater risks. The array had never been used in a human. Most experimentation had been done on cats, and when those studies were completed, the implant was removed and the animal was euthanized. That was definitely *not* an option for Kevin. What if his nervous system became infected and he lost the use of his hand? What if it caused excruciating pain? What if his nerve fibers were damaged while inserting the implant? What if . . . what if . . . what if?

When you're pioneering a new procedure, you have to anticipate all sorts of possible complications and understand there could be additional risks you haven't even imagined. Mitigating the potential downsides weighed heavily on the team. After practicing with "blanks," they decided that firing the implant into the nervous system with an injector gun at high velocity—just as James Bond experienced in *Casino Royale*—would give it the connectivity they wanted without any damage . . . *they hoped*!

Before going under the knife, Kevin felt the rush of excitement—and the hint of fear—that all trailblazing scientific researchers experience, especially those who dare to act as their own guinea pigs. Think of Sir Henry Head, a British neurologist who convinced a surgeon to sever the radial nerve in his left arm in 1903 so he could study pain.[12] Luckily, he eventually regained sensation, and the radical experiment led to important findings on the body's sensory system, but it also caused controversy among his peers, who questioned the ethics of self-experimentation.[13] Then there was Swiss chemist Albert Hofmann (not the same person as the 1960s social activist Abbie Hoffman), who was the first person to synthesize lysergic acid diethylamide, better known as LSD, and to experience its trippy effects.[14] In 1943 while mixing the powders, Hofmann accidentally ingested the chemical, which produced psychedelic hallucinations. To confirm what he'd experienced, he staged a second experiment, taking a small amount of LSD that left him feeling so anxious and dizzy he thought he might die, and he had to have his assistant take him home on a bicycle. And don't forget Australian doctor Barry Marshall, who wanted to prove that ulcers and gastritis were caused by the bacterium *Helicobacter pylori* but needed a healthy volunteer for the experiment.[15] In 1984, Marshall decided to bypass the ethics committee and drank a "brew" of the bacterium himself. After five days, he started feeling bloated after meals, had awful breath, and began vomiting clear liquid every morning. Talk about dedication to science! An endoscopy confirmed he had developed gastritis, but fortunately a round of antibiotics cleared it up. For Marshall's self-experimentation, he eventually shared a Nobel Prize in 2005, proving that being your own guinea pig, although risky, can pay off.

Happily, for Kevin's cyborg experiment, the second implant surgery was successful, and he emerged as a man–machine hybrid. Wires from the array snaked up the inside of his arm and poked out through the skin, where they were affixed to an external connector pad. From there, the connector pad could be hardwired to a computer, or in some cases, a digital radio transmitter. And with this human–tech connection, Kevin could transmit neural signals directly from his peripheral nervous system to the devices. On the flip side, the devices could also send signals to the implant, which would stimulate his nerve fibers, creating a closed feedback loop.[16] In a series of experiments, Kevin hoped to show that he could control a range of cybernetic devices with his mind when appropriately translated by the computer.

Before the planned lab experiments could begin, however, he had to do some brain training. He had to learn to recognize the external stimulation—delivered in the form of pulses—sent from the computer to the array. According to the cyborg, the only similar work that had been done before took place at the University of Utah, where researchers delivered pulses into chicken nerves. Kevin's team took their cue from those chicken experiments and used those levels as a starting point. But the current wasn't sufficient. Kevin's brain couldn't detect the low-level current, so they began upping the pulses. For about two weeks they delivered current into his nervous system, while Kevin responded with, "Yes, there's a pulse," or "No, not a pulse."

After six weeks, they'd established the right level, and he was sensing the pulses with 100 percent accuracy. With this tedious prerequisite out of the way, they could finally proceed with the scheduled experiments, all of which had both a therapeutic and an enhancement aspect. For the surgeons on the team, it was the therapy potential that sparked their enthusiasm. For Kevin, it was the potential of human enhancement that thrilled him. It was finally time to have some cyborg fun again!

Blindfolded, Kevin sat in the lab at the University of Reading and felt the rhythm of the pulses in his nervous system.

Ping! . . . *Ping!* . . . *Ping!* . . . *Ping!* . . . *Ping!* . . . *Ping!* . . . *Ping!Ping!Ping!*

"Closer, closer," he said.

Ping!Ping!Ping! . . . *Ping!* . . . *Ping!* . . . *Ping!* . . . *Ping!* . . . *Ping!* . . . *Ping!*

"Farther, farther."

Kevin was tapping into his new cyborg sensory ability to sense ultrasonic waves, similar to the way bats, dolphins, and whales use sonar to locate objects or hunt in total darkness. Even with the blindfold, he could sense if his research team was moving objects toward or away from him.

During this particular demonstration, one thing really took him by surprise. One of the researchers who was maneuvering a large board closer to and then farther from Kevin suddenly moved it rapidly toward him. "It was quite scary. I couldn't see anything, and I was quite scared from the ultrasonic signals. It was a reactive thing from this new sensory sensation, this extending of the senses or new sense. It was quite unexpected."

Kevin's brain was interpreting this fast movement as a potential danger. He didn't need to train his neurons to know that having sound whooshing toward him like a small tsunami might be a hazard. I can't help but imagine how useful being able to sense ultrasonic waves would be for a blind person navigating their world, and that's exactly what excited the medical professionals on Kevin's team. For years, scientists have been trying to develop sonar-based technologies for the blind, but they've primarily been external devices, rather than internal implants like Kevin's.

As part of his cyborg experiment, Kevin traveled across the pond to Columbia University in New York, where he met with computer scientists for a go at remotely controlling a robotic hand, located in his lab back in Reading, in real time.[17] With a visual linkup on a computer, he could see the experiment as it happened. Kevin moved his hand in New York, and his neural signals streamed across the internet like an extension of his nervous system to control the robotic hand, and then came back across the internet to stimulate his hand. "It was really cool! This was showing both ways—motor and sensory. I was controlling it *and* getting feedback."

Surprisingly, he found it very easy to learn how to control the robotic hand and make it open and close in sync with his own hand. In fact, he had mastered this new ability within a few days after getting the wrist implant. "Neural signals are very different from muscle signals," he explains. "If you're thinking about moving, the signals are clearly different. It's a lot easier than people might imagine."

The feedback part, however, required training. The feedback from the sensors in the robotic hand's fingertips sent sensory signals to Kevin's brain based on how tightly it was gripping an object. Grasp it firmly and it was *Ping!Ping!Ping!* in rapid pulses. With a looser grip, the rhythm was slower: *Ping! . . . Ping! . . . Ping!* Kevin noticed a delay of about one-third of a second from the time he initiated a movement to the response of the robotic hand, or from when the robot moved to sensing it in his fingertips. "But that's very good," he explains. "There's a bit of a time delay on the nervous system from the brain to the hand anyway. Very quickly my brain got used to that delay, so I didn't notice it any longer."

How did it feel operating a robot thousands of miles away? "When I was controlling the robotic hand across the internet, it really felt extremely powerful," he says. "Suddenly with your brain, you can do anything you want. You're not restricted to your body any longer." For Kevin's medical team, this thrilling experiment revealed the therapeutic possibilities for people with disabilities to control their environment with their mind.

It is incredible to think of a person sitting on one continent and moving a robotic hand on another continent via his nervous system. The practical possibilities seem endless. "A soldier could be a tank, a building, or any object," Kevin muses. "The body can be whatever and wherever you want it to be. There is a lessening of importance of the body and increasing importance of the brain." On the healthcare side, he believes there will be more emphasis on looking after the brain and research into keeping the brain alive separate from the human body. "People get cancer of the body and die. It's ridiculous. We can probably get rid of the physical thing and survive."

That wasn't the biggest revelation of Kevin's brief life as a cyborg. The part that really blew his mind was when he engaged in what almost might be described as a Vulcan mind meld by communicating telegraphically, nervous system to nervous system, with his wife. Ever since Kevin's first foray into cyborg territory, Irena had been urging him to let her be a part of the experiment. He acquiesced, and the brave woman had two electrodes—not the sophisticated BrainGate implant—injected into the nerve fibers in her arm in a fifteen-minute procedure. Like Kevin, she had a couple of wires protruding from her skin that could be connected to a computer.

Back at the lab, they got down to work. The goal was to take neural signals from Irena's brain—via her nervous system and those electrodes in her arm—and transmit them to a computer, which would then interface with another computer that would send them to Kevin's nervous system and into his brain via his wrist array.

After some practice, it was time for the moment of truth. Kevin put on a blindfold and waited. When Irena closed her hand, he felt a pulse in his brain. "Yes!" he shouted with a rush of adrenaline.

They had done it: the first communication between nervous systems had just occurred at 2:14 PM on June 10, 2002. Kevin could imagine it must have been the same way Alexander Graham Bell felt when he made the first telephone call in history in 1876, shouting to his assistant in the other room: "Mr. Watson, come here! I want to see you."

The pair continued with Irena opening and closing her hand and Kevin receiving an electrical charge in his fingers each time, achieving 100 percent accuracy. As primitive as the electrical pulses had been, he was filled with exhilaration and firmly believed it marked the debut of a whole new way of communicating for humans.

Now the deputy vice-chancellor of research at Coventry University, Kevin looks back wistfully on that heady optimism of nearly two decades ago. As he tells me, he thought by now we would be far closer to achieving pure brain-to-brain communication with neural implants. He's not sure why more scientists haven't been building on the human enhancement experiments he did years ago. "I guess it's like Dr. Jekyll trying to drink the potion, and you don't know what's going to happen," he says.

"But it's too bad other scientists haven't tried it out. I want other scientists to do it. It's disappointing it hasn't happened." He's even had to face some criticism from the scientific community blasting his human enhancement experiments as mere media stunts.

Nonetheless, some of the technology-fueled sensory abilities he tested have found their way into some incredible advances on the therapeutic side, such as walking canes for the blind that use sonar to detect objects, and those mind-controlled robotic prostheses from DARPA. Kevin still has his eye on continuing his cyborg life with one more pioneering experiment. "I'd love to do a brain-to-brain communication experiment. It is dangerous, though." He's already lined up a surgeon who would be willing to do the operation. Now he just needs a volunteer. Anyone?

When Will You Become a Cyborg?

That's the question serial neurotech entrepreneur William Rosellini asked the audience in a 2015 TED Talk.[18] His prediction? The year 2027. In part, Will chose that date because it coincides with the year the video game *Deus Ex: Mankind Divided* takes place. The game features a battle between natural humans and mechanically augmented people—cyborgs. A longtime gamer and fan of the *Deus Ex* series, Will acted as lead science consultant on the game and its main character, Adam Jensen, who has over sixty human enhancements, including emitting a sonar pulse from his fingertips, hacking devices remotely, and making things appear to move in slo-mo.

Will is the right guy to consult on future human augmentations. For years, he's been inventing devices that can turn real humans into cyborgs, and he's certain these neurotechnological advances are driving us to become an augmented species. Just ask him his thoughts about implants. "Active implantable devices will change more in the next ten years than any other industry, any other technology, and will change what it means to be human more than we've ever seen before," he says. His work in the field of neural implants earned him a spot in the *Human by Design* documentary alongside Neil and myself.

Although we didn't get a chance to meet while filming, Will and I have run into each other a few times at neurotech conferences. Watching him speak, I get the sense he's ready to hurtle humanity into the next frontier like a 105-mile-per-hour fastball. He definitely stands out in a field filled with lab types who likely hung out in science and computer clubs at school. Will took a curveball-like path to this small circle of mad science. A former Minor League pitching prospect for the Arizona Diamondbacks, Will was hurling fastballs when he realized that, despite his athleticism, talent, and hard work, he wasn't going to make it to the Major Leagues. At six foot two and 200-plus pounds of muscle, he certainly looked the part of a professional athlete. He had all the top-of-the-line training and biomechanics, but something was missing. "My nervous system was somehow different from guys that excel at the level of the big leagues," he told me when we finally connected.[19] "I thought that was really interesting, and I've been studying it for the past fifteen years." He hung up his glove, earned six college degrees, and started pitching neurotech projects through a number of startups he's successfully launched and sold.

Will's fascination with the nervous system never dwindled. To get a firsthand feel for how the nervous system works, he braved a brief stint as a cyborg when he had a neurosurgeon implant an electrode in his arm and run it out to a computer. He conducted some experiments with various inputs to see how his nervous system would feel. In a word? *Ouch!* These days, he's chairman and CEO of Nexeon MedSystems, where one of his latest transformative technologies is a neural implant similar to a cardiac pacemaker that is placed deep inside the brain to stop the tremor from Parkinson's disease.

But deep brain stimulation isn't new, you say? You're right. It earned FDA approval for the treatment of Parkinson's disease in 2002 and now ranks as the most common surgical procedure for people with the condition. To date, it has been performed on more than 40,000 individuals.[20] Its remarkable successes have been heralded in the media with stories of people formerly unable to leave home overcoming uncontrollable symptoms to regain their independence. The procedure has given hope to the ten million people worldwide living with the disease, in which electrical signaling patterns in the brain misfire and interfere with motor control.[21] It involves placing electrodes deep inside the subthalamic nucleus or the globus pallidus interna, two regions within the brain's basal ganglia that play a role in movement. Once the electrodes are implanted, they are wired to a battery-operated neurostimulator similar to a pacemaker that's embedded under the skin near the collarbone. The neural pacemaker delivers electrical pulses to the electrodes to regulate the abnormal electrical signals within the brain and control the shaking and involuntary movements associated with Parkinson's. And its users effectively become cyborgs, a blend of biology and technology. I would venture that anyone whose tremors are calmed by implanted technology would feel more human, not less, thanks to the machinery.

What makes Will's neurostimulator a next-gen device is it can record nervous system activity at the same time. Think of it as a "smart" stimulator in a closed-loop feedback system. "This will enable us to find biomarkers to more dynamically program and personalize the therapy for each patient," he says. With this kind of a system, the neural pacemaker would only deliver electrical stimulation when the brain actually needs it, rather than nonstop. And it could give a person more or less stimulation as needed.

"Where I think the industry is going is everyone is going to have the hardware, the implantable or external stimulators to activate the nervous system," Will explains. "The real challenge is going to be what's actually happening in the brain, in the autonomic nervous system, in the sympathetic nervous system, and in the organs such that we can drive a change in how diseases are currently managed with electrical versus chemical energy."

What's most exciting about closed-loop neural pacemakers like the ones Will is creating is the possibility to improve its effectiveness at warp speed. The closed-loop system can help drive the technology forward far faster than the progress of other devices, such as cardiac pacemakers. The first implantable pacemaker was surgically inserted into the body of forty-three-year-old Arne Larsson in Sweden on October 8, 1958.[22] Arne had a debilitating heart rhythm disorder called Stokes-Adams syndrome, which caused him to suddenly fall unconscious twenty to thirty times a day, necessitating resuscitation each time. Arne's dire circumstances are what prompted the physician-inventor Rune Elmqvist and the cardiac surgeon Åke Senning to take the plunge and perform the risky, first-of-its-kind operation. Arne survived the surgery, but the implant functioned correctly for only eight hours before needing replacement. He would require numerous replacements throughout his life, but he ended up outliving both his surgeon and the inventor of the device.

In the decades since Arne received his pacemaker, innovators got smart and started not just stimulating the heart but also recording data from it. Then they began using technology that records remotely from a home-based device that monitors the patient's pacemaker activity. Today, Will says these devices are "like rocket ships in terms of their intelligence."

The pioneers from the '60s and '70s followed the same concepts used in cardiac pacemakers and began applying electricity to the nervous system to treat chronic pain, Parkinson's, epilepsy,

and other conditions. For the last thirty years, the field of neural pacemakers has been using open-loop stimulation on a nerve
or in the brain to treat neurological disorders. "The era we're in
now," says Will, "is those nervous system functions will start to be
enhanced like the cardiac pacemaker functions by getting more
closed-loop information from recording," and he expects neuromodulation devices to get better, faster. The dataset gathered
by those recordings could provide a valuable window into the
brain, and applying machine learning to that dataset could reveal
unprecedented ways to explore the brain. The nature of these
recordings is similar to EEG, just deeper in the brain. They yield
a higher signal-to-noise resolution compared with EEG, which,
as you've already learned in this book, can be limited because
of the noisiness in the brain. I can't wait for the day when we
can combine datasets from deep-brain and surface-EEG recordings. At that point, buckle up for some really amazing discoveries
about how the brain works!

Will has been talking about a cyborg revolution for about a
decade. If you think that means an army of Terminators is on the
horizon, think again. According to Will, the Terminator character
popularized in James Cameron's 1984 sci-fi epic isn't a cyborg; it's
an autonomous robot with artificial intelligence. "I think we're a
long way from that," he says reassuringly. What's a lot closer, he
predicts, is your cell phone becoming a part of you. "We know
that you blink 70 percent less when you're looking at the screen,
and everybody's saying we need to have less screen time. Well,
there's a way that's going to happen," he says. "You're going to
have that information come through in a more pleasing environment for the nervous system." So forget about trying to solve the
screen-time problem. Will says we're going to have to do it by getting rid of the interface. Say goodbye to that handheld phone and
hello to an internal connection to the internet, a sort of biological
Bluetooth.

He admits the notion of an implantable internet sounds wild. "'Cyborg' sounds creepy and weird and futuristic and obtuse, but quite frankly, it's obvious we're heading in that direction," he says. "The idea that you could enhance your nervous system and loop it to the internet and not have a clumsy phone, it seems logical." I think Will is right when he says cyborgs will be humans merging with technology they're already comfortable with.

When I ask Will about the ethical issues associated with cyborg enhancement, he doesn't hesitate. "Would a soldier enhance themselves to be able to do their job as a soldier better?" he asks. "I would argue, it's unethical for the government not to do that. If you're sending a soldier into harm's way and you have the ability to enhance their X, Y, Z, you should be paying for it." Will is hoping to help make learning enhancement a reality for the military. One of his firms has been tapped to work on a DARPA program called Targeted Neuroplasticity Training, which involves stimulating the vagus nerve—the longest of the cranial nerves, which helps control blood pressure, heart rate, and digestion—to open up a window of learning. Such an approach is a more invasive version of the noninvasive tDCS neuropriming Brett Wingeier's headphones provide. The goal is to be able to teach soldiers to learn new languages two to three times faster than normal. "Is that unethical?" Will asks. "Why would we ever stop enhancing ourselves?"

The Cyborgs Among Us

While the notion of becoming a cyborg with enhanced human abilities still seems fantastical, you likely already have noticed that we have hundreds of thousands of cyborgs living among us. There could be one living in your neighborhood, on your street, next door, or it could be your mom, your dad, or maybe even you.

Just consider the 324,000 people worldwide who have cochlear implants that help them hear.[23] Or the 150,000 people with Parkinson's disease who have brain pacemakers to calm tremors.[24] Or the people who have improved sight thanks to artificial corneas, implantable telescopes, or retinal implants. They're all part human, part technology.

As a society, we have welcomed assistive technology that has helped people regain basic human senses or experience them for the first time. When you consider that about 466 million people worldwide live with disabling hearing loss—a number expected to double by 2050—the need for cochlear implants and other devices that restore hearing is critical.[25] In 2014, only 48 percent of deaf people were employed compared with 72 percent of hearing people.[26] With deference to opinions on the cultural impact of cochlear implants within the Deaf community, I believe that giving someone the ability to hear can be life changing on many levels. The same goes for the gift of sight. As many as ten million people suffer from corneal blindness worldwide, but only 100,000 transplants are performed each year because of a lack of access to donor tissue.[27] It's a veritable international public health crisis. Artificial cornea transplants offer an alternative to donor tissue, and mechanical implants are helping restore sight for other types of vision problems. For example, an implantable telescope is helping people with end-stage age-related macular degeneration improve their eyesight.[28] And retinal implants are helping blind people restore their vision. I can't help but hope that one of these visual implants could someday help Mark Pollock regain his vision.

The technology has already helped Rozina Issani, who shared her story of becoming a cyborg with a bionic eye in *Toronto Life*.[29] Rozina grew up with bad eyesight—really bad. She could distinguish shapes and some colors but couldn't recognize faces. They looked like the muted brushstrokes of an Impressionist painting—blurred patches of color and indistinguishable features.

When Rozina was twenty-two, the Pakistani-born woman's family moved to Toronto, Canada, where she finally got an accurate diagnosis. She'd been born with a condition called retinitis pigmentosa, which causes a person's sight to slowly dim until total blindness descends. In a healthy eye, retinal rods and cones convert light into tiny electrochemical pulses that are sent to the optic nerve and into the brain, where they are decoded as images. In people with retinitis pigmentosa, those rods and cones deteriorate.

Rozina had resigned herself to a life of darkness. Then in 2015, something she heard on the radio sparked a ray of hope. She heard about a revolutionary retinal implant that basically gives a person a bionic eye to restore vision.[30] Ophthalmologist and engineer Mark Humayun at the University of Southern California (USC) invented the chip, which became known as the Argus II Retinal Prosthesis System and earned FDA approval in 2013.[31] It was the success of the cochlear implant that inspired the physician-engineer to conceive a device for people with retinitis pigmentosa.

The procedure would involve implanting an electrode-rich chip on Rozina's retina, where it would take over the job her damaged rods and cones could no longer do. To activate the bionic eye, she would wear a special pair of glasses that don't look that different from a pair of designer sunglasses. But these glasses house a powerful system that includes a miniature camera that transmits videos to a small battery-operated unit that fits on a belt. From there, information is returned to the glasses via a cable and then sent wirelessly to an antenna on the retinal implant. The signals then travel to the electrode array, which emits small pulses of electricity to the brain, where it is interpreted as images. All of this activity happens in real time.

The implant comes with a hefty $150,000 price tag in U.S. dollars, so a philanthropic donor covered most of the cost for

Rozina's procedure. After healing from her surgery, the day came for her to test out her new bionic eye. She put on the glasses while a technician fired up the connection to the implant and gradually increased the electrical pulses. "And then it happened: I saw light for the first time in fifteen years—a soft, radiant glow that illuminated the room. It was overwhelming. I burst into tears." Rozina could make out the shapes of the doctor, nurses, and friends who had accompanied her, describing it like looking at a film negative. No color, no facial recognition, but enough to detect the people around her and to see the light. "I could see!" she exclaims.

Getting the most out of the device requires a lot of training. By practicing every day, her brain would get better at interpreting the signals from the receiver chip. Similar to the way Kevin had to train his brain to detect the pulses being pushed into his brain and the way Neil had to memorize which tones went with which colors, relearning to see with a bionic eye or to hear with a cochlear implant takes effort. Becoming a cyborg doesn't instantaneously give you superpowers or restore senses you lost. You have to work at it.

However, becoming a cyborg may help you regain lost powers more quickly than normal. For example, if you're a stroke survivor, being a cyborg could speed up your ability to relearn motor skills. A study on vagus nerve stimulation in stroke patients presented at the 2017 International Neuromodulation Society Conference in Edinburgh, Scotland, showed promising results.[32] After six weeks, 75 percent of patients who experienced vagus nerve stimulation while performing physical therapy tasks achieved a clinically meaningful benefit, compared with only 33 percent of patients who engaged in therapy only. After three months, the positive results of neuromodulation climbed to 88 percent. Preliminary results of a clinical trial published in 2016 in the journal *Stroke* pointed out the safety of the therapy and described the procedure.[33] For this study, surgeons placed electrodes on the vagus nerve in stroke victims with moderate to severe upper-limb impairment and wired the electrodes to a pulse generator inserted under the skin of their chests, similar to a cardiac pacemaker. While the participants performed rehabilitation exercises, a physiotherapist pushed a button to trigger a small jolt of electricity to the vagus nerve. That charge traveled up the nerve to specific regions of the brain, triggering the release of neurotransmitters that strengthen neural connections. The results show vagus nerve stimulation combined with rehabilitation promotes neural circuits in the motor cortex associated with physical movement. It's like opening up a temporary window of plasticity to retrain the brain to learn the movements faster. Remember how Mario, the classical musician in chapter three, wore headphones to enhance neuroplasticity while practicing Bach preludes? This is a similar concept but with implants directly stimulating the vagus nerve to promote that plasticity. And it's also similar to Will Rosellini's DARPA program to stimulate the vagus nerve in an effort to speed up new-language learning.

It is fascinating to see so many innovators coming at the same process from so many different angles. For example, take the researchers at University of California, San Francisco, who are using implantable electrodes to decode speech in the brain. In a remarkable triumph, the UCSF team deciphered the neural secrets required to create synthesized speech based solely on brain activity. The groundbreaking feat, described in a 2019 issue of *Nature*, raises the possibility of restoring speech in people who have lost verbal ability to neurological conditions, such as stroke, TBI, amyotrophic lateral sclerosis, Parkinson's disease, or others.[34] "For the first time, this study demonstrates that we can generate entire spoken sentences based on an individual's brain activity," said UCSF neurosurgeon Edward Chang, one of the study authors. "This is an exhilarating proof of principle that with technology that is already within reach, we should be able to build a device that is clinically viable in patients with speech loss."[35]

To perform this feat, the scientists needed subjects with a very specific prerequisite: they had to have a brain–machine interface already implanted. They found five such volunteers at the UCSF Epilepsy Center. The patients had temporary neural electrode arrays implanted prior to neurosurgery intended to help control their seizures. The scientists recorded the voices of the subjects, who did not have speech disabilities, and then used machine learning to reverse-engineer the linguistic process. The algorithms produced synthetic speech in full sentences, and crowd-sourced transcribers accurately identified 69 percent of the words spoken. Future steps will involve volunteers who are speech impaired to see if they are able to train the system to translate their internally spoken thoughts into synthesized vocalizations. In other words, people with speech disabilities might regain the ability to speak using brain-controlled artificial voice tracts. Of course, this would require the implantation of neural electrodes—an intricate and risky process—but for some people, the rewards of being able to communicate again could be worth the risks.

Gaining or regaining abilities isn't the only thing you can do as a cyborg. One of the most interesting aspects of becoming a cyborg is what it can help you forget. Did you know that achieving cyborg status could help alleviate PTSD, a condition that affects an estimated 6.8 percent of American adults at some point during their lifetime?[36] Animal studies show that vagus nerve stimulation could help reduce PTSD when combined with exposure therapy.[37] People can literally erase bad memories.

People with medical conditions aren't the only ones currently benefiting from cyborg status. Employers are inviting workers to join cyborg nation by implanting RFID chips under their skin similar to the way Kevin Warwick did back in 1998. In 2017, tech firm Three Square Market in Wisconsin began offering employees an unusual perk: an RFID chip implanted between the thumb and forefinger.[38] The chip, which is about the size of a long grain of rice, empowers employees to do some of the things Kevin did two decades ago—enter the office building and complete other tasks without lifting a finger. They can also log on to computers—no more typing in passwords—and get food from the cafeteria or vending machines without having to reach for their wallet. Initially, fifty employees volunteered to get chipped; by 2018, eighty had achieved cyborg status thanks to the RFID chip. Unfortunately, the chip doesn't elicit a personalized greeting the way Kevin's did.

Three Square Market isn't the only enterprise using implantable devices. A growing number of Swedish companies are exploring the cyborg route. One firm called Biohax has implanted microchips in several thousand customers to allow them to hop on board trains without waiting in a ticket line.[39] And, of course, millions of dogs and cats have been microchipped in the U.S. Does that make them "dogborgs" and "catborgs"?

The idea of implantable chips in the workplace could prove tricky. Could employers use the devices to track employees without their consent or knowledge? Could hackers steal personal information? What happens when an employee quits or gets fired? Having to undergo an implant removal procedure could make an awkward situation even more uncomfortable. State legislators have been slow to tackle the issue. As of November 2018, only eight U.S. states had RFID privacy laws prohibiting the mandatory implantation of an RFID chip.[40]

We may have millions more human–machine cyborgs if billionaire inventor Elon Musk has his way. When the tech pioneer isn't plotting his next SpaceX rocket launch, rolling out a new Tesla model, tunneling under Los Angeles with The Boring Company, or designing the high-speed Hyperloop train, he's delving into designing a brain–computer interface at his firm Neuralink, which he founded in 2016. Musk has often said humans are already superhuman cyborgs with magical powers thanks to our computers and cell phones. But he claims the present-day interface between the brain and the digital extension of ourselves is extremely limited because of low bandwidth. Increasing that bandwidth with a direct neural interface is the answer to helping humans keep pace with emerging AI.

In a crowded planetarium in San Francisco in July 2019, Musk divulged some of the first details about the ultra-secretive Neuralink devices.[41] Speaking to a rapt room of techies, the billionaire CEO of SpaceX and Tesla explained how that upgraded bandwidth will come via a small computer chip worn behind the ear that connects to miniscule "threads" implanted deep into the brain.[42] How will the implant procedure work? A surgeon-controlled robot will drill tiny holes—about 2 millimeters in diameter—into a person's skull and push the threads into the brain in a sewing machine–like motion. The behind-ear computer chip will allow the brain to connect wirelessly to a smartphone app, Musk said. He envisions the device being a boon to people with spinal cord injuries, amputees, stroke victims, and blind people, as well as those simply looking for a bump in memory. Musk is aiming to start clinical trials in humans by the end of 2020. Futurists, AI technologists, and anyone who cares about the evolution of the human brain should pay attention.[43]

Also joining in the cyborg race is Bryan Johnson, who founded neuroscience startup Kernel in 2016 to develop a neural interface that can read and write from the human brain.[44] Like Musk, Johnson and the small team at Kernel are looking to create a neural implant that pushes past repairing neurodegenerative disease to radically enhance cognition so humans can outpace or simply keep up with technology. With your brain linked to your laptop or cell phone, or a supercomputer, you could effectively upload or download information directly to or from your brain. The technology could help treat brain damage from a stroke or restore memories to reverse or prevent dementia and Alzheimer's disease.

These are certainly all noble efforts, but Kernel's real goal is brain enhancement. For example, you could link to your laptop and download new abilities just like Neo in *The Matrix*. Imagine how much more productive you could be if you could send texts and emails simply by thinking about them. How much more responsive could your business be if you could get real-time analytics downloaded directly to your brain? How much better could you do in the stock market if you could effortlessly access thousands of company statistics? How much faster could you complete projects if you didn't have to type on a keyboard and could simply translate your thoughts directly to your computer? In many ways, being a cyborg could make life a lot easier.

While these entrepreneurs are on a quest for a surgical implant that will take the human brain into a new frontier, those mad scientists at DARPA are seeking a nonsurgical option. In 2018, the organization requested proposals for a dramatic effort called the Next-Generation Non-Surgical Neurotechnology (N3) to create a noninvasive neural interface system to enable neural recording and stimulation.[45] DARPA scientists are seeking to create a neural interface that is completely external—that is, a nonsurgically delivered nanotransponder that will translate signals between neurons and an external recording and stimulating device. While previous DARPA programs like the prosthetic arm my friend Geoffrey Ling oversaw have been geared to restoring function to wounded warriors, this program is squarely centered on next-gen human enhancement. Considering the trickle-down effects of DARPA inventions, this could open the floodgates to the new era of brain enhancement.

Birth of a Cyborg

How much is the lure of superhuman senses, brain-to-brain communication, and brain–computer interface worth? Becoming a cyborg—even just temporarily—isn't easy. In fact, the transition from human to cyborg is likely to involve some pain. Neil Harbisson suffered headaches for months after undergoing surgery to implant the antenna in his skull. While Kevin Warwick was lying on an operating table getting the BrainGate implant jammed into his median nerve fibers, he remembers being "jolted by what felt like an enormous bolt of electricity blasting down every finger of my left hand at the same time. I flinched and swore at the top of my voice." His wife, Irena, had to undergo her procedure without any anesthesia, not even a local painkiller. She shrieked a couple of times as the physician used a pair of forceps to push the electrodes into her nerve fibers. And Will Rosellini also had to forgo anesthesia for his temporary trip into cyborg land.

Clearly, all implant procedures come with the possibility of a host of complications: infection, migration, nerve damage, and more. Just ask Jens Naumann. The most unnerving story I've found about the real price of becoming a cyborg comes from this Canadian who lost his sight after a series of traumatic eye injuries. I read Jens's story in his 2012 book, *Search for Paradise: A Patient's Account of the Artificial Vision Experiment*, and haven't been able to get it out of my brain ever since.[46]

In 2002, Jens became "Patient Alpha," the first person in the world to undergo an experimental procedure intended to give him artificial sight. The implantation procedure involved placing 140 electrodes across both sides of his visual cortex, connected via two pedestals, or jacks, that protruded from the back of Jens's head. The system worked with the aid of a computer processor and a small video camera. After twenty years of darkness, cyborg Jens could now make out shapes and outlines. His remarkable experience made international headlines that year when he demonstrated his artificial sight by driving a car.

But the dream didn't last. The equipment eventually failed, and Jens was plunged back into darkness. Even worse, the pioneering doctor who championed the technology died suddenly, leaving Jens and all that technology in his head on his own. By 2005, Jens began reaching out to other doctors for help, writing to one physician: "My antiquated equipment I was first issued in 2002 is presently practically useless, given that any adjustments necessary must be done through a master computer operated by specific software, as well as replacement parts, even batteries, are no longer available." The useless equipment remained in his head until 2010 when Jens finally had the two pedestals surgically removed because they were causing health problems. As he describes it in his book, "My scalp had been receding from the jacks, globs of infectious discharge oozing constantly out of them." Jens's pursuit of artificial vision had come with a heavy price, one any future cyborg must contemplate.

The neural implants such as those being developed at Neuralink and Kernel could pose risks we haven't even considered. Or they could create complications years after implantation. We just don't know yet. The promise of an enhanced brain that connects to the internet could cause problems in other ways we have yet to imagine. Could hackers tap into your brain and reprogram your memories? Could the government spy on your thoughts? Who owns your thoughts and memories? How will you upgrade your implanted technology? These are some of the questions we need to address now before we become a cyborg nation.

CHAPTER **6**

NEUROREGENERATION

Tools to Repair the Brain
on a Cellular Level

A S A YOUNG REFUGEE in the hardscrabble suburb of Footscray, I got to know so many of our neighbors. I will never forget the house on the corner of our street just a few doors down from us. It was a rooming house for seniors. I remember feeling very sad for these elderly people because they had to live with strangers while our family—all three generations—lived together under one roof.

My mum, sister, and I would walk to the Footscray Market every week, and as we returned home, we would often see our rooming house neighbors wandering up and down the streets looking lost, forgetting where they were, and asking for help. One gentleman I remember well was called Big Tony. It was hard for me to understand how such a large man could have so much trouble finding his way around the neighborhood. Another old, short Aussie man who lived in the rooming house was so forgetful he couldn't remember who we were from week to week. We would smile and say hello, and he would stare at us blankly as if he had never seen us before.

There was yet another resident called Hugh who was still alert when we first met him. One day when my mum was dropped off in front of our house, she unknowingly dropped her wallet. Hugh found it, saw Mum's driver's license with our address, and returned the wallet completely intact with the cash in it. We were grateful to him for his quick thinking and honesty. A few years later, however, Hugh's memory had faded, and he could no longer remember our names or even our faces when we ran into him on the street. I would try to remind him of the story about Mum's lost wallet, but he had no recollection of the incident we all remembered so clearly.

I didn't know it then, but these men were suffering from dementia, most likely Alzheimer's disease, the most common form of the condition. Years before they began forgetting who we were and losing the ability to navigate the neighborhood, their brains had begun to degenerate. As they went about their days, some of the 100 billion neurons inside their skulls were undergoing devastating changes. Abnormal clusters of sticky protein fragments known as beta-amyloid were forming plaques that squeezed into the spaces between the nerve cells and may have started disrupting their ability to communicate with other neurons. Inside their deteriorating neurons, tangles of twisted tau proteins were accumulating, hijacking the delivery of essential nutrients and other materials. This insidious process altered neurotransmitter activities and ultimately began killing off neurons and possibly activating an immune response, triggering inflammation that attacked and annihilated even more neurons. Their brains were literally shriveling up, with the shrinkage beginning in the hippocampus, a region involved in forming memories, and then spreading to other areas involving planning, judgment, behavior, language, and more. Unfortunately, the devastation devoured more and more of their brains, and within a matter of years, after it robbed them of their memory, it stole their very lives.

What if my rooming house neighbors didn't have to lose their memories? What if doctors had detected signs of those brain changes years earlier and had intervened with treatment to slow the cellular damage and prevent the symptoms from ever developing? What if these elderly men simply could have watched a movie that would have alleviated their symptoms and restored lost memories? What if they could have taken advantage of a neural implant to help them remember their neighbors and make new memories? What if there were a brain prosthetic as powerful as the robotic limb prosthetics you read about in chapter four that could have taken over the memory-making process in their brains? What if a neurotechnology device could have pushed their neurons into self-repair mode to reverse the progression of the disease? Sadly, my Footscray neighbors didn't have any of these options.

Although the hunt for an Alzheimer's cure is littered with failed drug trials—more than 150 attempts to develop a medication for the condition have crashed and burned since 1998—there is promise in other domains. Thanks to some next-level advances that neuroscientists, bioengineers, electrical engineers, and mathematicians are developing, we might be able to repair the brain on a cellular level. Such advances could arrive sooner than you might think. Forward-thinking innovators are creating early-detection tools and blending biological and artificial means for stunning next-gen cellular brain repairs.

This opens up a world of possibilities for the more than two million people who suffer traumatic brain injuries each year,[1] the more than 795,000 stroke victims each year,[2] and the more than 23,000 people who are diagnosed annually with malignant brain or spinal cord tumors.[3] But it is especially good news for the more than five million Americans currently living with Alzheimer's and other forms of dementia, as well as the 16 million expected to develop it by 2050.[4] Worldwide, 50 million people are living with dementia, and it is estimated this number will skyrocket to 76 million by 2030.

Part of the rise in dementia is an effect of health advances extending our life spans, such as prevention and treatment of cardiovascular disease. No matter the age at which dementia strikes, some experts call it one of the greatest threats facing humanity. For this reason, this chapter will focus primarily on tools that are setting the stage for cellular brain repair, with an emphasis on healing the damage associated with Alzheimer's disease. I'll introduce you to a dissonant chorus of voices—some frustrated with the struggles in the drug arena, others energized by advances in neurotechnology—to give you a realistic sample of the discourse.

The Problem with Brain Disorders

"When it comes to brain disease, there is a very long list of disorders—depression, Alzheimer's, Parkinson's, schizophrenia, bipolar disorder—and not a single cure for any one of them. Not a single cure!" Frank Tarazi sounds exasperated as he shares his thoughts about the state of brain health with me in the summer of 2018.[5] I've loved Frank's refreshing candor ever since meeting him a couple years earlier at the 2016 annual meeting of the WEF's Global Future Councils in Dubai. This elaborate affair is the ultimate think tank, convening more than seven hundred people at the absolute forefront of their fields, who descend on the ultramodern city known more for its luxury shopping and exciting nightlife than as an innovative hub for tackling geopolitical issues related to the Fourth Industrial Revolution.

Over the two-day event, we all broke off into smaller groups for each hand-picked committee, and I found myself sitting in a circle with about a dozen other people from the worlds of academia, industry, medicine, philanthropy, business, and economics. One of them was Frank, a burly Harvard Medical School professor and director of the Psychiatric Neuroscience Program at McLean Hospital in Boston, which focuses on the pathology and neurobiology of psychiatric disorders such as Alzheimer's disease, schizophrenia, ADHD, and depression. With his pedigree, you might think he'd be one of those stuffy academics who thinks innovation emanates only from within Ivy League universities. Instead, he's one of those rare individuals who also recognizes that breakthroughs can also come from outside those ivory towers. After his brief introduction, I could tell he had a remarkable grasp of the entire landscape of diagnosis, treatment, and prevention of brain disorders. That's why I tracked him down to talk about the current state of brain repair at the cellular level, particularly dementia and Alzheimer's disease.

Frank is frustrated that, despite the billions of dollars invested into research, we still don't have an effective treatment for Alzheimer's disease. The last drug approved for the disease hit the market in 2003. Since then, over one hundred "promising" drug trials have failed. "Some drugs are available to help manage the symptoms better, but they don't cure them," he says. "In the progressive diseases—Alzheimer's, Parkinson's—they don't stop or even delay progression. These patients will all eventually die from complications of the disease." Finding a pharmacotherapy that acts like a magic bullet is seeming like less of a possibility.

The issue isn't money. In 2017, business magnate Bill Gates announced he was personally funneling $100 million toward Alzheimer's research—$50 million immediately and another $50 million earmarked for start-up ventures.[6] It's a phenomenal gesture, but sadly, throwing money at the problem has yet to provide an answer.

Frank thinks the solution may lie in earlier diagnosis and intervention. As an Alzheimer's expert, he is acutely aware that by the time a patient with memory problems sees the doctor, it's often too late. The brain has already suffered inevitable damage, and we have yet to come up with a drug to reverse that damage. "In my research program, we're trying to identify patients who are at high risk of Alzheimer's and develop immunotherapies to intervene earlier in asymptomatic individuals. It's not an easy task," he admits. So far, the number-one risk identified for Alzheimer's is quite simply older age. The older you get, the higher your chances of developing the disease.

That's basically what the world's best researchers have come up with since 1906 when Dr. Alois Alzheimer first described the "peculiar disease" in a groundbreaking lecture at the Thirty-Seventh Conference of South-West German Psychiatrists. In his lecture, he shared that, five years earlier, he was asked to examine a fifty-one-year-old woman who had been admitted to the Hospital for the Mentally Ill and Epileptic in Frankfurt, Germany, where Alzheimer was a senior physician. The woman, Auguste D, was suffering from a strange cluster of symptoms: memory problems, disorientation, paranoia, and more. The doctor, who had a special interest in dementia, proceeded with a series of examinations. His handwritten notes of his remarkable exchanges with the patient were unearthed in 1995 when Auguste D's blue cardboard file, lost for decades, was finally relocated. The contents of that long-missing file were detailed in a 1997 paper in *The Lancet*.[7] When Alzheimer asked Auguste to tell him her husband's name, she responded with her own instead. While lunching on pork and cauliflower, she told Alzheimer she was eating "spinach." And she would forget objects he'd shown her just a short time before. Alzheimer recorded the progress of her disease until he moved to Munich in 1903, and after her death on April 8, 1906, he asked for her brain to be sent to him for examination.

In a 1907 paper he published of his now-famous lecture, he wrote that Auguste D displayed "as one of her first disease symptoms a strong feeling of jealousy towards her husband. Very soon she showed rapidly increasing memory impairments; she was disoriented carrying objects to and fro in her flat and hid them. Sometimes she felt that someone wanted to kill her and began to scream loudly . . . After four and a half years of sickness she died." Alzheimer went on to detail the shrinkage, neurofibrillary tangles, and plaques he found in her brain at autopsy, changes that have since become known as the hallmarks of the disease.

When Dr. Alzheimer, a psychiatrist and neuropathologist, first published his paper, nobody cared. The medical community didn't see the significance of his findings. "Even Alois Alzheimer didn't recognize the importance of what he reported," according to Frank. When you consider that the average life expectancy in the U.S. hovered around age fifty in the early 1900s,[8] it's no wonder doctors and scientists missed out on the gravity of the disease. The incidence of Alzheimer's at age fifty is significantly lower than at seventy-nine, which is the current life expectancy in the U.S. And these days, it's common for people to live well into their eighties, nineties, or even past one hundred. "It's not that the disease wasn't present, but people didn't live long enough to develop symptoms," says Frank. It wasn't until 1910 that Emil Kraepelin, a psychiatrist who worked with Alzheimer, first referred to the condition as Alzheimer's disease in the eighth edition of his book *Psychiatrie*. The pioneering doctor died in 1915, long before anyone would realize that the symptoms he first described would one day become one of the greatest threats to human cognition and would launch an international research effort to understand, treat, and prevent the disease.

Today, rates of Alzheimer's disease are surging. It's unlikely to find a person who doesn't know someone or have someone in their own family who is affected by Alzheimer's. It's so pervasive and devastating, it has entered the political arena. Much like when the AIDS virus became epidemic, and the world said, "We have to have an intervention," government leaders are determined to have a treatment for Alzheimer's by 2025. But experts still don't know what causes Alzheimer's—what triggers the death of neurons. They've hypothesized that it's the buildup of toxic proteins, but this remains only a hypothesis. Identifying biomarkers of the disease, such as neurofibrillary tangles and plaques, is possible with current brain imaging technologies, but it isn't being done in clinical practice. Why not? The cost—about $4,000 to $5,000 for a positron emission tomography (PET) scan. "Think about it. If I order a PET scan for a patient in practice and find a high accumulation of beta-amyloid, what am I going to do for that patient? At this time, nothing!" says Frank. These biomarkers will only become more useful if they can be coupled with effective treatments that can prevent or at least delay the progression of the disease.

What makes treatment trickier is that, even if a person has an accumulation of beta-amyloid, it remains unknown if they will develop symptoms in five years, fifteen years, or ever. Frank has seen patients with abnormal beta-amyloid and no symptoms, as well as people with unremarkable levels of beta-amyloid who do have symptoms. In his opinion, the beta-amyloid hypothesis is on life support. There's another camp in the Alzheimer's field that thinks beta-amyloid may actually be neuroprotective and that removing it could make the condition worse. With sadness in his voice, Frank admits, "After fifteen years and billions of dollars, we're at square one." Our conversation left me feeling a bit frustrated that researchers and Big Pharma have yet to find the molecules or the therapeutic interventions needed to reverse or halt the progression of Alzheimer's, but even Frank alluded to the fact that neurotechnology has the potential to change that.

Revolutionary Tools for a Cellular-Level View of the Brain

I've been following the latest advances in neurotechnology tools for years, and in my world, the developers of these new tools are like A-list celebrities. Some people lose control or get tongue-tied when they see a movie star or a famous musician. Me? I get excited when I run into the people behind the latest and greatest innovations in brain science.

In 2016, I headed to Davos, Switzerland, for the World Economic Forum's Annual Meeting, which was teeming with the biggest names in the industry. Along with navigating the bustling throng of WEF members and high-powered guests, I went from speaking on one panel to listening in on other fascinating presentations, then decided to take a quick break. Such a flood of data about the latest breakthroughs and most promising technologies can get overwhelming, so I looked for a quiet nook to let my brain relax for a few minutes. That's when I spotted a bearded man whom I instantly recognized, and my plan to relax was washed away by a surge of adrenaline.

That's Ed Boyden! I thought.

Ed is the neuroscience prodigy and MIT professor I briefly mentioned in chapter four who co-developed optogenetics, arguably one of the most important brain research tools to emerge in the twenty-first century. The monumental discovery of the technique was named the 2010 "Method of the Year" by the journal *Nature Methods*.[9] The development also earned him what is considered to be the Academy Award of science, a Breakthrough Prize in Life Sciences, in 2016,[10] as well as the 2018 Canada Gairdner International Award.[11] And that's barely scratching the surface of all the accolades he's earned. Forget about taking a break—I couldn't let this opportunity slip past me.

I struck up a conversation and soon discovered Ed isn't the single-minded researcher I had expected. He may have the mind of a scientist, but he has the heart of a philosopher. From the time he was a kid—maybe eight or nine years old—he's been wondering about the meaning of life. While his schoolmates were racing around the playground and struggling to learn fractions, Ed was pondering what causes human suffering and happiness. Eventually, he decided he wanted to tackle these existential questions through science.

Advanced beyond his years, Ed started college at age fourteen and began working in a lab where researchers were attempting the impossible. "They were trying to create life from scratch in a test tube," he told me during an interview for this book.[12] Obviously, that experiment didn't work, but Ed was enthralled by the process and has been aiming for the loftiest of goals ever since. By the time he entered grad school, he had decided to take everything he'd studied—chemistry, physics, quantum computing, neuroscience—and blend it to approach brain science from a novel angle. He realized the history of science is really the history of tools. "Science is taking the invisible and making it visible. With the telescope, you can see distant stars, but without it, it's hard to imagine how the origin of the universe would have been worked out," he muses. "Without the microscope, how would we ever know about bacteria?"

So, while most of his fellow neuroscience students were contemplating the amazing new discoveries they hoped to make with existing technologies, Ed chose an alternate course, focusing instead on building a whole new set of more powerful tools that could help unlock the mysteries of the brain. Many scientists spend their entire lives chasing promising hypotheses in the hopes of making one big breakthrough, only to be thwarted again and again. Not Ed. Since he was a quick starter in everything, it didn't take long for him to land on a groundbreaking discovery. In fact, he co-developed optogenetics as a "side project" while working on his PhD in his mid-twenties. As I said, the guy's a prodigy.

As briefly mentioned in chapter four, optogenetics helps control the brain with light. Most existing technologies that map or control brain activity take a shotgun approach, encompassing the whole brain or major regions within it. By contrast, Ed and fellow medical student Karl Deisseroth were trying to activate or shut down specific neurons while leaving nearby nerve cells unaffected. They turned to nature for inspiration, specifically photosensory or photosensitive molecules from bacteria and algae that convert light into electricity. Borrowing these molecules from nature and using tricks from the field of gene therapy, they implanted them into neurons. "It worked almost on the first try," he recalls. "We took these genes, put them into brain cells, and made them light sensitive. And that allowed us to turn them on or off."

Activating or deactivating specific cells gives researchers the opportunity to figure out how they contribute to behaviors and diseases. "They can hunt down the specific cells that play a role in a brain disorder and which cells, if deactivated, will remedy that disease state," says Ed. This was a real breakthrough because current drug therapies can affect the entire brain, and many neurotechnologies impact large swaths of nerve cells, altering not only the targeted cells but also billions of other healthy neurons. By determining the specific cells involved, scientists might be able to target medications or other technologies to just those individual cells responsible for brain disorders, leaving the normal neurons untouched. Since optogenetics burst onto the scene in 2005, more than one thousand neuroscience groups around the globe have been using the technique to study the brain, making explosive discoveries in the areas of recalling lost memories, restoring sight, recovering after stroke or TBI, suppressing depression, and more.[13]

The success of optogenetics fueled Ed's quest to create high-powered tools for next-level brain science. True to form, he isn't simply refining existing techniques to inch research forward. He's remaking the way we can view and control the brain, so we can leapfrog into the NeuroGeneration. This is evident in his latest innovation: expansion microscopy. While most scientists have been tethered to the microscope as a method to zoom in on biological tissues, Ed and his team turned that notion upside down: Could they enlarge the tissue samples for easier viewing? This innovation grew out of the frustration that, as much as we know about the brain, there's even more that we don't know. Ed lamented that we don't even have a complete list of the different cell types within the brain, nor a grasp of their shapes or molecular composition.

To make it happen, they brainstormed how to swell the brain and read papers by the MIT physicist Toyoichi Tanaka, who studied swellable polymers. Later they discovered that these same polymers were found in a product Ed was very familiar with—diapers. As the father of two young children at the time, Ed had seen the way baby diapers swell when they get wet. So Ed's team tried embedding brain tissues in a really dense polymer matrix that expands in a similar way. They discovered this method could enlarge brain tissues a hundredfold in volume, evenly pushing molecules apart.[14] Rather than pumping up the power of a microscope, they were able to enlarge the biological specimen. "Expansion microscopy lets you do 3-D imaging with nano-precision resolution. Essentially, what we are doing is making a map of the brain," he says. "Once you know the locations in the brain that change in a brain disease, you can try to repair the brain." That's the next step.

To achieve that step, Ed is making this technology—along with other tools he's developing—freely available to neuroscientists worldwide. His team has already trained more than four hundred research groups—and the number keeps growing!—on expansion microscopy, and they're already churning out new findings for Alzheimer's disease, Parkinson's, epilepsy, and glioblastoma brain cancer. As exciting as it is to imagine a world with treatments to end these brain disorders, it isn't the final goal for this philosopher at heart. "If we cure all the brain diseases," he says, "but we humans still don't feel meaning, we still don't have enough empathy, and we still have unnecessary suffering, then I would consider that only a partial success."

Repairing Impaired Brainwaves

Pass the popcorn, please! These days, most of us head to the movies for a little escapism with a superhero blockbuster—or the latest installment of my personal favorite, *Star Wars*—but in the not-too-distant future we could be watching a movie to help reverse memory problems. You won't find the "directors" of this movie listed on IMDB or hobnobbing with Hollywood types. They're more familiar with lab rats than A-list actors. Behind the scenes of this scientific production are Ed Boyden and Li-Huei Tsai, a neuroscientist at MIT. The two colleagues have co-founded Cognito Therapeutics, which is committed to developing device-based therapies—such as this movie—for Alzheimer's disease and other brain disorders.

Let's rewind a bit to understand how a movie could potentially help people with this devastating brain disorder. Li-Heui (pronounced "Lee-way"), the director of MIT's Picower Institute for Learning and Memory, noticed that research has shown that people with Alzheimer's disease tend to have impaired levels of gamma brain waves,[15] the frequency associated with higher-order cognitive functions. Along with a team of researchers, Li-Heui embarked on a series of studies on mice that had been genetically programmed to develop the distinctive amyloid-beta plaques and the accumulation of tau proteins that become tangles. In her

2009 study, collaborating with Ed Boyden's group to use optogenetics and to record how they changed brain rhythms, they implanted optical fibers into the mice brains and then stimulated and synchronized the gamma oscillations at 40 hertz (the number of cycles per second) in the hippocampus, unleashing a cascade of biochemical reactions and changes in gene expression. Microglia, the immune cells that act like janitors to clear out debris in the brain, changed shape and went into overdrive, effectively removing 40 to 50 percent of the amyloid-beta from their tiny brains.[16] "If you drive the brain at a certain frequency," explains Ed, "the brain's immune system turns on and cleans up the junk in the brain."

The astounding results inspired the team to look for a noninvasive method to use instead of optogenetics, which Ed had developed as an invasive tool for research, not therapy. Optogenetics involves genes that come from microbes, such as bacteria and algae. "You aren't supposed to have those in your brain," explains Ed. "If we introduced them into the brain, there's a chance, however small, that the body would think they are foreign invaders and the immune system would attack the brain." The solution? Li-Huei's team lit up the lab with LED strobe lights and a pulsing beat, creating a sort of EDM rave for the mice, and tuned the flickering lights and sounds to 40 hertz.[17] Subjecting the rodents to this makeshift rave for one hour a day for seven days produced a 67 percent reduction in amyloid-beta plaques and also minimized the presence of tau proteins.

This is great news for mice, but as you've seen in this book, what works for the mouse brain doesn't necessarily translate to the human brain. That's where Cognito Therapeutics comes in. They're conducting tests now on humans with Alzheimer's disease, who basically watch a movie with flickering lights and clicking sounds at 40 hertz, to see if the therapy can reduce the symptoms of memory loss. "With a neuroscience experiment, you can think all you want and plan all you want, but the experiment can fail. The question for any of these experiments is . . . where's the data?"

Li-Huei and Ed can't wait for that data to arrive. "If this works, it's going to be a major breakthrough," he says. In the age of digital electronics, he adds, a device that delivers light and sound that's modulated forty times a second wouldn't be that complicated to create, and it could be quite cheap. I can't help but think how amazing it would have been if my Footscray neighbors could have simply watched a movie for an hour a day in order to remember their loved ones' names and find their way home again.

An Artificial Memory Prosthesis to Offset Neural Damage

As you've seen in earlier chapters, researchers, engineers, and biotech developers have already pooled their massive talent to edge biological beings into cyborg territory with prosthetic devices like cochlear implants, retinal implants, and bionic limbs. What's the next frontier? Prosthetics for the brain. That's right, humanity lies on the verge of truly mind-altering neural devices that target the part of the brain most often damaged in people with Alzheimer's disease. For years, star-studded teams of researchers led by Robert Hampson, a professor of physiology/pharmacology and neurology at Wake Forest Baptist Medical Center, and Theodore Berger at USC, have been working feverishly toward an artificial memory prosthesis. Buoyed by funding from DARPA as part of a program launched in 2013 called Restoring Active Memory (RAM), in 2018 the researchers took a giant leap forward in their quest to develop a device that can restore memory function. In this remarkable, first-of-its-kind, proof-of-concept trial in humans, the researchers stimulated electrodes implanted in the hippocampus, resulting in 35 to 37 percent improvement in short- and long-term memory.[18]

"This is the first time scientists have been able to identify a patient's own brain cell code or pattern for memory and, in essence, 'write in' that code to make existing memory work better, an important first step in potentially restoring memory loss," says Hampson about the study, published in the *Journal of Neural Engineering*.[19] For DARPA, this represents the culmination of two decades of investments in neurotechnology. On the day the results of the study were released to the public, Justin Sanchez, the director of DARPA's Biological Technologies Office and the program manager for RAM, said, "[It has] brought us to an extremely exciting point today where we're testing tangible technologies that have the potential to alleviate some of the worst effects of brain injury and illness."

If we someday have a neural prosthetic to reverse memory loss in people with Alzheimer's disease, stroke, or TBI, we'll have people with epilepsy to thank for it. As you saw with the world's first cyborg, Kevin Warwick—the scientist desperately searching for someone to engage in a brain-to-brain communication study with him—it isn't easy finding volunteers who are willing to have electrodes surgically implanted in their brain in the name of science. That's why the Wake Forest team enlisted the help of eight people who already had electrodes in their brains—epilepsy patients. These brave individuals—not the same epilepsy patients you read about in chapter five—had undergone a procedure to place electrodes throughout their brain, including in the hippocampus, to determine the cerebral source of their seizures. When they weren't undergoing testing for that primary purpose, they participated in the memory study by playing a computer game. They performed two tests—a short-term memory test that lasted about two minutes and another one that went on for up to one hour and fifteen minutes. In the first test, the patients were shown a simple image, such as a color block, and after a brief delay where the screen was blanked, were then asked to identify the initial image out of four or five on the screen. In a second test, participants were shown a highly distinctive photographic image, followed by a short delay, then were asked to identify the first photo out of four or five others on the screen.

As they played the game, Hampson's team recorded the activity in their hippocampal neurons to identify the brain patterns involved in encoding memory. This is where the USC team led by biomedical engineer Theodore Berger came in. For years, he has been trying to unlock the mysteries of the hippocampus to discover how it transforms short-term memories into long-term ones. The hippocampus, a horseshoe-shaped structure deep in the medial temporal lobe, is one of the most misunderstood parts of the brain. It's common to mistakenly think of this area as a storage unit for memories: a mental Rolodex that allows you to remember the name of that CEO you read about when you actually come face-to-face with her, the fact that your high school mascot was a tiger, or that the bishop in chess can only move diagonally. In fact, the hippocampus is responsible for *forming* new memories, not necessarily storing them. All facts (a.k.a. inputs) coming to the hippocampus are short-term memories, but as they are routed through the hippocampus, signals encode them so they become long-term memories. Along the way, the information undergoes a number of important transformations.

Much of what we understand about how memories are formed in the brain can be traced to over five decades of studies on H.M., the renowned amnesia patient I mentioned in the introduction to this book whose postmortem brain was famously sliced by neuroanatomist Jacopo Annese in 2009. From the age of ten, H.M. suffered from epileptic seizures that became so debilitating over time that, in 1953, at the age of twenty-seven, he agreed to undergo a radical treatment.[20] That year, a surgeon sliced open his scalp, drilled into his skull, and removed a portion of his brain in a procedure called a bilateral medial temporal lobe resection. The surgery proved successful in calming his seizures, but it came with a major side effect: severe memory impairment. According to a 1968 study by Brenda Milner, the British Canadian researcher who spent years investigating his memory loss, H.M. could no longer remember events that happened only moments earlier, couldn't recall the names of people he just met, couldn't state his own age, and could only "make wild guesses as to the date."[21] As Brenda described it, "His experience seems to be that of a person who is just becoming aware of his surroundings without fully comprehending the situation, because he does not remember what went before." H.M. said his new life was "like waking from a dream." The years of studying H.M. and his curious memory loss laid the foundation for what we know about the formation of memories and the importance of the hippocampus in that process.

USC's Berger explained the process in a keynote at EmTech 2013 at the MIT Media Lab in Cambridge, Massachusetts.[22] The input converges on the entorhinal cortex, which (functioning somewhat like a hub) sends the information to the dentate gyrus (DG) in the hippocampus. From there, the DG communicates with an area within the hippocampus called CA3, which then talks to a region called CA1. (These regions are named using the initials for "*cornu Ammonis*"—Latin for "Ammon's horn"—which refers to the ancient Egyptian god who was depicted with the horns of a ram that resemble the curved shape of the hippocampus.) The final transformation occurs when CA1 sends the revised info back to the entorhinal cortex, completing the loop and sending it out to wherever it will be stored. For over a decade, Berger has been trying to decode the signals that take place at each of these junctures. Neurons communicate with one another using a form of pulse, and Berger's studies have shown that it's not actually the pulses themselves, but rather the time between the pulses that carries the pertinent information. The space-time codes are altered with each one of the transitional stages of long-term memory formation. Berger wondered if they could identify those codes.

Like so many in the science community, he turned to some thirsty lab rats for answers. His team implanted electrodes into the CA3 and CA1 zones in the animals' brains while they were being trained to choose between two objects. It was a very simple task. They presented the rats with one of two items; then, after a delay, the rats were presented with both items, and they had to choose the opposite of what they had chosen the first time. The rats had to hold that initial memory—was the object they originally saw on the left or on the right?—and show they remembered it by pressing the opposite bar. If they got it correct, the thirsty rats got to drink some water. "They did this about one hundred times a day," says Berger, whose team recorded and stored the input and output codes every time.

Then came the next big step in the process—creating an artificial hippocampus to enhance the memory process. The researchers gave the rats a drug to shut down the hippocampus so the animals could no longer transform short-term memories into long-term memories. They could remember the object they chose for five to ten seconds but no longer than that. Using the space-time codes they'd recorded, the researchers stimulated the electrodes and the rats successfully retrieved a long-term memory. The rat's brain hadn't created the memory; the recorded space-time code created it. The process restored long-term memory function. "Even though they couldn't create it, we created it for them," says Berger.

Taking things even further, the team redid the experiment, this time minus the drug that shut down hippocampal activity, effectively with the rats in a normal state. "He's got electrodes in his head, but otherwise he's normal," says Berger, adding with a chuckle something every neuroscientist can relate to: "That's what we call normal." In this experiment, stimulating the rat's normal brain with the encoded signals enhanced its long-term memory formation. In Berger's words: "So, we can improve memory quite substantially."

The trials continued with rhesus monkeys who, according to Berger, "will work all day for grape juice because they love grape juice." The researchers showed the monkeys a single picture and then, after a delay, showed them two to seven pictures, and the monkeys had to choose the picture they had originally seen. Everything the researchers found in rats also worked in monkeys. You can imagine the researchers' excitement when, after toiling away in labs with rats and monkeys, they moved on to human trials.

In the 2018 study with the Wake Forest team that involved twenty-two epileptic individuals with implanted electrodes, Berger's crew analyzed the recordings from the correct responses on the memory tests and synthesized a multi-input, multi-output (MIMO)–based code for correct memory performance. Then the Wake Forest team retested the participants' image recall ability while stimulating the hippocampal electrodes with the code the USC team had devised based on the patterns in the participants' own hippocampal nerve cells. In both tests, the people showed a significant improvement. The fact that it worked didn't come as a surprise. These Wake Forest and USC bioengineering rock stars have been placing electrodes into the brains of mice for many years and eliciting a boost in memory. "What surprised us was how successful it was," Hampson says. "Thirty-five percent improvement in memory is huge!"[23]

This stunning demonstration showed that it is possible to tap into a person's own memory-making process and feed those neural codes back into the hippocampus to reinforce them. According to Hampson, even in people with impaired memory, we can differentiate the neural codes that represent proper long-term memory formation from the faulty patterns that prevent short-term memories from lasting more than a few moments. Feeding the healthy codes into a person's brain boosts their ability to form new memories. "In the future, we hope to be able to help people hold onto specific memories, such as where they live or what their grandkids look like, when their overall memory begins to fail," he says.

DARPA's Sanchez thinks the end zone is in sight. "We're closing in on our goal of an implantable, closed-loop memory prosthesis," he says. And while DARPA's primary goal lies in creating powerful technologies to counter memory loss in the nation's service members and veterans, in the coming decades the implications of such a device could reshape all of humanity.

Transplanting Memories into Brain Cells

Many of us think memory manipulation is the stuff of sci-fi movies like *Total Recall*, *Inception*, or *Eternal Sunshine of the Spotless Mind*. But next-level researchers are already exploring how to replace lost memories, transplant them from one person to another, and even edit them. Imagine someday being able to erase painful memories—your first heart-wrenching breakup in junior high, the wildfire that burned down your family home, or even the IED explosion that killed your fellow Marines. What about implanting new memories about events that never happened to you but that you wish had? Could you fill your brain with fantastic memories about making the Forbes 400 list, winning Wimbledon, or earning the Nobel Prize in Neurotechnology? Or what about replacing lost memories? For now, these experiments are restricted to mice, but they're making some remarkable progress and, according to Duke University Medical School professor Murali Doraiswamy, "we're getting closer and closer to where you can actually transfer different types of memories from one mouse to another."

Along with Murali, one of the researchers at the forefront of some of these memorable efforts is Boston University's Steve Ramirez, a guy who's so smackdown funny and exuberant he almost seems like he could have been a character in the movie *Superbad* (his favorite, by the way) rather than a lab geek. Steve made headlines when he and his late colleague Xu Liu successfully implanted a false memory into a mouse.[24] For this landmark trial, Steve dropped a mouse into a small box and watched as it froze in fright, recalling a previous event when it received an electric foot shock in that box. This is a common fear response elicited in lab experiments, except in this case, the mouse's memory of that negative event was completely false. The little guy had never gotten a shock in that box. The research team had identified the specific brain cells that were active when the mouse was making a particular fear memory in a different box. Then using optogenetics, they tricked those brain cells into responding to pulses of light, and after surgically injecting narrow filaments from a laser into the mouse's hippocampus, they shot light into the brain to re-create that fear memory in a new box. The mouse was remembering something that had never happened—now that's sci-fi reality.

News of the mouse with the false memory spread rapidly. The *New York Times* covered the study, and the rest of the media world followed. In 2014, the pair won the Smithsonian American Ingenuity Award and were runners-up for *Science*'s Breakthrough of the Year. Their TED Talk on the achievement notched over a million views, and Steve landed a spot in the Forbes 30 Under 30 Innovators in Science. Since then, Steve has continued his explorations into memory, flipping the switch from instilling fear memories into mice to reactivating positive memories in the creatures to minimize negative feelings. He foresees a day when these techniques could be used to help people overcome a variety of brain disorders, such as Alzheimer's disease, anxiety, depression, and PTSD. Forget traditional drug therapy—he's excited about the revolutionary concept of memory itself as a therapy. In his view, it's just a matter of time until memory manipulation in humans happens. "Because the proof of principle is there that we can artificially reactivate memories and create false memories in animals," he told *Smithsonian Magazine* in 2014, "the only leap left between there and humans is just technological innovation."

Can Stem Cell Transplants Create New Brain Cells to Replace Damaged Ones?

As you have seen in this chapter, despite the setbacks and struggles that researchers like Frank have noted to develop medications to treat Alzheimer's disease, progress is being made in other arenas. From the experts I spoke to, technological breakthroughs appear to be lighting the way. To continue my exploration of the most promising advances, I turned to another fellow WEF Global Future Councils member, the aforementioned Professor Murali Doraiswamy at Duke. From the moment I met Murali, I felt an immediate kinship with him. With a slight build and an easy laugh, he has this warm and engaging way of speaking that makes you feel like you're the only person in the room, even if you're in the middle of a busy conference hall with hundreds of neuroscientists, entrepreneurs, and tech developers noisily bustling around. He's also one of those impressive types who have the mental bandwidth to tackle a range of brain-related topics rather than focusing on a narrow slice of research. As Duke's director of the Neurocognitive Disorders Program, this Renaissance man is known for his work in imaging biomarkers and Alzheimer's disease, but he also delves into human consciousness, mental well-being, and yoga and its effects on the brain. He's so well respected in the field that he serves as an advisor to leading government agencies, biotech and health companies, and patient advocacy groups. He's the kind of guy who can make other Type A people feel like slackers. I reached out to him to talk about the future of diagnosis, treatment, and the global effort to find a cure for Alzheimer's, and I came away feeling more hopeful than I'd expected.

As an expert in the arena (he co-authored the popular book *The Alzheimer's Action Plan*), Murali points to a number of breakthroughs we need in order to make progress in fighting Alzheimer's: early detection before symptoms develop, technology to understand the biochemical process and steps involved in the breakdown of neuronal communication and cell death, technologies to develop targeted treatments, and tools to monitor whether or not the drugs are working. Digging even deeper, he says treatments for the disease need to be targeted to its stage of development. "At a very late stage, ideally, you want treatments that can potentially restore lost cells or lost connections. At earlier stages, we need technologies that prevent further damage. Each of these is slightly different technology, and there are many kinds of tools that are being developed," says Murali. In terms of early detection, he quickly rattles off close to a dozen technologies in the works, including PET scans; digital tools; at-home tests; and blood, genetic, metabolic, proteomic, and microbiome biomarkers.

When it comes to repairing damaged cells, he tells me that a number of pilot studies point to promising potential for stem cell transplantation to prevent, delay, or slow the progression of brain disorders, such as Alzheimer's disease. Think of stem cells as a sort of multipurpose cell that can differentiate into any specialized type. "The hope is that, if you can get stem cells into the brain, perhaps they will either result in new brain tissue or in repairing the connections that aren't working properly," says Murali. So far, studies with lab animals have seen stem cells boost the release of neurotrophic factors that support the growth and survival of neurons, produce immunomodulatory effects, increase expression of synaptic proteins, and even replace diseased cells.[25] In Florida, a clinical trial is underway in which researchers are infusing stem cells into people with Alzheimer's.[26] The results could change everything.

Repairing cellular damage to a brain that has been ravaged by Alzheimer's, TBI, or stroke could offer hope to millions of people who hope to regain lost cognitive and physical capabilities. But what about repairing cellular damage that *might* one day lead to symptoms? Thanks to progress in the field, doctors are now able to identify people who have a "silent" buildup of amyloid-beta and tau proteins, which means their brains show the damage associated with Alzheimer's disease, but they don't display any of the symptoms. This is what experts call preclinical Alzheimer's. According to Murali, it is estimated that about 30 percent of all people over the age of sixty-five have preclinical Alzheimer's. As mentioned, what's so troublesome from a research standpoint is the fact that not all people with preclinical Alzheimer's will ever develop symptoms, so we don't yet have a perfect predictive test.

We learned this in part from the famous Nun Study that David Snowdon began in 1986 in Mankato, Minnesota.[27] Snowdon wanted to determine why some people fell victim to age-related brain deterioration and others didn't. The study, which ran for decades, grew to include 678 Roman Catholic nuns around the U.S. between the ages of 75 and 107. The women participated in annual cognitive assessments and other medical workups, and they all agreed to donate their brains at death for examination. One of the most surprising findings of the lengthy study was that some of the women who had a genetic predisposition to Alzheimer's, and whose brains at autopsy showed an abundance of the lesions associated with the disease, nonetheless remained cognitively sharp up until their death at an advanced age. Researchers are racing to develop more accurate predictive tests and test a variety of novel approaches—such as antibodies targeting amyloid-beta and tau—in prevention trials.

But it begs the question: What will happen if and when neurotechnologies that can successfully repair brains become available? Would people with preclinical disease be encouraged to undergo potentially hazardous procedures *in case* they might develop symptoms years or even decades later? We're already seeing this dilemma play out in other arenas—think of women who undergo prophylactic mastectomies, for example. Are humans ready to undergo brain surgery, stem cell transplants, or other procedures simply to mitigate long-term risk? Especially when these procedures present far more immediate dangers, such as seizures, strokes, brain swelling, stem cell rejection, and more? Is the promise worth the risk?

When pondering the exciting possibilities explored in this chapter, consider as well the cellular-repair endgame. Could scientists someday discover a way to reanimate brains after death? It sounds like the stuff of a bad sci-fi movie, but a 2019 study could make you think twice. Researchers from Yale University made headline news when they restored some function in the brains of pigs that had died up to four hours earlier.[28] The team of scientists pumped a solution into the brains of the deceased pigs that jump-started microcirculation as well as some molecular and cellular activity. However, there was no evidence of higher functions like consciousness—yet. While scientists hope it could open up a whole new set of possibilities for people with Alzheimer's disease, traumatic brain injuries, or stroke, what this ground-shaking experiment ultimately will mean for the human brain remains to be seen.

CHAPTER **7**

CREATING SMARTER ARTIFICIAL INTELLIGENCE

How the Human Brain and AI Will Coexist

S CIENTISTS SAY THE BIG BANG set the universe in motion, and it took over 13 billion years for that primordial soup to become the cosmos as we know it today. Some religious leaders say God created the heavens and the earth in only seven days. Tech experts say that, in the age of artificial intelligence, the speed of invention will happen at such an accelerated rate that when we look back at this time period, it will seem as if everything started in an instant—an AI Big Bang. But what will that AI future look like?

Researchers predict that, within the next decade, AI will outperform humans in language translation, writing high school essays, and driving a truck. By 2049, AI is predicted to outclass humans in writing a bestselling book, and be better surgeons than their flesh-and-blood counterparts by 2053. Experts in the field say it's a coin flip—a fifty-fifty chance—that AI will outperform humans in every task by approximately 2063 and that in the next 120 years, every job will be automated.[1] I disagree.

Some people imagine killer robots will wipe out humankind. Some envision an AI utopia where automatons solve all of life's ills. Others, myself included, hold an alternative view of how AI is more likely to develop (*hint:* it won't be the proverbial "us vs. them"). Yes, there will be robots, but AI will also become part of an extended, augmented human organism—part of us, part of our brain. In other words, "humanistic intelligence" will prevail, with humans integrated in the feedback loop with computers, allowing the analog and digital systems to work together. In the NeuroGeneration, human–machine hybrids will combine the high-speed processing powers of computers with the creativity that is uniquely human, transforming us into something much greater than the sum of our parts. And in my view, it is this powerful combo that will outperform all others.

Taking this concept to the extreme is Dutch neuroscientist Randal Koene, who has spent years investigating the notion of "whole brain emulation," or uploading the human brain to a computer.[2] If he succeeds, this could effectively allow us to live forever in a virtual world where biological bodies built for life on Earth are no longer required. Other innovators, including Elon Musk, are focused on doing the reverse—uploading computer processing ability to the human brain in an effort to allow humans to keep pace with the machines. While the ultimate blurring of human and machine has yet to arrive, AI is beginning to spread at a quickening pace into nearly every arena imaginable.

In any discussion about AI, it's important to clarify terms because there is a lot of confusion surrounding the concept. Some people automatically associate the term with a catchall for artificial general intelligence (AGI), or superintelligence, in which machines can perform any task—repetitive, creative, or intellectual—as well as or better than humans. This is only one type of AI, however, and it is still in the pipe dream stage. "Narrow

AI," such as deep learning or machine learning, is already being used today for thousands of practical applications. With deep learning, computer systems can perform specific tasks by recognizing patterns and sifting through mountains of data at lightning speeds no human can match—all unsupervised. In this chapter, you'll see the many ways humans are harnessing the power of narrow AI to extend our cognitive capabilities while working to safeguard a future for our biological species and the human brain in the event general AI becomes a reality.

How Big Data and the Human Brain Are Driving AI

Gary Flake adjusted his brainwave-reading headset and tuned his attention to the floating cube on the computer screen in front of him. The former CEO of Clipboard, which was acquired by Salesforce, Gary was attempting to manipulate the cube using mind control for my company's Focused Mind Challenge at the 2013 TED conference. Like all the contestants, he had eight seconds to perform a baseline recording and then another eight seconds to train the machine learning algorithm to recognize his mental commands to push, pull, rotate, or lift the virtual cube. He then had sixty seconds to get back into that train of thought and hold it for as long as possible.

Even without all the commotion and distractions at TED conferences, it's extremely difficult to maintain a singular thought for sixty seconds. The person who could exert the greatest mental control over that virtual cube would win a prize. Each year, the much-coveted TED Prize of $1 million is given to a thought leader with a bold idea to spark global change in a positive way. Our contest may have had a decidedly smaller award—a free EEG headset—but it promoted so much buzz within the tech crowd, it earned the title of "The Other TED Prize" that year.

Superstars like Google's Sergey Brin, World Wide Web inventor Sir Tim Berners-Lee, and parallel computing innovator Danny Hillis queued up for a chance to control the cube with their thoughts. Sergey notched an impressive, near-perfect score on his first try, and Danny zoomed up the leaderboard, but Gary wasn't about to let anybody beat him. He came back over and over and over, taunting his pal Danny with photos of his scores in a friendly competition. By the end of the conference, he had surpassed close to one thousand people who had taken the challenge to claim the top spot. (A grad student who meditates a lot took second place, and Sergey landed in third.)

Elated, Gary walked away with the prize, and I had gained a new friend. "I'll be honest; I cheated in multiple ways," he admitted to me years later when he became an advisor to my company. "I'd been working in machine learning and signal processing for decades at that point, so right away, I started thinking about it through the lens of a machine learning system and trying to figure out what it was trying to figure out about me. So, I kind of used what little expertise I had in machine learning to try to game the system a little bit."

When I wanted to delve into machine learning and AI to see what they mean for the future of the human brain, I went straight to Gary, who led the world's largest enterprise search engine at the CRM giant Salesforce. Now officially retired, he invests in and consults for innovators with the coolest new technologies. In my opinion, he's among some of the world's greatest minds on big data. He thinks of AI as being on a path similar to the evolution of big data and the internet.

Think about the internet for a moment. In 1989, when Berners-Lee invented the World Wide Web, the average person couldn't grasp how it would change our lives. It has since evolved into billions of users, and many of us feel like we couldn't live without it. AI is heading in the same direction. Thanks to all those internet users, a lot of data has been generated as a side effect. That's a good thing for product development, according to Gary, who says if you're really clever in how you architect a system, you can get away with releasing a product that's good but not great. Then you harness the stream of user data to quickly make powerful improvements to that product. "If you can do that in a way that's very dynamic, where you're basically adapting in real time, you can make a product that is almost evolving outside of the normal shipping cycle," he says.[3] He cites speech-to-text as a prime example.

In the early 2000s, decades of progress in speech recognition technology had reached a plateau, and getting to that final stage of comprehension was considered a near-impossible problem to crack. For years, experts had been tackling the concept with techniques based on peer signal processing and linguistic communities. At the rate they were developing improvements, they figured it would be another ten or twenty years before they arrived at anything that seemed fluid and natural.

Enter the propeller-head crowd. "Google paved the way for how you design and architect systems like this," according to Gary. "What they did was come out with a crappy little smartphone mobile app for doing voice searches." With that Google Voice Search app, people could speak into the phone and do a search. It sounded cool and sometimes it worked, but it was wrong a lot of the time. But the ingenious brains at Google came up with a smart user interface. When the system stumbled on a word—you said "cat," but it understood "caught"—it would offer a variety of alternatives you could tap to make the correction, or you could supply your own correction. "The beautiful thing about that was, it made an okay product good enough because even when it was wrong, when it failed, there was an escape hatch," says Gary. The user taught the system how to work better. It's as if the users' brains were acting as both the R&D and quality control departments for the product. This allowed the tech giant's system to leapfrog the traditional industry, and now we're conversing with Google Home, Alexa, and Siri far sooner than if developers had continued with the usual iterative steps to improvement. Gary sums it up: "We're able to take state-of-the-art machine learning systems, bolt them on top of that stream of user data, and yield machine learning solutions that are oftentimes better than what specialized AI techniques were producing a generation before."

With specialized AI, developers hand-code systems with narrow abilities, such as understanding language or playing games. Remember when IBM's Deep Blue outmaneuvered chess master Garry Kasparov in 1997[4] or when the Roomba robot vacuum cleaner made its debut in 2002? They were basically one-trick ponies without a clear path to generalization. Today, instead of these highly specialized systems, developers can produce more generic off-the-shelf systems, and they'll eventually outperform the narrow AI. The first generation will have a very simplistic form of brain–computer interface in which the user will have the device attached, and as you're performing an action—say, turning the page in an ebook—you'll be giving explicit directions: "Turn the page for me." Further in the future, the first generations will give you a simplistic way of thinking those commands instead of actually taking physical action. They won't be 100 percent accurate, but just like with speech-to-text, they will have some feature that allows users to correct mistakes. "Think of these billions of corrections as training exemplars that are going to create a virtuous cycle of data," says Gary. "It will allow us to improve brain–computer interfaces and start leapfrogging older ways of doing things."

In the near future, Gary thinks we can expect a convergence of the hardware technologies and data collection in which human brains essentially train machine-learning systems until they reach levels that will improve the end users' lives in some way. Whereas traditional ways of running businesses and advancing science have been iterative—you go from an experimental phase through a theoretical phase, and each of these informs the other—innovations in business and scientific research will hit light speed. "The cycle for improvement, the cycle for an insight in the scientific community or the business world, typically follows social or business cycles," Gary says. "You have to publish a paper. It has to be validated by the peer community. There's supporting research later on, and finally, it becomes part of the canon of what society knows. That takes years." But letting these cycles happen in real time will prompt a collapse of outmoded business, scientific, and social cycles; rather, the models will become highly fluid. In other words, if you can turn a formerly step-by-step process into something much more continuous, you can actually turn the crank on that process. Instead of it taking years, it might take seconds.

Using AI to Have a Brain That's Forever Young

It's a fact of life that as your birthdays add up, your cognitive function goes down—blanking on your neighbor's name, forgetting where you put your keys, taking longer to hit the brakes when a car stops short in front of you. As discussed in chapter six, it's one of the most dreaded aspects of aging. Declines in memory, processing speed, attention, and conceptual reasoning are all considered normal effects of aging, according to a 2013 review in *Clinics in Geriatric Medicine*.[5] And it sets in earlier than you think. Processing speed—how fast your brain performs cognitive and motor functions—starts to diminish in your twenties and continues its gradual downward spiral throughout the rest of your life.[6] By the time you hit seventy, there's a decrease in visual confrontation naming, meaning you may see everyday things like a dog, a tulip, or a pair of scissors and have trouble recalling their names. About this time of life, mental flexibility, idea formation, and abstraction also take a hit.

Some of these seemingly inevitable drops may stem from structural changes in the aging brain. Starting at about age twenty, the brain's gray-matter volume starts to shrink, with most of the loss occurring in the prefrontal cortex and, more moderately, in the hippocampus. Aging takes a greater toll on the brain's white-matter volume. People over seventy have up to 20 percent less white matter than younger people, according to cadaver research that appeared in a 1992 issue of *Annals of the New York Academy of Science*.[7] With all of these brain changes, it's no wonder it can be so hard to teach Grandma how to use a smartphone. But what if AI could help you slow the brain aging process? You could stay sharper for longer and possibly ward off neurodegenerative diseases like dementia and Alzheimer's.

That's one of the goals of anti-aging researchers like Alex Zhavoronkov, the CEO of Insilico Medicine and chief science officer of the Biogerontology Research Foundation. Alex is harnessing the power of deep learning to zero in on the biomarkers of aging and speed drug discovery to turn back the biological clock. Considering the number of Americans age sixty-five or older is projected to soar from 48 million in 2016 to over 98 million in 2060, and that one in four Americans will fall into this age group by then, the need to find ways to preserve cognition and prevent age-related disease is greater than ever.[8] Among anti-aging researchers and tech innovators, the search is on for the greatest geroprotectors. And with Insilico Medicine receiving the Frost & Sullivan 2018 Technology Innovation Award, it's clear Alex is racing to the head of the pack.

I first met the fast-talking, bespectacled scientist, who has multiple degrees in physics, biotechnology, and computer science, in 2008. That was back in the early days at EMOTIV, when I personally got to know many of our initial customers. Alex was one of them. He was looking for affordable EEG equipment he could use in his experiments, like one study in which he used EEG and fMRI to recognize the cognitive differences when a person was thinking about a face or a house, and then used a machine learning algorithm to recognize those patterns and predict which object a person was imagining. This study landed in a 2011 issue of *Plos One* and, since then, Alex has been putting those deep-learning algorithms to work in the anti-aging realm.[9]

Although Insilico is based out of the Johns Hopkins Emerging Technology Center in Baltimore, Maryland, it has tapped the genius of dozens of scientists hired through hackathons and competitions worldwide in the U.S., U.K., Poland, Belgium, Russia, South Korea, Taiwan, and Africa. And it works with over 150 academic and industry collaborators worldwide. It's one of the reasons why it's so hard to catch up with Alex. Like the Energizer Bunny, he is constantly on the go: traveling over two hundred days per year, visiting labs around the world, and crisscrossing the globe to speak at the world's most mind-blowing conferences on AI in healthcare, machine learning, aging, and longevity.

The last time I saw him in person, he showed up for a quick visit in our office in San Francisco. For this book, I managed to track him down after his recent trips to Hong Kong, Philadelphia, London, and Germany and just before he jetted off for Sweden, Boston, and Glasgow. I felt privileged to get the whirling dervish to sit down for a phone chat to delve into the latest advances in AI and anti-aging and what they mean for the future of the human brain.

"One of the most exciting breakthroughs I've seen over the past five years is in the area of aging biomarkers," he says. "In order to be able to intervene, we need to understand how to measure aging and how to compare ourselves when we are twenty, twenty-five, thirty, thirty-five, fifty, seventy, and eighty. We can see aging in pictures, but it was pretty much impossible to measure it on the biological level."[10] Alex and his team have been using deep-learning techniques to hunt for those aging biomarkers. One of the first they've identified is the blood, the nine pints in the average woman and twelve pints in the average man that course through the body's circulatory system.[11] They looked at millions of blood tests and trained deep neural networks to recognize which features in the blood are associated with youth and which are linked to older people. Now, they can predict your age within a few years just by looking at your blood. The next step, according to Alex, is to determine what adjustments can be made to make the blood biochemistry levels look younger. And if they can make your blood look younger, could it make you look and feel more youthful? Even more exciting, will looking younger on a molecular level translate into physical and cognitive health benefits?

In Alex's view, the idea of anti-aging is less about knocking ten years off your looks and more about fighting diseases of the brain and body before they begin. As discussed in the last chapter, by the time Alzheimer's disease is diagnosed, the damage to the brain has already been underway for years, and it may be too late to reverse it. "If you want to diagnose these processes earlier," he says, "you really need to look at aging as a central, driving factor behind Alzheimer's and many other age-related diseases."

Drug interventions to slow the aging process are percolating in labs around the world, and there are some promising ones in the pipeline. Imagine if you could zap your aging body's tired old cells to put them out of commission, leaving the peppy young cells to do all the work. That's the idea behind the emerging field of senolytics, which studies chemical cocktails designed to kill senescent cells—basically, old cells—that contribute to cellular dysfunction and aging. These impaired cells, dubbed "zombie cells" because they refuse to die, spew out harmful pro-inflammatory cytokines that contribute to age-related conditions, such as heart disease and diabetes. The zombie cells infect neighboring cells, turning them into zombies and leading to a veritable army of the undead. Researchers may have found their silver bullet to kill the zombie cells.

In a 2018 study published in *Nature Medicine*, scientists from the Mayo Clinic found that injecting healthy young mice with senescent cells compromised their health and function.[12] But treating the mice with a senolytic combo of drugs—dasatinib and quercetin—eliminated zombie cells and restored physical function. And giving the senolytic cocktail to chronologically old mice increased their life span by 40 percent and enhanced their "health span." That is, rather than being sick, frail, and slow in their bonus golden years, the mice were zippier, stronger, and had greater endurance. For anti-aging researchers like Alex, that's the ultimate goal—not just living longer, but living healthier for a longer period. Who wants to live to one hundred if you're going to be bedridden, saddled with chronic disease, and struck with dementia for the last twenty years of your life? You want to be kicking up your heels at the local dance contest, spending time with your great-grandchildren, launching a new business venture, and playing Words with Friends.

Alex thinks the results of the senolytics study on mice are staggering, but he doesn't trust the lab rodents, which only live about two years in captivity. "They don't have the time to accumulate all the damage humans do," he says. "For example, if you open up a seventy-year-old on an operating table and touch the aorta, it actually feels stiffer and kind of like an eggshell when compared to the aorta of a twenty-year-old. And the importance of that is because there are all kinds of mineral deposits that build up in the heart muscle and connective tissue, and the mice just don't have the time to accumulate this damage." Humans live an average of 78.6 years,[13] giving us many more years to build up harmful gunk in our bodies. And time to lose more neurons.

Considering the adult human brain loses about 85,000 brain cells a day, we've typically lost hundreds of millions of them by the time we reach retirement age.

This is why Alex is keen to use machine learning to create "virtual humans" to take the place of mice in research. Literally, it's what his company's name, Insilico, means: scientific experiments conducted using computer modeling or simulation. Not only could this approach significantly cut down on the over 100 million rats and mice that are sacrificed each year in the name of science,[14] but it would also provide truer results. By tracking the aging process at every level—from blood biochemistry to transcriptome to behavioral data—his team could then mine data pipes to create a virtual human. "The idea is to actually build humans from scratch," he says. "So I can say, 'Create a human male, who is a fifty-year-old Asian with a specific issue,' and the lab will give me that from the data pipe."

In the meantime, Alex tracks his own biochemistry to test his biological age. Considering he's at the cutting edge of anti-aging research, you might think his biochemistry would look younger than this calendar age. But he's quick to admit that he's in step with his chronological age or even slightly older. "To be honest, I don't take care of myself as I should," he admits. He blames his heavy travel schedule, which exposes him to radiation and throws off his circadian rhythms. Our master biological clock lies deep within the brain's hypothalamus, and when it is off kilter it can disrupt production of neurotransmitters and hormones, which is associated with a greater risk for cancer, depression, and obesity.

Does Alex think he'll live long enough to benefit from his research? "I want to live as long as possible, but if I don't get to enjoy the benefits, I think it's going to be all right because it's the most altruistic thing anybody can do. You save more lives than preventing World War II." That's a true scientist talking. I, for one, hope Alex gets to take advantage of some of his findings so he can find the fountain of youth that will keep our bodies and our brains looking and performing their best.

A Tool for the NeuroGeneration

Remember reading in chapter six how Ed Boyden, the co-developer of optogenetics, said that the history of science is really the history of tools? In some ways, AI is simply a next-generation tool, one that is already showing promise in a variety of industries, with some of the biggest advances arriving in the medical field. At the 2016 International Symposium of Biomedical Imaging, a competition pitted pathologists against a machine learning algorithm to see who could most accurately detect breast cancer in images of lymph nodes.[15] The AI won in two categories and had a final accuracy rate of 92 percent. In a separate trial, U.K. researchers found that a deep-learning algorithm accurately spotted 7.6 percent more patients at risk of heart disease than physicians did, and it came up with 1.6 percent fewer false positives.[16] Google has now teamed up with doctors to develop AI that can detect diabetic retinopathy, which can prevent people with diabetes from going blind.[17]

Frank Tarazi, the Alzheimer's researcher you read about in chapter six, sees a host of advantages in using AI to diagnose brain disorders, including Alzheimer's, Parkinson's, and Huntington's disease, an inherited disease that attacks nerve cells in the brain and can emerge in juveniles. "[AI] can determine if a patient is at risk and can find them when they're asymptomatic," Frank says. "We're seeing more and more use of AI in brain imaging. The biggest one I see is in accurately diagnosing brain cancer without the need for more invasive approaches such as brain biopsy." The current way doctors diagnose brain cancer starts after a person experiences symptoms, such as headaches, blackouts, seizures, numbness, tingling, or vision changes. Generally, after ruling out other more ordinary causes, an MRI is scheduled. Although this neuroimaging tool can reveal if there's a tumor, it can't tell you what kind of cancer tissue it is, if it's an aggressive form of the disease or if it's confined to the tumor and hasn't spread to other organs. The only way to determine what type of tumor it is? Biopsy. This entails slicing through the scalp, drilling through the skull, and removing tissue from the brain. It's risky, but the pathology report from a biopsy is crucial in determining the best treatment plan.

Thanks to advances in the use of AI in medical imaging, this standard method of diagnosis could be banished to the medical history catalog of barbaric procedures, like frontal lobotomies or the ancient practice of trepanation, which involved using a rock to scrape a hole into a person's skull for health reasons (although a British woman, Amanda Feilding, famously drilled a hole in her own skull in 1970 in search of higher consciousness).[18] AI will be able to dissect images of a tumor, sift through thousands of other images, and determine the type of cancer without having to do surgery. "It's not going to happen tomorrow, but maybe in ten years, maybe less," says Frank. "One big thing for AI is it analyzes images in a way that radiologists may not be able to."

For example, people with brain tumors who undergo radiation may develop necrosis, the death of tissue that leaves small scars in the brain. On a subsequent MRI, a radiologist might discern something new, but be unable to tell if it's necrosis or a new tumor. "We're talking about millimeters here—very small amounts—but that's enough to raise an eyebrow," says Frank. "Let's say the radiologist finds two millimeters of tissue that has changed since the last brain image. Is it necrosis or is it a new tumor or recurrence of cancer? The radiologist can't eyeball it even with enlargement and magnification." This could mean a person has to undergo another biopsy with all the risks involved.

In the not-so-distant future, AI medical imaging and emerging deep-learning programs would be able to differentiate between new tumor growth and necrosis, avoiding unnecessary procedures if the tissue changes arise from the latter. In Frank's opinion, the medical field is going to become increasingly dependent on AI. Before a radiologist sends a report, they will run it through AI, which can detect things the human eye can't see. "This will change medicine," Frank says.

These advances may come at a cost. In the business world, these developments threaten to replace millions of human laborers with comparatively more efficient mechanized alternatives. Think about those radiologists who are being outperformed by AI, for example. "It's man versus machine," says Frank. "We've created the machine, but the machine will win in the end. In thirty to forty years, there will be no need for radiologists, or we won't completely eliminate them, but there will be far fewer of them. We will have more dependency on these programs."

My take is that rather than throwing our hands up in despair at the "rise of the machines," industry leaders can harness the developments that have the potential to dramatically increase human efficiency. Nimble companies that adopt emerging AI technologies early may gain an unsurpassable competitive edge over slower legacy firms. In a workforce dominated by automated devices, workers who don't want to become obsolete may have to upgrade their brain's software to stay relevant.

AI for All

Tech experts, researchers, and healthcare professionals aren't the only people who can take advantage of deep learning, according to Rachel Thomas, who co-founded Fast.ai with her husband, Jeremy Howard.[19] This power couple looks at AI through a very different lens and is breaking down barriers surrounding the technology. "We want people to know that it is possible for them to get involved with AI even if they don't think they have the right background or didn't go to the right school, or if math makes them anxious," says Rachel.

I'm not surprised at all that the two of them are bucking industry trends by encouraging people from all walks of life to take a sort of DIY approach to deep learning. I heard about Jeremy years ago from a mutual friend back in Australia, who told me I had to meet up with him because he was doing some really amazing things. When we finally did meet in 2011 in San Francisco, where he and Rachel are now based, it was one of those classic "small-world" moments. It turns out he went to one of the top boys' schools in Melbourne, not far from the girls' school I attended. In fact, we both took the same tram line and got off at the very same stop to head to our respective schools. Even though he's a few years older than I am, we very well might have been on that tram at the same time at some point. I wouldn't have noticed him, since back in those days, I was far more interested in my books than in boys!

After falling into the comfortable back-and-forth of two kids from the same circle, I realized our mutual friend was right. Jeremy, one of those scary-smart types who topped the state at the high school level, was up to some fascinating things. A philosophy major, he had taught himself how to code and began dominating the competitions on Kaggle—the competition platform now owned by Google where anyone can try their skills on real-world challenges using machine learning. At one point, Jeremy raced up the rankings to grab the top spot as the number-one Competition Grandmaster. The guy was so good, he was eventually tapped to become Kaggle's president.

A few years later, he met Rachel, who took a slightly more traditional route to the AI field. With a PhD in mathematics, she spent some time as a quant in the finance world before switching to software engineering and then being a data scientist in the tech industry. When she started exploring the AI field, it was almost impossible to find much practical information, and she was struck by the harsh reality that the field is highly exclusive—"unnecessarily so," she says. "I went to a meet-up where one of the stars in the field was speaking, and he gave this very theoretical talk. I asked a simple, practical question during the Q and A, and he said, 'That's part of a dirty bag of tricks that nobody writes down.' He didn't answer the question, but it was this really explicit message that if you're not in the inside crowd, nobody's writing this information down, and you're not going to be able to get it." Most of deep learning is rooted in the academic world, where publishing your research in the top journals is the goal. Rachel and Jeremy were both interested in looking at it from a completely different angle. They wanted to find ways to use deep learning to help solve real-world problems and make it more accessible and easier to use for people who don't have "PhD" after their name.

Around the same time the University of San Francisco was starting its Data Institute, Rachel and Jeremy proposed teaching a course with only one year of coding as a prerequisite and no advanced math required. Most instruction in the AI field assumes students have graduate-level math backgrounds—a major barrier to the vast majority of people. When they first proposed the course, they weren't even sure if it was possible. "Are we really going to be able to pull this off?" they wondered. They created a plan based on the principles in David Perkins's *Making Learning Whole* book, which advocates introducing students to the "whole game" rather than bits and pieces of knowledge generally taught before doing anything fun. "We wanted to get people using deep learning as quickly as possible to solve problems even if they didn't understand the underlying details," Rachel says. "We wanted to get people hooked on how exciting it is to use it first."

That's exactly what happened. They actually had students deploying apps in their second week of the class. One student used deep learning to help identify whether a big cat was a cougar, a bobcat, or something else. The app won an award at a hackathon just one week into the course. Another student trained a classifier to tell the difference between cricket and baseball, using a relatively small dataset of about forty images. And then there was the Canadian dairy farmer, who wanted to use deep learning to identify the health of his goats' udders. Poor udder health is a huge factor in dairy farming and causes more economic loss than any other factor, so it's extremely beneficial to identify udder infections early. It's hard to imagine that any ivory tower researcher would have landed on udder health as a topic for inquiry. The couple now films the course so people from anywhere around the world can log in and participate. Their students have logged in from as far away as Pakistan and India.

According to Rachel and Jeremy, it's critical to get more people from diverse backgrounds—in terms of gender, race, geo-diversity, etcetera—involved in deep learning. The industry has created some unexpected negative outcomes. For example, researchers at MIT found that Amazon's facial-recognition technology, called Rekognition, misidentified dark-skinned women as men 31 percent of the time compared to just 7 percent of the time for lighter-skinned women.[20] This is not an isolated occurrence and remains an unfortunate side effect of the homogeneity of the people currently working in the field. The lack of diversity results in everyone racing to build solutions for the same few problems because they can't even imagine the vast majority of real-world issues people outside the tech industry might be trying to solve.

Rachel says there are a few things that scare her about deep learning—among them, people implementing algorithms without any sort of mechanism in place to catch errors, or with no meaningful appeals process when there are mistakes. "We get some chilling stories coming out of that," she says. "It concerns me that the large tech companies seem to have this disproportionate unchecked power and no real accountability. We need to have smart policies and smart regulations to respond as a society to these huge changes that are coming." While major corporations and policymakers grapple with those issues, Jeremy and Rachel are continuing to spread the message that AI is for everyone and that it's important for people outside the usual developers to get involved. "We need you to be a part of it because we need people from all backgrounds," Rachel implores. "We need journalists, politicians, and lawyers to understand the capabilities of AI because their expertise is really valuable."

The Fear of General Intelligence and AI Safety

"AI is far more dangerous than nukes." Elon Musk didn't mince words at the 2018 SXSW Conference when asked about the future of artificial intelligence.[21] Although most AI devices currently have very limited competencies, it isn't far-fetched to think that they could aggregate competencies to develop a form of general superintelligence—superior to human cognitive function and performance in multiple or even all areas. There's a looming existential risk that AI could be intentionally programmed to turn against humans, or be developed with the best intentions to benefit humanity but take an unpredictable and unexpected detour that threatens civilization or even our existence. But while some people like Musk, who's already given us self-driving cars, fear that we're hurtling toward a doom-and-gloom future with AI, most experts in the AI community disagree. In fact, according to a 2016 survey of experts in the field, only 5 percent fear that human-level machine intelligence will have an extremely bad long-term impact on humans—as in wiping out the human race. Another 10 percent think it will have a net negative effect on humanity, but 45 percent envision it will have a good or extremely good impact.[22]

My hope is that we can infuse AI devices with intelligence that is rooted in humanity—with an understanding of emotions, motivations, value systems, and morals. If we can do this, then it's likely that AI will remain a benefit to humanity. A growing cadre within the tech community is banding together to use their brainpower to promote AI safety as a way to prevent these existential risks. Jaan Tallinn is one of them. You may not have heard of the organizations he has co-founded—the Centre for the Study of Existential Risk and the Future of Life Institute—but ten or twenty years from now, you'll probably be thanking him for it. You've undoubtedly heard of the programmer and physicist's other contribution to the world of technology and communications: Skype. As one of the co-founders of the communications tool that boasts 300 million monthly active users and one billion downloads,[23] Jaan holds a lofty place in the tech world. I met him in 2014 at an international conference called Dialog, an invitation-only, weekend-long think tank at the Sundance Mountain Resort in Utah, hosted by angel investor Auren Hoffman and Peter Thiel of PayPal fame, where 150 global leaders get together to hash out radical ideas that could change the world. Forget the usual panels and keynotes you find at most conferences; the gloves come off at Dialog, where it's all breakout sessions and group discussions that tend to get heated.

Everything Jaan said at the conference resonated with me, so when he visited the San Francisco Bay Area some time after that, we made plans to meet for dinner. As a foodie, I wanted to take him somewhere that showcased the best of San Francisco dining and went through my repertoire of outstanding restaurants. I soon learned that all that effort was only for my own benefit, as Jaan is one of those rare people who simply doesn't care what, when, or even if they eat. Dining with Jaan made me stop and wonder whether, when we become human–AI hybrids, we'll have the ability to turn on and off our desires for things like food, cigarettes, alcohol, and drugs. Personally, I would never want to give up great food. When I was researching this chapter, I knew I wanted to get his perspective, so I scheduled an interview with him.[24] His preferred method of communication? Skype, of course.

From his hometown in Estonia, which was still behind the Iron Curtain when he first began tinkering with computers, Jaan discussed two main challenges we need to solve regarding AI. The first is ensuring that AI is developed in a way that is beneficial to humans. The second is ensuring that, once intelligent AIs themselves begin developing next-generation technologies, they don't veer from that beneficial path. At a conference a few years ago, he likened AI to a rocket launch. At first you're just trying to get enough acceleration for liftoff, but you're also going to need someone to steer it, and you're going to have to plot its trajectory, and importantly, you must to do the plotting *before* takeoff. So Jaan is trying to help steer AI in a direction that benefits humanity before the countdown. At the Centre for the Study of Existential Risk, he and his colleagues are developing prevention and mitigation strategies in collaboration with a global community of technologists, policymakers, industry figures, and academics to reduce the potential risks from these emerging technologies.

There is no denying that if AI development goes off track, the risks could be catastrophic. Just think about the environment we live in, Jaan says. For millions of years, evolution shaped our planet, but in the last one hundred thousand years and especially the last five millennia, humans have taken over for evolution and reshaped our environment. Almost everything you see in our cities and suburbs is a product of the human brain. "Humans are smarter than evolution, and humans have been able to create things that evolution never could, for example, radios," says

Jaan. For generations, humans have been at the helm in shaping the future of the planet, but our influence could be waning. In five, fifty, or one hundred years, things could begin to change in ways we didn't anticipate—and dramatically so. This could spell trouble for humans, who are biological creatures with a very narrow range of environmental parameters in which we can survive. "If AI were to take over the environment, it's very possible that it would do very drastic things, like getting rid of the atmosphere, for example," he says. "It could raise the temperature by 100 degrees or lower it by 100 degrees" because the temperature doesn't affect AI as much as it affects biologicals. Humans, though, would be wiped out.

Aligning AI with human values is essential to creating technology that stays on course to benefit humans. Like almost everybody who interviews Jaan about this topic, I ask him, "Whose values are we talking about?" He reminds me that humans have far more in common than we might think. We all like breathing. We all need to eat (although a few people, like Jaan, can go without it for a while). And as he likes to say, "We all like our planet to be roughly at about room temperature."[25] You get the picture. But Jaan also admits we have a major problem aggregating values. And we can't simply ask each other what our values are, because what we say we value may not be what we truly value. You'll recall from chapter two that we viewed this disconnect at work in EEG marketing studies looking at what consumers say they want versus what they actually choose. In 2017, Jaan proposed designing mechanisms to "transparently and robustly aggregate global opinion about what a good future should look like."[26]

To some extent, the AI industry is akin to the so-called Wild West of frontier days. Unlike the medical and pharmaceutical sectors, which fall under the FDA's regulatory grasp, the computer-technology and AI industries operate unchecked. As of this writing, there is no regulation to stop someone from creating

AI that is capable of wiping out humanity. As government leaders begin to understand the far-reaching impacts of AI, they may seek to pull the reins on the unbridled development. Until then, it is up to us—tech innovators—to voluntarily abide by some code of ethics or a sort of Hippocratic oath that will ensure that the AI technologies we create serve the greater good.

Fortunately, some industry heavy hitters are rising to the challenge. OpenAI, a nonprofit organization sponsored by Elon Musk, Peter Thiel, Microsoft, and other big names, boasts sixty full-time researchers and engineers who are on a mission to build safe artificial general intelligence. "By being at the forefront of the field, we can influence the conditions under which AGI is created," the group states on their website.[27]

They aren't the only ones tackling the tough questions and attempting to steer the future of AI in a positive direction. In 2016, AI researchers from tech giants Microsoft, DeepMind, Apple, Google, Amazon, Facebook, and IBM joined forces to launch the Partnership on AI to Benefit People and Society. The collective—now including over fifty member organizations, researchers, academics, businesses, policymakers, and other diverse stakeholders—aims to develop best practices for AI, advance public understanding and awareness of it, provide an open and inclusive platform for discussion and engagement, and support efforts for its benevolent application. "By working arm in arm with multiple stakeholders, we can address the important topics rising at the intersection of AI, people, and society," says Eric Horvitz, director of Microsoft research and co-founder of the partnership. His co-founder Mustafa Suleyman, who is head of applied AI at DeepMind, insists, "We must work collaboratively to hold AI to the highest ethical standards and make sure it has the broad and transformative impact we all want to see."[28]

At the Beneficial AI 2017 conference, a five-day gathering dedicated to AI best practices that included AI researchers and thought leaders in diverse areas, the attendees came up with a set of guidelines.[29] The 23 Asilomar AI Principles address research issues, ethics and values, and long-term concerns and provide a blueprint to AI that offers a shared benefit to as many people around the globe as possible.[30] As of December 2018, the principles have been signed by 1,273 AI/robotics researchers and 2,541 others, including people like the late Stephen Hawking, Elon Musk, and Jaan. I recently added my name to the list. With so many technologists and other stakeholders signing on, it appears we're heading in a positive direction.

The Promise of the Human–AI Hybrid

Every time my friend Gary Flake hears an example of what a powerful AI could do—something that seems to be on the brink of new levels of intelligence—he always finds it inferior to what could be achieved if a human were part of that entity. Like many of us, Gary doesn't buy into the binary view that the future of AI will either destroy humanity or save us. "The future of AI is entirely dependent on the future of brain–computer interfaces because what I believe will happen is not the AI apocalypse, not the AI utopia, but something that's actually a lot more human and arguably a lot more interesting," says Gary. "It's going to be very intimately involved with humans."

He offers up the legal field as an example. Let's say we have an AI that can digest the entire body of legal knowledge in existence and then do a massive search of prior legal arguments to find the one that has the greatest probability of winning a case—and do it in a matter of minutes, not days, weeks, or months as it would take a human. It sounds impressive, but the AI advantage may stop there—AI isn't going to be able to argue the case in court. The process of convincing someone that something is true or

false or compelling or not compelling is based not just on present-
ing a body of evidence but also on engaging someone—a judge
or jury—in a back-and-forth dialogue. That lightning-fast legal AI
might put some legal researchers out of a job, but it's not likely to
replace that trial lawyer who is adept at crafting compelling arguments that can win over a courtroom.

Rather, in a human–AI hybrid future, those two entities could
blend together into something even more outstanding. "Imagine
that you had a good lawyer who had the super AI as an advisor
whispering in their ear," Gary says. "What would they be capable of
doing then?" Think of Matthew McConaughey as Mickey Haller
in *The Lincoln Lawyer* (based on Michael Connelly's book of the
same title), with what amounts to a supercomputer legal assistant
seamlessly feeding him case reports at the ideal moments in his
opening statement. This scenario would allow a brilliant lawyer to
enhance their creative argument without all the drudgery.

Let's revisit the 2016 biomedical-imaging contest I mentioned. The AI had a 92 percent accuracy rating when detecting breast cancer, but even though it won in two categories, the
humans still outperformed it with a 96 percent accuracy rating.
What was most remarkable, according to study author Andrew
Beck, a researcher at Beth Israel Deaconess Medical Center, was
that when they combined the efforts of AI and the pathologists,
the accuracy rating rose to 99.5 percent.[31] The human–computer
combo outclassed them all.

As AI progresses, it will continue to conquer individual
domains—think of those expert systems from the field of medicine, such as interpreting MRI scans, detecting cancer from
pathology reports, and diagnosing diseases before symptoms
develop. Retail, manufacturing, and service industries will all
adopt some form of AI to tackle specific aspects of labor where
the AI system is seemingly superior to a human. But it's far more
exciting to envision a future where humans collaborate with these

AIs, for example, where game developers use AI to create elaborate games that respond and even change dynamically in response to player feedback. "Imagine an interface where the AI has access to everything I see and hear, and then it can overlay audio or video privately to me with something like Google Glass and earbuds," Gary muses. "With that scenario, we will be able to realize human–AI combinations that will seem like superheroes."

Remember analog astronaut Dr. Susan Ip-Jewell from chapter two, whose mission to simulate life on Mars involves memorizing a telesurgery protocol to handle medical emergencies? What if she and other crew members didn't have to memorize anything? What if they were connected to an AI version of an EMT that could see and hear everything they're viewing and direct them through patient care? The AI EMT could tell them where to apply pressure, how to slice into the skin with a virtual scalpel, how to suture a wound, and more. On a much more earthly level, what if it's a holiday and you would really like some help cooking that celebratory feast? You could have cooking pros Rachael Ray, Bobby Flay, or Luke Nguyen whisper the recipes in your ear so your holiday meal comes out looking divine and tasting even better. And this sensory overlay would feel completely natural, like an extension of your own senses.

"In the future, I'll walk into a room, and there will be annotations floating above people's heads to remind me who they are and what the last thing we talked about was," says Gary. "I'll be able to think, 'Ah, what company do they work for?' and it will appear." Even better, it won't feel like a robot is responding to Gary's questions. It will feel like it's coming from his own brain because the integration between how a person interacts with the world and how they interact with AI will be seamless. We will think of it as part of the human organism.

Here's yet another example. Most commercial jetliners use autopilot to take off and land the plane and to handle almost everything in between as human pilots supervise. In Gary's view, humans will act much like a pilot of an ensemble of AIs, a combo more powerful than any one AI or any one human. The AIs are going to feel like an extension of the human organism, and your brain will control all of it. As developers figure out how to mass-produce millions of these AI workers and advisors and people start using them, the side effect will be a flood of data. And just as we saw with speech-to-text systems, improvements will accelerate at such a rapid pace that we'll reach a tipping point when these "advisors" become a part of us and we will effectively become human–AI hybrids.

As exciting as it sounds, the promise of becoming a super-powered hybrid presents a host of risks. Will we become so reliant upon this way of experiencing the world, similar to how we've bonded to our smartphones, that we'll feel incomplete when disconnecting from our AI advisors? Will we become unwilling or even unable to detach from our machine-driven advisors? Will our brains suffer from this mind–machine meld, losing the ability to perform certain functions we've relegated to our AI? When it comes to human brains, their functionality is "use it or lose it." For example, if you actively practice speaking French every day, you will strengthen the neural pathways in your brain to make it easier to remember how to ask, *"Où sont les toilettes?"* the next time you're in Paris and you need to use the restroom. On the other hand, if you arrive in the City of Lights and simply ask your AI to translate your thoughts into French, your brain isn't actually learning how to speak. Take away your AI, and you'll be in big trouble when you need to go *now*. Developers need to start addressing these issues so that in the future we can integrate AI with our biological brains without becoming slaves to it. In our ongoing quest for the advancement of humankind, we must continue to ponder what we want the evolution of the human brain to look like, and strategically map our trajectory to get there.

PART II

EXPLORING THE RISKS AND ETHICAL DILEMMAS OF BRAIN ENHANCEMENT

CHAPTER **8**

ALL BRAINS MATTER

Why Neurodiversity Could
Be the Great Equalizer

I N A SMALL VILLAGE IN INDIA—a place so remote it has no electricity, no telecommunication system, and no cars or buses—a research worker prepares to place an EEG headset on a female villager's head.[1] The woman, who earns the equivalent of $3.75 a day laboring in a nearby rice paddy and who has never ventured outside her village, eyes the futuristic device with trepidation.

"Is it going to hurt my head?" she asks.

Sathish, the research worker, has heard this question before. In fact, he's heard several similar queries from villagers who grew anxious when they saw the brainwear.

"Will it give me a headache?"

"Is it going to give me an electric shock?"

He assures the woman the headset is painless and explains that all she has to do is sit quietly and allow her mind to wander. Sathish gently adjusts the array of electrodes on the woman's head and turns on the device that will read and record her brainwaves. Unsure what to expect, the villager does as Sathish asked. She closes her eyes, sits in silence, and starts to daydream.

This woman is just one of hundreds in close to fifty settlements in India who agreed to take part in a trailblazing research project. Launched by the nonprofit organization Sapien Labs to study neurodiversity among people from all walks of life in every corner of the earth, this study included people in areas ranging from small, remote villages to urban hubs with daily incomes ranging from less than $1 to more than $400. The results reveal the profound impact that modernization has had on the human brain and show that the brains of villagers who live without electricity are fundamentally different from those of white-collar professionals in urban centers. This spotlights why it is imperative in the NeuroGeneration that researchers and brain-enhancement innovators take the approach that "all brains matter."

The Untenability of Normal

What's normal? When it comes to the brain, it's hard to say. Although the major physical architecture of the brain is something we all have in common, the way in which each individual brain is wired is influenced by each person's life experiences. The brain's mysterious folds and trillions of connections become as unique as each and every one of the 7.5 billion individuals living on this planet.

For decades, however, neuroscience research has taken a shockingly narrow-minded approach. Over 75 percent of human neuroscience research has been conducted in the U.S. and Western Europe, mainly on university-educated students.[2] And neuroscience research has largely ignored females in animal studies. This bias comes in two forms: neglecting to include females in studies, and neglecting to report the gender of the rats or mice used in trials. This is slowly changing. In 2017, a team of researchers reviewed 6,636 articles that involved rats or mice and found that an increasing number of studies are reporting gender.[3] Although the percentage of studies reporting both male and female animals rose from 17 percent in 2010 to 35 percent in 2014, the percentage of articles using males only jumped from 31 percent to 40 percent in that time period. And relatively few studies showcase findings that differ based on gender. The research on people who are transgender or who identify as nonbinary is even more sparse.

Although the research on the differences between female and male brains remains skimpy, a 2014 analysis revealed that some areas in the frontal lobes (involved in executive function, impulse control, and decision making) are larger in women, while other areas (including those involved in fear and anger as well as spatial perception) are bigger in men.[4] One study showed more activity in the female brain in seventy of eighty brain regions tested, indicating that women tend to have busier minds.[5] What exactly all these differences mean is still being hotly debated. I believe it simply means that men's and women's brains are equally intelligent and capable, just wired differently so they problem-solve in unique ways.

But the neurodiversity between birth genders matters. Studying brains on a massive scale may help us understand why birth gender influences the risk of developing certain brain-related diseases and psychiatric conditions. It could also tease out why males and females exhibit different symptoms of conditions like ADHD and depression. For example, in boys, one of the markers of ADHD is hyperactivity and an inability to sit still. Girls with ADHD, however, are more likely to exhibit inattentiveness or to cry more frequently. When you consider that boys are diagnosed with ADHD at nearly three times the rate of girls, one might ask, are some girls not being diagnosed because physicians and parents are missing the gender-based differences in symptoms? A 2017 study in the *Journal of Child Neurology* found that boys and girls with ADHD had smaller-sized cerebellums, an area associated with attention.[6] But the boys and girls differed when it came to *where* in the cerebellum they had less volume. Could brain imaging be the future of diagnosing what we consider "mental" health conditions? Could it effectively close the gender gap associated with certain conditions by allowing for a more objective way to diagnose males and females?

Similarly, researchers have found differences between female and male brains when it comes to depression.[7] Women are diagnosed with the condition at twice the rate as men,[8] and once again, symptoms differ between the sexes. Females are more likely to express the sadness we typically associate with depression, whereas males may exhibit anger or aggression. So, are women really more prone to depression, or is it just that men aren't being diagnosed—due, again, to the differences in symptoms—or because they are less likely to talk about their feelings or seek help for emotional issues? Gaining deeper understanding of the brain may help us answer these important questions and more effectively diagnose and treat people.

The fact that women have been historically underrepresented in medical research[9] also means that the bulk of our pharmaceutical treatments for brain-related disorders and psychiatric conditions have been created based on the male brain. It's possible that a greater understanding of the female brain could usher in new treatments targeted for the female brain that are more effective for them. Although there has been a concerted effort within the scientific community to include more women in clinical trials,[10] the fact remains that researchers largely continue to gather data from only a tiny proportion of the types of brains that exist. There is a danger that by relying on research that largely studies the neurons, axons, dendrites, and synapses of just one narrow band of the population, tech innovators may inadvertently build bias and inequality into their development cycles, and ultimately, their brain-enhancement products.

To mitigate this risk, we need to understand the whole gamut of neurodiversity. We need to study the brains of children, women, and men in Africa, Latin America, and Asia. We need to study the brains of people in tiny villages as well as urban environments. We need to explore the developing brain and the aging brain. We need to look at the female brain across the hormonal cycle. We need to study all of humanity. It's an enormous task, but we are making inroads.

Tara Thiagarajan, the founder and chief scientist of Sapien Labs, is on a mission to make it happen, and I've been helping supply EEG headsets and software for the project as she lays the groundwork to open one hundred neurolabs worldwide to study human brains on a broad scale. This radical concept of studying brainwaves in people from places ranging from the world's tiniest rural villages to urban settings is making waves of its own in the industry. At the inaugural Brainnovations Pitch Contest at the 2017 SharpBrains Virtual Summit—a sort of *Shark Tank* for neurotechnology innovators—Sapien Labs took home the prize as the Top Brainnovation Harnessing Big Data. This annual summit is teeming with the most cutting-edge thinkers, experts, innovators, and investors in the brain health and performance space. The 2017 event alone attracted more than 250 pioneers from twenty-three countries. In fact, it was through one of these summits that I was first introduced to Tara courtesy of SharpBrains CEO and editor-in-chief Alvaro Fernandez, who also happens to be a fellow Young Global Leader and a member of the WEF Council on the Future of Human Enhancement. The lanky, dark-haired woman who favors simplicity and facts over flash gives off a no-nonsense vibe that I find refreshing. In this male-dominated space, it's rare to meet another woman who is helping lead us into the NeuroGeneration, and that may have been part of why we immediately bonded.

A world adventurer with a penchant for destinations less traveled—she once ate nothing but millet and a smelly root on a voyage through Timbuktu—Tara is equally comfortable at conferences in the world's most sophisticated cities or on her own in the middle of nowhere in the farthest reaches of the globe. She's one of those quant types who tracks her calories, water intake, sleep, exercise, and even her mental consumption (what she's reading, time spent on the internet, and so on) to gauge their effects on her productivity, moods, focus, and metabolic system. Her biohacking results have shown that she performs better when she shuns sugar and avoids social media. Considering she has an undergraduate degree in math—along with an MBA from the Kellogg Graduate School of Management at Northwestern University and a PhD in neuroscience from Stanford University—it's no wonder she likes to measure things. She has spent years in labs at Stanford as well as at the National Institutes of Health and the National Centre for Biological Sciences in Bengaluru, building algorithms from brain signals, such as electrocorticography and EEG, in order to understand what they mean. For all of her mental horsepower, what I'm really drawn to is her dedication to understanding all brains and her commitment to sharing neuroscience research on a collaborative platform. I couldn't be more thrilled to play some small part in helping her reach her goals.

If you merely looked at her curriculum vitae, you might guess that Tara would have stayed on her original trajectory and landed in a lab within the hallowed halls of academia. But this superwoman was living a parallel life, splitting her time between the most esteemed institutions in the U.S. while building a microfinance company her late father had launched in India. She helped expand the micro-lender into a company that employs over 2,500 people and to date has provided more than $300 million in microloans to low-income communities across 20,000 villages and towns. Her customer base in these tiny rural areas has low levels of literacy and education, and no electronic footprint—no cell phones, no internet trails. As part of her studies and efforts with the business, she realized that many of the paradigms neuroscientists ascribe to human behavior were not playing out in these areas. "There was a big contrast between doing neuroscience at Stanford and being in the small villages in India," she said when we discussed Sapien Labs and the need for greater exploration into brain diversity.[11]

Tara wanted to understand the dynamics and behaviors of the people in these impoverished ecosystems, and her mathematician's brain couldn't resist the desire to start quantifying things. She had set up a small lab within the company to study her rural customer base and to understand the dynamics and behaviors in those environments. At that time, her initial goal was to understand the drivers of economic outcome. So, she assembled a team to start collecting and analyzing a variety of data. They'd started looking at cognitive metrics when one of her team members threw out a suggestion: "Why don't you start measuring their brain activity?"

It was one of those electrifying "aha!" moments that changes everything. The light bulb flicked on, and Tara could see how to combine her neuroscience background with her drive to understand her customers in these impoverished remote villages.

That's when Tara reached out to me regarding EMOTIV's EEG headsets. She wanted a brain-measurement device that was both affordable and portable so it could be used in the field. I found the whole concept fascinating, and as someone who grew up in a refugee community where many of the people now find themselves with low incomes and with educational degrees that are not recognized in their new country, the project resonated with me. I remembered some of those Vietnamese refugees I had helped at the resource center my mom had started, and I wondered what an EEG of their brains would have looked like. I was thrilled to get involved in Sapien Labs' Human Brain Diversity Project by shipping some EEG headsets and software to Tara.

With headsets in hand, Tara's team visited a couple of villages in India and performed initial recordings from about fifty people. Then they headed to the city to record the brainwaves of college-educated, white-collar professionals. When she saw the results, Tara was thunderstruck. "Oh, my God," she recalls thinking. "When we started looking at the brain activity, we saw that, fundamentally, the two did not look like the same thing at all. You would expect to see a continuum. I've worked with so many biological systems and you look at two groups, and you see small percentage differences." As she explains it, scientists are usually trying to determine if the subtle differences they notice are statistically significant, but this was something else entirely. "The distributions were barely overlapping and so distinctly different." That's when it dawned on her: the view neuroscientists (and, thus, the world) has of the human brain lacks data on the vast majority of the human population and is therefore skewed.

The rebel inside her said to reject the typical neuroscience practice of using small sample sizes in studies, to abandon the long-standing bias of studying the brains of college-educated Westerners, and to find a way to overcome the lack of standardization across data. She was ready to disrupt the status quo in these areas, but the quant inside her kicked into gear, nagging at her to ensure the study would hold up to the most rigorous scientific standards. First, she needed to expand the study. To do that, she needed an affordable tool you could use in the field. But could the portable EEG equipment—EMOTIV's EPOC—do the job? As a neuroscientist who worked in academic labs, Tara had grown accustomed to powerful, clinical-grade $50,000 EEG devices. "What can you measure reliably with a $799 device, and what can't you measure with it?" she wondered. She got to work testing the portable headsets against clinical models, noting certain measurement paradigms that worked really well with the portable models—such as working memory, pattern recognition, and rapid recall—while ruling others out.

This gave birth to the Human Brain Diversity Project, and the researchers hit the ground. Researchers like Sathish, introduced previously, visited forty-eight different settlements of varying sizes and levels of remoteness in the southern Indian state of Tamil Nadu. These settlements ranged from villages with just three hundred residents and no electricity or motorized transport to a metropolitan city with five million people and all the modern technological amenities. They tested more than four hundred people between the ages of twenty-one and sixty-five with annual incomes ranging from $300 to approximately $150,000. Some had no formal education while others were college graduates. Some had never ventured beyond the reaches of their village while others had traveled extensively to international destinations. Each one permitted a researcher to place an EEG headset on their scalp, and then they closed their eyes and started daydreaming while the device recorded their brainwaves.

Doing neuroscience research in the field presents some unexpected challenges that don't occur in sterile lab environments. For example, in the most remote villages, residents usually wash their hair with herbal powders rather than the shampoo most Westerners use, then they apply coconut oil or some other oil the way Westerners might use gel. These oils on the scalp confounded efforts to get accurate readings from the EEG equipment. Eventually, the researchers resorted to handing out packets of shampoo with instructions on how to use it and then returning the following day after the volunteer had given their hair a good, sudsy scrub. This solved the oily-scalp problem.

The recordings started pouring into the Sapien Lab headquarters, and the team applied those readings to the volunteers' living contexts. The results turned up unprecedented findings. For example, some features of the EEG varied up to a thousand-fold across global populations, suggesting there is no "normal brain." The team found such an exceptionally strong link between context and brain dynamics that Tara now firmly believes you can't research the brain without taking its living environment into consideration. "The brain, unlike the heart or any other organ, is an experience-dependent organ. Your heart will beat the same way from the time you're born. Your lungs will breathe the same way from the time you're born. But your brain will not. It doesn't function the same way when you're born as it does when you're an adult. It's going to evolve based off the context you're in and the stimulus in the environment. And you can see that, absolutely starkly," she says of the study results. According to the stream of data pouring in, the fundamental complexity of brain activity scales in relation to access to elements of modernization, education level, and a measure Tara calls the geofootprint—the degree to which a person has traveled.

The single most shocking finding? A feature that neuroscientists have long considered the archetypal human brain rhythm—the alpha oscillation—was virtually undetectable in remote villagers. The alpha oscillation is also called Berger's Wave, named after EEG pioneer Hans Berger, whom you read about in chapter two and who first discovered alpha waves back in the 1920s. Since his landmark study was published in 1929, the alpha oscillation has been hailed as the dominant brainwave pattern in humans and a reflection of the most basic cognitive processes.[12] "In Western neuroscience studies, when a person closes their eyes, you can see this rhythm. Everybody has it, and it's very pronounced," says Tara, whose findings very clearly showed the contrary: "Except when you look at people who are very remote with no access to technology—it's not detectable." Sapien Labs' study didn't show the alpha oscillation doesn't exist in these people, only that it isn't present at a level the equipment can pick up. This upended one of the most basic long-standing beliefs about the fundamental activity of the brain. If the foundation of what we consider normal doesn't exist or isn't detectable in certain populations, what other beliefs about the human brain don't apply across all of humanity? What other aspects of the human brain are different depending on context?

Tara's team at Sapien Labs ran the numbers to see how income affects brain dynamics. After all, income is what allows a person to travel, access higher education, and buy technology. The global poverty line is $1.90 a day, according to the World Bank, and an estimated 700 million people live below that line,[13] which applies mainly to calorie sufficiency and physical survival. "But when you look at cognitive parity in terms of all the dynamic features of the brain," says Tara, "what we were seeing in that measurement is that you need to hit $30 a day before you can afford what it takes to increase that cognitive complexity." A quant at heart, she quickly did the math and concluded that there are billions of people on this planet who fall below that income level, which means there are billions whose brains are functioning completely differently from those of college-educated Westerners.

Searching for a New Normal

These astonishing revelations gave Tara a jolt. Studying small samples of college students in a U.S. or European academic lab is a context relevant to only 10 percent of the world population.[14] This is woefully insufficient to understand the mysteries of the human brain on a global scale. It just doesn't add up: "There's no representation of brain activity in most of the world," Tara says.

This data jump-started Sapien Labs' efforts to expand studies of the human brain in developing nations and remote regions around the world. But how could they advance neuroscience in these areas without trained neuroscientists or expensive equipment? Tara devised a plan to seed neurolabs in Asia, Africa, and Latin America—no neuroscience experience required! Sapien Labs would provide existing labs studying medicine, sociology, or public health with the equipment, tutorials, and tools necessary to start investigating the human brain within their own populations quickly and cost efficiently.

Take Nadia Justel, for example, who has a PhD in psychology. Her lab in Buenos Aires, Argentina, which studies the connections between emotion, memory, and music, has partnered with Sapien Labs to become one of its first neurolabs. By adding EEG into the mix, the psychologist's team can link certain brain activities to her psychology research outcomes. Tara says the preliminary work coming out of Argentina is showing results similar to those from the study in India—that brain dynamics are dependent on context. In Argentina, tribes that live up in the mountains without electricity are showing some of the same brain dynamics found in remote villages in India. She cautions that the findings are very preliminary, but they suggest the foundational differences observed weren't just something unique to India.

The Argentina experiment also confirms that Sapien Labs' plan to partner with a lab that has never done EEG or neuroscience before and quickly turn them into a productive neuroscience lab actually works. Other neurolabs have been announced in Rwanda, Sudan, and Brazil, and many more could be dotting the landscape soon. I can't wait to see the research that emerges from these underrepresented areas, and I hope we can find ways to use it for the betterment of humanity and to inform the way neurotechnology inventors and AI developers approach their work. It's one thing to point out differences in our brain function, but the bigger question is—what can we do about it? A major redistribution of wealth is highly unlikely, and although a push to develop micro-grids in rural areas around the world is underway, electricity may not be on the near horizon for many more-remote areas. So, what can be done to ensure cognitive parity among populations?

As Tara pushes to open neurolabs around the world, she is also drawing on her mathematical brainpower to improve the analytical paradigms associated with EEG to make them more effective for these research purposes. During her years in academic labs, she was involved in research using the data from electrodes implanted inside the skulls of monkeys and other animals. Thanks to those electrodes, the signals from the brain were clear and strong, and researchers harnessed the power of computers to create sophisticated ways to analyze the signals. Analytical paradigms for EEG, on the other hand, were created in the 1930s, before computers, and stayed stuck in that mode for decades. And the signals from the scalp just don't have the same strength or clarity as when you put electrodes directly on the brain. As someone who's been in this field for over a decade, I know firsthand that EEG was one of the technologies that was stuck in a time warp. We devised a new array of analytics to boost what we can measure with it, and Tara is doing the same, so the neurolabs can gather more and more viable data.

A New Kind of Brain Trust

Ramping up neurolabs to study local populations in underserved regions represents a giant step in taking a more inclusive approach to human brain diversity. But how much good can we do by gathering data in remote areas if the findings don't reach further than the local population? Wouldn't it be better to offer open access to the data, so researchers can learn from the global body of findings?

Tara is acutely aware that most neuroscience datasets remain siloed within academic and lab walls. Yes, researchers publish their findings, but they don't typically make their datasets available to other scientists, largely because files are created using specialized software and platforms don't permit sharing. Sadly, a wealth of valuable raw data on the human brain is hidden away on computers, gathering virtual dust rather than being used to its full potential. This hampers scientists' ability to reproduce experimental results—vital to a robust scientific process—in what they call a replication crisis. But this is finally starting to change.

A team of researchers at the University of Washington is aiming to democratize neuroscience by making experimental data easier to share. In a 2018 *Nature Communications* article, the UW team detailed an open-access browser they'd developed to make big data research on the central nervous system available to fellow researchers.[15] Scientists can use the tool, which runs in any web browser, to display, analyze, upload, and share neurological data from studies using diffusion-weighted MRI. The AFQ-Browser, which stands for Automated Fiber-tract Quantification, is publicly accessible and doesn't require any specialized software—just a computer and an internet connection. According to the paper, "AFQ-Browser facilitates exploratory data analysis, fueling new discoveries based on previously published datasets."

Similarly, a community of scientists, researchers, engineers, artists, designers, and innovators has created an open-source brain–computer interface called OpenBCI. The operation has already provided the hardware, software, and other tools necessary, including 3-D printable EEG headsets that provide research-quality recordings, to researchers—and anyone else interested in biosensing and neurofeedback—in more than sixty countries. The people behind this community understand that the only way we'll ever be able to understand who we are and how the brain works is through massive collaboration. "These discoveries will only—and should only—be made through an open forum of shared knowledge and concerted effort, by people from a variety of backgrounds," states OpenBCI's website (https://openbci.com/). In its community forum, people can share their projects and learn from others. These types of collaborative platforms are expanding our capacity to harness the power of big data for improving our understanding of the human brain and to use this data to build better neurotechnologies and refine them rapidly. Tara's Sapien Labs is also fostering collaboration with a web-based platform called Brainbase.

It's mind-boggling to think of the extraordinary discoveries that could arise from a globally shared platform. Yet Tara anticipates a slight snag in the concept: How can you share data without infringing on privacy? She's seen reports of individuals being re-identified from anonymized data. In an explosive 2015 investigation, Latanya Sweeney, the director of the Data Privacy Lab at Harvard University and editor of *Technology Science*, tested patients' vulnerability to re-identification. She focused her study on Washington State, one of thirty-three U.S. states that legally share or sell anonymized patient data. Using newspaper articles about traffic accidents, assaults, and other incidents that resulted in hospital visits, Sweeney was able to correctly match 35 of 81 individuals—43 percent—who were identified by name in the news stories to the anonymized information released by the state.[16] In 2018, Sweeney and a team of researchers performed a similar test on anonymized patient data from Maine and Vermont. With information gleaned from local news articles, they were able to match 69 of 244—over 28 percent—of the names in the media to hospital data from the state of Maine. In Vermont, they matched 16 of 47 names—34 percent—in local news reports to hospital records.[17] What's troubling is that the hospital records correlating to the incidents described in the news articles sometimes included diagnoses unrelated to the event—diabetes, depression, anxiety, alcoholism, substance abuse, even a history of domestic violence. Having such information made public poses numerous potential consequences for the re-identified individual. Sweeney's study suggests anonymized data requires additional safeguards to prevent re-identification.

With this in mind, Tara is trying to anticipate and sidestep any future risks associated with an open-access database. One possible solution she's contemplating is making the data accessible but not downloadable. Instead, a researcher could search the database, compile a dataset based on certain criteria, and then do the analysis on Brainbase itself, rather than having all the data in hand. "This way, you'd get results back without actually being able to see each record individually. That's a way to make it open access without compromising anyone's privacy," she says. I hope other neuroscience labs have taken note of this. Think how valuable it would be to have pooled brain data available to the brightest scientific minds.

The Time Is Now

It's more important than ever to understand brain function across the global population: seniors, women, children, men, urban dwellers, people in remote villages, those who are highly educated and those with no education, those of high wealth and low income, the poverty stricken, and more. The future of human society depends on our cognitive capability. The next generation of jobs will be increasingly technical in nature. The number of people expected to have neurological disorders is skyrocketing. And the leap into artificial intelligence requires a deep understanding of brain function. The brain is at the crux of our future as a species.

It's why forward-thinking leaders launched the BRAIN (Brain Research Through Advancing Innovative Neurotechnologies) Initiative in 2013—to deepen our understanding of the most complex entity in the universe and to facilitate the development of next-gen neurotechnological tools and systems to reimagine the way we treat and heal disorders or to prevent them in the first place. This far-reaching project encourages scientists, engineers, physicians, and government agencies to collaborate across fields, industries, and geographic boundaries to stretch our knowledge about the final frontier—the brain. In the U.S., government agencies such as DARPA, the NIH, the National Science Foundation, and the Intelligence Advanced Research Projects Activity[18] are pouring money into the project. In the first five years of the initiative, the NIH alone has invested nearly $560 million in the research of over five hundred scientists.[19] Researchers have already made significant inroads into mapping the inner workings of the brain, thanks to new imaging tools that show the neurons of lab animals communicating with each other in real time. Unique public–private partnerships that match scientists with companies developing neurotechnologies are speeding the delivery of a new breed of devices aimed at treating neural disorders. They're ushering us into an era with brain–machine interface devices like the BrainGate array Kevin Warwick had implanted, as we learned in chapter five. Expected to continue through 2026, the BRAIN Initiative will continue to strengthen our understanding and unleash new technologies that will potentially heal disorders and enhance our capabilities.

The primary reason for understanding the human brain in all its diverse forms is to ensure that we create new technologies and AI that are beneficial to all of humanity, not just one small segment of it. The other overarching reason why we must study the human brain on a large scale relates to brain health. "When you go to an annual checkup, they'll listen to your heart, and they'll listen to your lungs. No one listens to your brain and tells you your brain's okay, too. The reason is, no one knows what to say about it. What is okay?" asks Tara. The challenge lies in the fact that there are no standards. Since we don't know what normal looks like, and we have only just begun to scratch the surface of what brain activity looks like across different populations, what would a brain health checkup achieve? Think back to the dilemma of those tangles and plaques associated with Alzheimer's disease. Although they are seen in people with the disease, their presence in the brain is not a reliable predictor that someone will develop symptoms of memory loss. What would healthcare professionals do with this information? Tara predicts these large-scale datasets will be the game-changer that overhauls the brain health field, diverting it from symptom-based diagnoses for brain disorders like depression, ADHD, or autism and toward physiological definitions.

All People Matter

As fascinating as it is to contemplate *Star Wars*–like advances that can treat or prevent brain disorders and enhance cognitive capabilities to levels our ancestors could barely have imagined, it's equally important to consider how accessible they will be. In the same way it's critical to study all brains to better inform the new technologies we are creating, we must ensure that these brain-enhancement innovations benefit everyone. How do we prevent a small, wealthy segment of society from monopolizing the benefits? How do we avoid the creation—or, arguably, continuation—of a neuro-elite class? How do we make sure the majority of the population is not left in the margins? How do we make the NeuroGeneration a great equalizer rather than a force for widening disparity?

Tara thinks understanding the brain across global populations is the first step to creating technology to benefit all. She's not alone. University of San Francisco neuroscientist Bill Bosl also sees the need for "lots and lots of data" in the healthcare field if we want to improve access to care. While many neuroscientists are enamored with using big, expensive machines like fMRI to study small numbers of brains and then using machine or statistical learning methods to find patterns in the data, Bill would prefer practical tools that can be used in a doctor's office or a community health center. Those fancy imaging machines? They're never going to work for clinical use, says Bill. "Just imagine going to the doctor for a routine checkup or taking an infant for a regular well-baby checkup and the doctor says, 'Oh, by the way, we're going to do this extra forty-five-minute test that's going to cost $2,000, and we're going to do it every time you get a checkup.'" He adds that a brain checkup has to be more like taking your blood pressure: "painless, easy, simple, and takes only a minute." In his view, brain imaging tools like that are what we need to enable brain monitoring throughout the life span as part of routine care. A significant part of Bill's research has been to develop new uses for EEG as a tool for monitoring mental health and cognitive function.

To make routine brain health checkups effective, you would need all that data Tara is trying to accumulate to show what's normal within a given context. And we need that data across all populations, ages, and genders. And we need to detect patterns that indicate neurological conditions, as you saw in chapter six. And we need to provide access to the necessary data and tools to the global population, not just to wealthy nations or individuals. Take autism, for example, which is typically diagnosed around age four in the U.S. In underserved populations, however, children generally aren't diagnosed until two years later, according to the CDC. They simply don't have access to the same quality of healthcare, so the window for early intervention is missed, which results in poorer outcomes. Bill believes the technology that's being developed—a pediatric EEG device—would be an affordable solution for community clinics.

The emerging technology Bill's been working on could also help to close the healthcare gap around the world. He's been collaborating with pediatric neurologists in Kenya and South Africa where technology could make a big difference. "In Africa, 80 percent of the people with epilepsy get no treatment even though drugs that would control the majority of epilepsy cases are available cheaply. Cost is not the problem," he says. What's keeping them from getting the medication? According to Bill, they don't have enough neurologists to diagnose their condition as epilepsy. "You can't have a community health worker handing out drugs for epilepsy. They're strong drugs, and you don't want to give them to somebody if you don't know what's really wrong." Technology could change that. "If we had EEG devices connected to algorithms that could reliably tell you if a person has epilepsy, then even a lightly trained community health worker could make that diagnosis and get the medicine for that person. There's a cheap, easy solution that would affect millions of people and get them the medicine they need." Bill says we're very close to being able to do this.

So many of the innovators, scientists, and tech gurus I spoke to while writing this book have kept accessibility in mind when creating their technologies. Sharing that perspective is Adam Gazzaley, the neuroscientist we met in chapter one who is the chief science advisor at Akili Interactive Labs, which is developing closed-loop, therapeutic video games intended to treat ADHD and other brain disorders. "I think one of the big challenges of our medical system is that pharmaceuticals are priced very high, and they have lots of side effects. All of these things decrease global accessibility and accentuate inequity issues," says Adam. "I would love to have treatment that really helped the people that need it most, regardless of their socioeconomic status or where they are in the world. I'm really enthusiastic about having truly global treatments out there."[20]

Improving access to treatment is likewise one of the main drivers inspiring Tom Insel at Mindstrong to develop mobile-based apps for mental health. "For mental health, where so much of what we do is not surgical, it doesn't necessarily require a brick and mortar presence. So much of it could be done remotely, including forms of psychotherapy and aspects of diagnosis," says Tom. "As you think about that, you think, 'Wow, this could be an area that would really be transformed by technology and could address problems of access and quality.'"[21] He cites companies that are already using technology to create platforms for anonymized online peer support as well as other kinds of help available 24/7. "They're seeing millions of people each month. And those companies that don't use any brick and mortar are, in fact, serving a population that more than 80 percent of the time is not in the care system." He views this arena as one of the ways technology is completely overhauling the mental health field and breaking down the barriers to access.

Neal Kassell at the Focused Ultrasound Foundation is equally passionate about improving access to treatment with the groundbreaking therapy he's been promoting for years. "Number one, it will allow treatment for patients for whom there is currently no treatment available. Number two, the hope, the aspiration, is it will be a more effective and safer treatment for all these neurological disorders. Number three, it will decrease the cost of care," Neal says, adding, in his dry sense of humor, "Other than that, there's not much."[22] Over at Halo, Brett Wingeier expects the price of their tDCS headsets to come down over time the way it typically does for any new technology, which he says will increase access to it. More importantly, he sees great promise in its potential as a medical device. Currently, transcranial magnetic stimulation as a medical treatment involves a $60,000 device and requires patients to go to a clinic and sit in a sort of dentist's chair while a healthcare professional arranges all the electrodes and wires. It's a very precise and time-consuming process. "For technology like electrical stimulation, the reason why this is such a big part of the democratization of treatment is because you wind up with an easy-to-use product that you can take home," he says. "With a product like this, it's not as constrained by geography as something where you need to go to a clinic within a few miles of your home, and you don't have to try to figure out how to get there if you're disabled."[23] He sees at-home electrical-stimulation medical devices as a way to increase access to treatment around the globe and in underserved areas.

And then there's Mark Pollock, the blind, paralyzed endurance athlete pushing the boundaries by using a robotic exoskeleton and electrical stimulation to voluntarily move his legs again. "As someone who can access a lot of these things, I'm constantly asking myself, yes, it's good for me that I can do all this, but how do we get these great interventions out of the confines of the lab and into the clinics?" he asks. "There are many in the U.S. who can't access any kind of healthcare or can't even get a wheelchair. How do we try to make this [technology] affordable? And if not for the individual, then how do we make a business case for the national health services in Europe or the insurance companies in the States?"[24]

In my own company, we keep these questions top of mind as we develop our technology. Our mission is to democratize access to brainwear by creating products that are affordable. From a business standpoint, we have found that marketing to the 99 percent rather than the 1 percent can offset the R&D costs that accompany tech development. Only by making technologies available to *everyone* can we really unleash the potential of the brain. When every teacher, every student, every lone inventor and tinkerer in every part of the globe is able to tap into the awesome resources of the brain, we will see an explosion of new applications, new knowledge, and new advances. When this technology is in the hands of hundreds of millions, rather than hundreds of thousands, then the world will truly begin to transform in a revolutionary way.

CHAPTER 9

MIND SHIFT

Shaping the Ethics and Policies
of the NeuroGeneration
into Our Shared Future

A S I STEPPED OUT OF THE AIRPORT in Dubai in November 2017, I was greeted with a furnace blast of 90°F heat—stifling compared to the cool, damp, foggy San Francisco weather I've grown accustomed to, but nowhere near as insufferable as the 115°F it had hit a few months earlier. Despite the heat, I always love visiting this ultramodern city because it's like a looking glass into the future. Already home to the world's tallest building, the Burj Khalifa, construction is well underway on the globe's tallest Ferris wheel. I got an early peek at the city's Museum of the Future, a one-of-a-kind incubator for futuristic innovation.

As eye-opening as these landmarks are, it's the seemingly impossible sci-fi projects on the docket that really intrigue me. For example, the United Arab Emirates is throttling into *Star Trek*–like interplanetary travel with plans to build the first city on Mars as part of its Mars 2117 project.[1] Before landing on the red planet, it intends to develop the Mars Science City, a mind-boggling 1.9-million-square-foot space-simulation project in the desert.[2] Think of it as a supersized version of the analog missions people like Dr. Susan Ip-Jewell, whom you read about in chapter two, are conducting. Other futuristic endeavors for the region include a hyperloop and even flying taxis like on the animated series *The Jetsons*.

On this occasion, I was in town for the annual meeting of the Global Future Councils. Less than one month earlier, the Emirates had taken a bold leap into the NeuroGeneration by appointing the world's first government minister of AI, twenty-seven-year-old Omar bin Sultan Al Olama. "We want the UAE to become the world's most prepared country for artificial intelligence," UAE Vice President and Prime Minister and Ruler of Dubai Sheikh Mohammed bin Rashid Al Maktoum said about the appointment, according to *Gulf News*.[3] The appointment coincided with the launch of the UAE's official AI strategy, a global first.[4] This ambitious AI strategy focuses on nine areas: education, space, environment, transportation, traffic, healthcare, technology, water, and renewable energy.

But what inspires me most isn't their plans for jaw-dropping landmarks and logic-defying feats of engineering. What's most intriguing is that their interest in the future relies heavily on answering the questions being asked by millions of youth around the world: What kind of education will they have? What kinds of jobs will they have? How will they be able to follow their dreams? Their strategy is about making a call to shape the future in a participatory fashion. It's about proactively creating legislation for neurotechnologies. I was excited to meet briefly with the new minister, and I remember hoping other countries would take notice and follow the UAE's lead in this arena—not just in focusing on the future of AI but in developing comprehensive strategies at all levels for neurotechnologies that will impact the future of the human brain.

The Neuroethics Question

Before this transformation rocks our world, we need to ask ourselves the deep philosophical questions, or we could be left trying to put the genie back in the bottle. In this chapter, you'll discover this range of queries—from alarmist concerns about the possibilities of a post-AI world to explorations into practical strategies that will help us navigate our way forward. Fortunately, a global cadre of neuroethicists is already pondering ways to ensure that we minimize the potential downsides and maximize the gains of neurotechnologies for the benefit of all humanity.

In a 2017 issue of the journal *Nature*, a group of twenty-seven neuroscientists, neurotechnologists, ethicists, physicians, and AI experts who call themselves the Neurotechnology and Ethics Taskforce (NET) raised a red flag.[5] They warned that some of the transformative brain–computer interface technologies explored in this book could pose a variety of threats. For example, they suggested that BCIs intended to help people with spinal cord injuries perform everyday tasks could "exacerbate social inequalities and offer corporations, hackers, governments or anyone else new ways to exploit and manipulate people." They take a rather doom-and-gloom view of things, fearing that existing ethics guidelines are woefully inadequate to address the sort of technologies that may profoundly alter the brain and what it means to be human.

In their paper, they point to four main areas of concern:

▸ **Privacy and consent:** As I've described, it may become possible for people's data trails to be tracked for potential diagnosis of brain disorders and mental health conditions. But we are still a long way off from seeing BCIs that are able to open us up to brain manipulation, hackers, and corporate or government agencies spying on our brains. NET says, "We believe that citizens should have the ability—and right—to keep their neural data private." They advocate regulating the sale or commercial transfer of neural data and limiting a person's ability to sell their neural data or accept payment to have neural activity downloaded to their brain.

▸ **Agency and identity:** Neurotechnologies have the potential to change our sense of identity and could blur the lines of personal responsibility. NET contends that agency must be protected as a basic human right, and they suggest adding "neurorights" to international treaties.

▸ **Restoration to enhancement:** As you've seen throughout this book, neurotechnologies have the capability of not only healing brain disorders but also enhancing and augmenting the human brain in new and exciting ways. In addition to issues of access, this tech could cause new forms of discrimination between haves and have-nots and could lead to an "augmentation arms race," according to NET. To counteract this, they recommend that national and international governing bodies set limits on how neurotechnologies can be used.

▸ **Bias:** This book has discussed issues of bias when technologies are designed by a narrow subset of the human population. Ethicists advocate having probable users, including those who are marginalized or from low-income or developing areas, be included in the earliest stages of development.

Some of the issues NET raises are extremely far-reaching and don't apply to the neurotechnologies currently available. Frankly, some of their worries border on scaremongering, which does this emerging industry a disservice. Still, as a developer in this arena, I'm deeply sensitive to many of the issues they broach and have a strong desire to be part of the movement to create tools that will better humanity.

To gain more insight into this arena, I turned to a woman who is quietly taking the lead on many of these issues—Karen

Rommelfanger, the director of Emory University's neuroethics program at the Center for Ethics. Although she may speak softly, her voice carries tremendous weight in some of the loftiest organizations around the world—the BRAIN Initiative's neuroethics division, the International Neuroethics Society, and the advisory council to the director of the NIH for BRAIN 2025. And that's just a start. I know this deep thinker from the OECD Workshop on Neurotechnology in Shanghai where I presented an opening keynote. I was pleased to find out later that the unassuming, dark-haired, bespectacled neuroscientist had been appointed to our new Global Future Council on Neurotechnologies.

As Karen told me, like many in her field, she gravitated to neuroethics because it offers a chance to shine a light on how "neuroscience might inform us about the things we hold most precious in life, like the life of the mind, our personalities, our emotional responses to things, our sense of humor."[6] Early in her career, when people asked her about possible societal implications of futuristic neurotechnologies, Karen found herself saying "no" a lot, reassuring people that the seemingly impossible sci-fi scenarios they dreamed up weren't possible. But now, years later, as she has become more deeply immersed in the field and its cutting-edge advances, the more she finds herself thinking, "Wow, things we didn't think were possible before really are possible." This has fueled her interest in laying the groundwork for ethical development of the emerging neurotechnologies that could change all of those things we hold precious in life.

Karen makes it clear that tackling these issues doesn't mean putting up roadblocks to stall or derail neurotechnological progress. In fact, she insists that good ethics can actually accelerate development by anticipating future problems and addressing them early so the innovation can flow with fewer bumps in the road. Ethical mindfulness can improve how scientists design research studies, developers create their neurotechnologies, and researchers collect and use data. In 2017, she co-chaired a group of close to forty leading neuroscientists, policymakers, ethicists, sociologists, and academicians involved with national brain research projects who converged in Daegu, South Korea, for the Global Neuroethics Summit. They wanted to generate a universal list of overarching questions to help guide neuroscientists in researching these brain projects. They spelled out these questions in a 2018 *Neuron* article:[7]

1. **What is the potential impact of a model or neuroscientific account of disease on individuals, communities, and society?**
   a. What are the possible unintended consequences of neuroscience research on social stigma and self-stigma?
   b. Is it possible that social or cultural bias has been introduced in research design or in the interpretation of scientific results?
2. **What are the ethical standards of biological material and data collection and how do local standards compare to those of global collaborators?**
   a. How can human brain data (e.g. images, neural recordings, etc.) and the privacy of participants from whom data is acquired be protected in case of immediate or legacy use beyond the experiment?
   b. Should special regard be given to the brain tissue and its donor due to the origin of the tissue and its past?
3. **What is the moral significance of neural systems that are under development in neuroscience research laboratories?**
   a. What are the requisite or minimum features of engineered neural circuitry required to generate a concern about moral significance?
   b. Are the ethical standards for research conduct adequate and appropriate for the evolving methodologies and brain models?

4. **How could brain interventions impact or reduce autonomy?**
   a. What measures can be in place to ensure optimal autonomy and agency for participants/users?
   b. Who will have responsibility for effects (where responsibility has broad meaning encompassing legal, economic, and social contexts)?
5. **In which contexts might a neuroscientific technology/innovation be used or deployed?**
   a. Which applications might be considered misuse or best uses beyond the laboratory?
   b. Does this research raise different and unique equity concerns and, if so, have equitable access and benefit of stakeholders been considered?

Asking questions is at the heart of a neuroethicist's profession, but in my sweeping conversation with Karen, we were both posing the queries. One of the concepts that I find most intriguing is neurotechnology's potential for altering our sense of identity. If the brain is the seat of the self, then neurotechnologies could have implications for all aspects of our lives. Should we be allowed to seek means to improve ourselves in ways that might fundamentally change who we are? "If we purchase one of these wearable devices or we have an implantable stimulator, might it change us in ways where we might not recognize ourselves, and is that okay?" Karen asks. Nowadays, in some instances, personality changes come as part of a treatment for a brain disorder or mental health issue. With mental health especially, a change in personality or behavior is often the goal of the treatment; in other cases, personality changes are more of a side effect.

Consider deep brain stimulation and medications for Parkinson's disease. As noted in chapter three, in some people these treatments have been linked to new and unwanted compulsive behaviors.[8] Research published in a 2018 issue of *Neurology* found that half the people taking certain Parkinson's drugs will develop some form of impulse-control disorder over time.[9] "People might be ashamed to tell their doctor about their problems, they may think these issues are not related to their Parkinson's disease, or they may not even consider the disorders a problem," writes neurologist Laura S. Boylan in an editorial in the same issue.[10] This indicates we could undergo fundamental personality and behavior changes without realizing what's behind them, sometimes with major life consequences—financial ruin, divorce, or additional health disorders. How can we avoid triggering these types of unexpected and unwanted changes as we continue to explore the neurotech realm?

When it comes to agency and responsibility if you're connected to a BCI or operating with neurotechnological enhancements, Karen asks, "Are you culpable for certain crimes you commit or laws that you break?" It's fascinating to think about the implications; they make me wonder about court cases in the future. Echoing some present-day legal defense strategies, could a person accused of a crime claim they were innocent because their BCI put an idea into their head? And what about all those corporations and marketers? As Karen muses, could they use these kinds of technologies to persuade people to buy things beyond their consciousness or underneath their consciousness? This possibility sounds frightening, but to some extent, we are all already subjected to the power of persuasion from marketers. Commercials tug at our heartstrings. Ads across all types of media attempt to convince us that this or that product is the only thing that can protect us from the dangers of X, Y, or Z. Food manufacturers use the science of crunch factor, melting points, and fat content to trigger our neural pathways to eat more, more, more. Are neurotechnologies that could manipulate neural data really that much different from these other methods?

Where the future could take a much more invasive turn is in decoding a person's thoughts and also mind control.

Frontier-science experiments by Jack Gallant, a UC Berkeley psychology professor and head of the Gallant Lab, showed that scientists can reconstruct crude images that you've seen based on your brain activation patterns as seen in brain scans.[11] Over at Carnegie Mellon University, psychology professor Marcel Just and his team have been using brain imaging technologies and machine learning techniques to uncover the structure of human thought. In a series of studies, his team was able to predict categories of words or numbers the participants were thinking.[12] "Those kinds of things," says Karen, "they start to make me feel uneasy."

As I've mentioned earlier, the medical community is making progress in early detection of brain diseases. Is there a line between surveillance and prophylactic care? And what about all that neural data that will be collected—and some of it that's already being collected? Think of brain-training games that test your cognition, or voice diagnostics or keyboarding activities that might one day predict mental health issues. A person might sign up for this and willingly allow companies to gather this data. Karen ventures that the data, combined with behavior tracking, could lead to people being identified, as Harvard's Latanya Sweeney revealed. That particular individual might not care if the world knows they have a mental health disorder or genetic disease, "but what will happen next is connecting that to family members, siblings, and children who may not want that information out there," says Karen. "There's bystander damage from that." One possible solution is to limit what a person can do with their personal neural data, including establishing limits on where and with whom they can share it.

To find these solutions and others for the most pressing neuroethics questions, Karen thinks we need to engage the public in these discussions so we can begin thinking more collectively. She's currently working on a few projects to facilitate engagement so consumers can plug in and become part of the process. It is only when we broaden the field to all stakeholders from diverse populations—scientists, developers, policymakers, marketers, and future users—that we will find the best ways to move forward with neurotechnologies that enhance the brain and humanity.

Fast-Forward

Decades from now, when our augmented brains have enhanced our cognitive function and transformed nearly every aspect of our lives, many of us will look back and wonder why we didn't do more to prepare for these inevitable changes. Government leaders may grapple with the runaway effects of AI and brain enhancement on geopolitics. Companies that fail to incorporate neurotechnologies and BCI into their operational flow could lose significant market share and be forced to scramble in an attempt to regain a foothold in an industry they once dominated. Workers who don't heed the advice to re-skill or upskill may find themselves out of a job as entire industries disappear. Graduating college students may discover their field of study is no longer relevant in the business world, leaving them unprepared for the changing job market. Tech innovators could be subject to fierce competition to snap up employees from a limited talent pool, driving up the cost of innovation and hampering its development. And everyday citizens may be wrestling with the unexpected consequences of unintentionally giving away the rights to their neural data. Rest assured, it doesn't have to be this way.

Alongside rigorously asking the deep ethical questions we must ponder, there are a number of areas where we can take a practical approach to address the changes already underway and lay the groundwork for a more seamless transition.

Local and global policymakers: Now is the time for governments and lawmakers at every level to create positions to drive policies regarding neurotechnologies, AI, robotics, the Internet of Things, blockchains, drones, and a whole host of other emerging technologies. Addressing these new advances with a one-size-fits-all approach won't do; each is inherently nuanced in the matrix of opportunities and potential risks it presents. Noninvasive technologies—such as EMOTIV's EEG headsets, the tablet-based games coming out of Adam Gazzaley's labs, the proposed smartphone-enabled concepts at Tom Insel's Mindstrong, and the potentially memory-boosting movies Ed Boyden is researching—lie at one end of the spectrum. On the other end are invasive tools—deep brain stimulation, neural implants, and transplanting memories into the hippocampus—that pose greater physical risks. In addition, some neurotechnologies merely monitor brain activity, while others alter the brain in some way: influencing neurochemistry, stimulating or inhibiting electrical activity, or impacting cellular function. Similarly, medical neurotechnologies differ from consumer devices. The most effective policymaking will encompass all of these differences. It makes sense that invasive medical neurotechnologies that alter brain function should call for more stringent restrictions and guidelines than "read-only" consumer devices.

Policymakers also must take into account how neuro-data is being collected, stored, and shared. Alongside the concept of informed consent that most of us recognize, there is a pressing need to adopt the concept of "informed risk." Patients and consumers should be made aware of a variety of issues associated with neurotechnologies and should expect certain protections. Users must be informed about the differences between *privacy* (the concept that your neural data is available only to you), *security* (the idea that your neural data won't be inadvertently shared), and *anonymity* (the understanding your neural data may be shared but without the possibility of your being identified).

Putting in the legwork to understand the multitude of ways these advances will impact work, education, training, and privacy will help develop comprehensive policies that ensure a low-friction transition. Policymakers must anticipate the impacts of automation and search for solutions, such as the possibility of countries introducing a Universal Basic Income—a living stipend for citizens to ensure they can maintain a reasonable, basic standard of existence even if future developments remove them from the job market completely. World leaders must come together to create a global framework for regulating AI and other brain-enhancement technologies to ensure they serve the greater good. At the same time, it's important to consider local context and communities in policymaking. In my view, this means educating the public with awareness campaigns and looping end-user feedback into the process, as Gary Flake discussed in chapter seven. To facilitate input that all stakeholders can access and analyze, we must standardize data collection and sharing at a global level, efforts pioneered at EMOTIV and by my friends, Tara Thiagarajan's Sapien Labs and OpenBCI.

Education: Nations will have to rethink their educational systems, retooling the focus to provide the building blocks for the future by emphasizing STEAM (science, technology, engineering, arts, and mathematics) programs and encouraging greater proficiency in these important areas. Ongoing refinement of these programs will help them remain current, reflecting fast-changing advances in technology. Educational systems will stay ahead of the curve by offering a number of options for disseminating information and providing collaborative, interactive learning programs. Educators have a tremendous opportunity to produce better results by taking advantage of the latest advances in neurotechnology in a variety of ways: tailoring education to individual learning styles, allowing students to use technology that facilitates learning, and offering tools that promote better focus and attention. Four-year colleges may become a thing of the past: as the economy starts to change at a breakneck pace, professionals may need to upskill more quickly and more often throughout their careers. I see the concept of higher education moving away from the traditional teacher–pupil model of learning a subject from the master and shifting toward the facilitation of lifelong learning. Our educational efforts will be better suited by focusing on complex problem solving, critical thinking, and creativity so we can acquire and implement the skills needed for the Fourth Industrial Revolution. Educators must begin creating programs now to re-skill and upskill the large numbers of talented individuals who will soon be displaced from their previous jobs.

Business: With brain enhancement on the horizon, business leaders who start planning now for these major shifts will fare better in this new era. As discussed in the introduction, the entire business landscape is expected to change dramatically in the coming years. Machines and algorithms could displace 75 million jobs by 2022, according to the WEF Future of Jobs Report 2018.[13] But the news isn't all dire. AI is also expected to create 133 million new jobs for a net gain of 58 million new positions. The report says that, in 2018, humans handled 71 percent of tasks with machines taking on the remainder, but this will shift dramatically by 2022, when it is expected that humans will only do 58 percent. By 2022, over half of all employees will require significant retraining. A 2017 jobs report from McKinsey suggests that, by 2030, 75 million to 375 million workers will be forced to switch occupational categories.[14] Even more important, the report indicates that all workers will need to adapt as job definitions evolve along with machine capabilities. Some workers may need additional education while others may need to focus on creativity, social and emotional skills, and other high-level cognitive functions that are more difficult to automate. The time to begin investing in alternative training is now.

Take a cue from one of the superstars in the field who is creating an AI blueprint for businesses. Andrew Ng, a Stanford University professor, co-founding leader of Google Brain, and former chief scientist at Baidu, is the founder of several teaching enterprises to integrate AI, including Landing AI, Coursera, and deeplearning.ai. In 2018, he released the *AI Transformation Playbook: How to Lead Your Company into the AI Era* to help guide companies into the field.[15] In it, he identifies five steps to ease into the arena and gain a competitive advantage:

1. **Start with a few pilot projects.** Get your feet wet by undertaking some small AI projects that you can realistically achieve. Getting successes under your belt helps gain familiarity and builds confidence in AI's possibilities.
2. **Start hiring an in-house AI team.** Create a centralized team that can service your entire company and consider hiring a Chief Artificial Intelligence Officer (CAIO) to lead the team.
3. **Start providing training in AI.** AI talent is scarce, so you may be better off upskilling your existing employees. Take advantage of MOOCs (massive open online courses)—similar to what Rachel Thomas and Jeremy Howard are doing with individuals but for enterprises—to upgrade your existing team.
4. **Start developing an AI strategy.** Wait until your team has had some successes with initial AI projects and better understands its capabilities to identify the best ways you can benefit from deep learning on a company-wide basis.
5. **Start communicating your strategy** with all internal and external stakeholders.

In addition to following Andrew's playbook for AI, companies should address head-on the ethical concerns of neurotechnologies by building trust through transparency, especially when it comes to collecting, managing, and sharing neural or mental data. Developing policies regarding employee access to and use of new neurotechnologies constitutes another area of concern. Will brain-enhancement tools or nootropics become a part of corporate wellness programs the same way gym memberships and massages are? Will companies offer access to brainwear or neural implants to increase worker productivity? How will businesses deal with human–AI interactions in the workplace? Business leaders will be faced with some tough decisions about the workforce. Do we owe it to humanity to maintain some percentage of human employees even though automation could reduce costs? Or will we be faced with "robot taxes" intended to avoid the elimination of human workers?

Technologists: As tech innovators, we are in the driver's seat, thrusting the world into the Fourth Industrial Revolution that will define the NeuroGeneration. Rather than tinker individually on shortsighted technologies, our focus should be on full-scale collaboration. I recommend stepping out of our silos and working together toward intentionally creating something that has long-term benefits for society at large. Central to this effort will be a commitment to develop democratically accessible technologies that will augment and empower the human brain. We will also benefit from retooling our own industry. By simplifying the tools, platforms, and technologies we use, we can enable more people to participate in the work we do. If we fail to confront this challenge, we will find the skills gap widening and our own projects held back by a lack of viable workers.

At EMOTIV, we work hard to create tools that allow users to connect their brains to the digital and physical worlds on their own terms. A lot of people out there have great ideas but aren't programmers; others are in unique situations and have important but very niche needs for the technology that are unlikely to be filled at a commercial level. For instance, a caregiver might want to enable the person they work with to do something very specific, like control a particular wheelchair or use a computer in a certain way. Or a middle schooler might develop his own way of controlling a 3D printed arm. To enable such everyday users, we've created extremely simple drag-and-drop interfaces that allow *anyone* to program one of our devices—*even I can do it*, and that's really saying something. Simplified, intuitive interfaces can help bridge the skills gap we face in the workplace as millions of people transition from traditional industries to emerging high-tech professions. By making technology easy to use, we make it accessible, and in doing so empower individuals to create their own places at the heart of our new Industrial Revolution.

Healthcare and insurance: As neurotechnologies, machine learning, and algorithms become integrated into the field of preventive, diagnostic, and therapeutic healthcare, it is critical to begin mapping out a deployment strategy. Healthcare providers and diagnosticians, typically slow to adopt new technologies, will require training to be able to transition quickly and maximize the benefits of the tools being developed. Medical schools may want to add neurotechnology and AI to the course list, and medical boards may want to consider offering certifications or continuing education credits in new technologies and data science. Assuring patients that healthcare professionals are adequately trained in emerging neuro-devices will be critical for widespread acceptance of these therapies. In addition, although some therapeutic neurotechnologies are already within the FDA's purview, many other direct-to-consumer wellness enhancement technologies have little to no regulatory oversight. Developing an independent industry body to provide stewardship for these types of devices could boost consumer confidence regarding safety and privacy issues.

With a growing number of neurotechnologies on the horizon that will detect and share data on a patient's biological or mental health status, it is critical to craft and adopt broad privacy policies. Patients must be made aware of who has access to their data and how it will be used. This isn't just some social media platform sharing information on your posting and search habits so marketers can target ads to you. This is data on the inner workings of your brain: cognitive abilities and failings, mental health issues, and, perhaps someday, even a window into your darkest thoughts. Healthcare organizations must address these privacy issues with great care.

Healthcare leaders should consider strategies to implement neurotechnologies that can monitor and reduce medical errors from mental fatigue. Tracking waning focus or reduced reaction times could prompt medical workers to take breaks when necessary, ultimately protecting against burnout, reducing employee turnover, and decreasing the labor costs associated with hiring and training new employees. Those cost savings could trickle down to patients.

Although the medical industry is already undergoing an AI revolution in the field of diagnostics, it could also invest in automated tools that can handle administrative tasks, giving healthcare professionals the ability to spend more quality time with patients. The industry is dragging its heels in terms of using neurotechnologies and big data to address patient behavior. The field could take a cue from retail giants like Walmart and Amazon, which are already using neurotechnologies and neuroscience findings to understand and influence consumer behavior. Doctors are routinely harping on their patients to take their medication and follow their treatment plans in order to improve their health and enhance their quality of life, with dismal success rates. Up to 50 percent of medications aren't taken as prescribed, and noncompliance claims as many as 125,000 lives each year and costs up to $289 million, according to the *Annals of Internal Medicine*.[16] Instead, doctors could use the same automated tools that provide reminders about the items still in your online shopping cart to encourage patient compliance. Organizations in the health and wellness field must step out of their comfort zone, adopting new technologies and taking advantage of AI and big data to measure and improve patient outcomes while lowering costs. By leveraging the power of the NeuroGeneration's new tools, healthcare providers will also speed up their ability to provide more accurate diagnoses as well as more targeted, personalized, and effective treatment plans.

I would like to see insurance providers craft policies regarding reimbursement for emerging neurotechnologies and AI diagnostics that will make them available at all income levels, rather than just the wealthiest echelon. Reimbursement is key for the further development of neurotechnological devices that can revolutionize healthcare and how we diagnose and treat physical and psychiatric diseases. If insurers fail to grasp the importance of these new technologies, they could languish underutilized, and the promise they hold to heal in remarkable new ways could fizzle.

Individuals: For anyone who wants to succeed in work and in life, emerging brain enhancement technologies offer tremendous promise. The same way we have taken control of our physical health with digital devices that track our heart rate, blood pressure, exercise, and nutrition, we will be able to harness and strengthen the power of our brains with tools that enhance cognitive function, creativity, productivity, mood, memory, and more. Adapting to the new technologies won't occur without friction. The reality is that individuals who dedicate themselves to learning how to make their brain sync with the new tools will outperform those who aren't willing to invest the hours necessary. To more smoothly transition to augmented human status, we can start training our brains now by engaging in new experiences, diving into mentally challenging tasks, including diversity in our everyday lives, practicing some form of mindfulness, and sharpening our attention. Most importantly, we must open our minds and accept the reality that we will most likely need to learn how to incorporate some of these tools into our daily lives.

The Ultimate Mind Meld

As you've seen throughout this book, the NeuroGeneration will be a time when the integration of the physical, digital, and biological realms will blur the distinctions between human and machine, between individual and environment, and, ultimately, between self and other. To fully grasp the changes that are possible, we must cast off the limits that constrain our own ways of thinking and be open to a more fluid conception of the world. This will mean challenging the distinctions between the near and the far, between the collective and the individual, between the privileged few and the excluded many. The task will not be easy, but it is only by tearing down these barriers that we will be able to unleash the full potential of the coming paradigm shift.

If these technologies are to provide the greatest possible benefit for humankind, then policymakers, technologists, and industry have to put in place structures to ensure these advances are accessible to all. And not just accessible but truly inclusive. A world in which humans live happy and healthy lives is the only goal worth pursuing. That means putting the lived experience of every individual at the heart of how we think about the future. If we are to do this, then we need to be committed to putting the lived experience of the individual at the center of everything we do. To build a future fit for humans, we must develop systems and technologies that empower, rather than exploit. This is not a world in which workers sacrifice their health and happiness for the benefit of the few, and not a world in which only the privileged are able to benefit from these remarkable technologies. We need to create a world that works for everyone.

Taking an inclusive approach to the development of disruptive technology means channeling the tech toward individually empowering ends. One way of doing this is to shift our perspective away from the idea of individuals as passive consumers of technology and treat them instead as plugged-in stakeholders, co-creators, and shared authors of the products they use.

The market is already beginning to adapt to this move away from old-fashioned, top-down mindsets, and in doing so it's showing that human-centric models don't need to involve sacrificing the bottom line. Bringing together open, accessible platforms, the power of big data, and the capabilities of brain enhancement allows us all to become co-creators of the new trajectories our society is charting. It is this shared experience, this universal participation, that will make the coming NeuroGeneration something truly unique. As the boundaries between the physical and digital worlds begin to blend, and as feedback and responsiveness speed up, we will all benefit from having as many minds as possible plugged into our evolving systems. If we make the journey into the future a *shared* project, we'll be able to draw on the cognitive power of every brain around the world to support our long-term well-being. By empowering the individual and putting them at the center of the collective, we can build a world that works for each of us, together.

With all the stakeholders in our society working cooperatively to usher in this new era, we'll gain faster and more democratized access to the tools and technologies that will enhance the human brain in positive ways. We'll have the option to fire up our neural networks with nootropics and other brain enhancers from people like Geoffrey Woo at HVMN. Our ability to learn more quickly and efficiently with technology, like Brett Wingeier's Halo tDCS headphones, will put us on a path to accomplishing things we never dreamed possible. And brave souls like Kevin Warwick, the world's first cyborg, will take the plunge with implantable devices to become superhuman by augmenting sensory perceptions or unlocking the doorway for brain-to-brain communication.

As our global society embraces the promise of neurotechnology and safeguards its development, the floodgates will open for powerful tools like Ed Boyden's optogenetics and expansion microscopy—as well as ones that have yet to be imagined or invented—to lead us to a deeper understanding of the billions of neurons inside our skulls. Based on this evolving knowledge, we can more rapidly devise better ways to prevent and cure brain disorders. With forward-thinking scientists like Adam Gazzaley, Tom Insel, and Neal Kassell, we're poised to make major inroads in preventing and treating brain-related conditions such as ADHD, depression, and Parkinson's. And thanks to the pioneering researchers finding ways to plant memories in the brain, we could minimize the devastating effects of Alzheimer's.

In this new era, it isn't hard to imagine a day when people like Mark Pollock, the blind ultramarathoner who was paralyzed in a fall, will harness the power of robotics and neurotechnology to walk again and possibly even see again. Advances in mind-controlled prosthetics will give individuals with physical disabilities a harmonized way to navigate their environment and live more independently. Just think of my friend Rodrigo Hübner Mendes, the quadriplegic Brazilian who drove a race car with his mind. If he can maneuver a powerful vehicle with his thoughts, it opens up a world of possibilities for people with physical limitations to improve their everyday lives.

In other eras, these feats would have been viewed as nothing short of miraculous. But to those of us living in the NeuroGeneration, they will simply become our new reality, the science faction of our daily lives. These tools will become such an integral part of human society and so enmeshed within our own biological beings, we will one day wonder how we ever managed to live without them. When that day comes, let's all be ready.

ACKNOWLEDGMENTS

I WOULD LIKE TO EXPRESS my heartfelt gratitude to the following people who have been instrumental in making this book a reality.

To my longtime friend and business partner, Dr. Geoffrey Mackellar, along with Kim Old and Vinh Pham who have been by my side since the earliest days of the EMOTIV journey. To the uber-talented team at my company, EMOTIV, who display their genius on a daily basis in developing and introducing our brainwear to the world.

To all of the innovators, scientists, and thought leaders who graciously offered their time and shared their compelling insights for this book: Dr. William (Bill) Bosl, Dr. Ed Boyden, Dr. Suzanne Dikker, Dr. Murali Doraiswamy, Dr. Gary Flake, Dr. Adam Gazzaley, Dr. Tom Insel, Dr. Susan Ip-Jewell, Dr. Neal Kassell, Dr. Geoffrey Ling, Phap Linh, Mario Marzo, Roslyn McCoy, Rodrigo Hübner Mendes, Dr. Olivier Oullier, Mark Pollock, Dr. Karen Rommelfanger, Dr. Will Rosellini, Jaan Tallinn, Dr. Frank Tarazi, Dr. Tara Thiagarajan, Dr. Rachel Thomas, Dr. Kevin Warwick, Dr. Brett Wingeier, Geoffrey Woo, and Dr. Alex Zhavoronkov. You are breathing life into the neurotechnological inventions, neuroscientific advances, and medical breakthroughs that will shape our brains and our world in the coming NeuroGeneration and I am in awe of your contributions.

To my World Economic Forum and Young Global Leaders communities—I am humbled to be in your company, and without you I wouldn't have had the opportunity to connect with all of these amazing people from around the world.

To my amazing writing partner, Frances Sharpe, who seemed innately able to read my mind—*without a brain-machine interface*—and translate my thoughts in such a remarkable way.

To my brilliant literary agent, Frank Weimann, who has championed this book at every stage. I'm honored to be among your esteemed authors.

To my publisher, Glenn Yeffeth, and the entire team at Ben-Bella, who believed in my vision for this book and were brave enough to take a chance on me.

To my extraordinary editors, Laurel Leigh and Alexa Stevenson, who exquisitely polished the manuscript to make it shine.

To my incredible team at BigSpeak for the encouragement and ongoing support of this book.

To my husband, Chris, who is a constant source of support in everything I do, this book wouldn't have been possible without you in my corner. There isn't anyone I would rather have by my side as we transition into the NeuroGeneration.

NOTES

Introduction

1 Adlaf, E. W., et al. "Adult-Born Neurons Modify Excitatory Synaptic Transmissions to Existing Neurons." *eLife*. 2017;6:e19886. doi:10.7554/eLife.19886

2 McGowan, Kat. "The Art & Science of Slicing Up a Human Brain." *Discover*, May 3, 2010. http://discovermagazine.com/2010/the-brain/03-art-science-slicing-up-human-brain

3 Grady, Denise. "The Vision Thing: Mainly in the Brain." *Discover*, June 1, 1993. http://discovermagazine.com/1993/jun/thevisionthingma227

4 Robie, A. A., et al. "Mapping the Neural Substrates of Behavior." *Cell*. 2017;170(2):393. doi:10.1016/j.cell.2017.06.032

5 Seung, Sebastian. *Connectome: How the Brain's Wiring Makes Us Who We Are*. New York: Houghton Mifflin Harcourt, 2012

6 Swanson, Larry W. "Mapping the Human Brain: Past, Present, and Future." *Trends in Neurosciences*. 1995;18(11):471–74. https://doi.org/10.1016/0166-2236(95)92766-J

7 Will, Tyler R., et al. "Problems and Progress Regarding Sex Bias and Omission in Neuroscience Research." *eNeuro*. 2017;4(6). doi: https://doi.org/10.1523/ENEURO.0278-17.2017

Chapter 1

1   Solecki, Ralph. "The Implications of the Shanidar Cave Neander-
    thal Flower Burial." *Annals of the New York Academy of Sciences.*
    1977;293(1). https://doi.org/10.1111/j.1749-6632.1977.tb41808.x

2   Bolton, Dan. "Tea Consumption Second Only to Pack-
    aged Water." *World Tea News*, May 1, 2018. https://
    worldteanews.com/tea-industry-news-and-features/
    tea-consumption-second-only-to-packaged-water

3   Cappelletti, S., et al. "Caffeine: Cognitive and Physical Perfor-
    mance Enhancer or Psychoactive Drug?" *Current Neuropharmacology.*
    2015;13(1):71–88. doi:10.2174/1570159X13666141210215655

4   Pase, Matthew P., et al. "The Cognitive-Enhancing Effects
    of *Bacopa Monnieri*: A Systematic Review of Randomized, Controlled
    Human Clinical Trials." *Journal of Alternative and Complementary Medi-
    cine.* 2012;18(7):647–52. doi:10.1089/acm.2011.0367

5   Neale, C., et al. "Cognitive Effects of Two Nutraceuticals Ginseng and
    Bacopa Benchmarked Against Modafinil: A Review and Comparison of
    Effect Sizes." *British Journal of Clinical Pharmacology.* 2013;75(3):728–37.
    doi:10.1111/bcp.12002

6   Reay, Jonathon L., et al. "Single Doses of Panax Ginseng (G115)
    Reduce Blood Glucose Levels and Improve Cognitive Performance
    During Sustained Mental Activity." *Journal of Psychopharmacology.*
    2005;19(4):357–65. doi:10.1177/0269881105053286

7   Lee, Chang H., et al. "Effects of Sun Ginseng on Memory Enhance-
    ment and Hippocampal Neurogenesis." *Phytotherapy Research.*
    2013;27(9):1293–9. doi:10.1002/ptr.4873

8   Scholey, A., et al. "Effects of American Ginseng (Panax Quinquefolius)
    on Neurocognitive Function: An Acute, Randomised, Double-Blind,
    Placebo-Controlled, Crossover Study." *Psychopharmacology (Berl).*
    2010;212(3): 345–56. doi:10.1007/s00213-010-1964-y

9   Ossoukhova, Anastasia, et al. "Improved Working Memory Performance
    Following Administration of a Single Dose of American Ginseng (*Panax
    Quinquefolius* L.) to Healthy Middle-Age Adults." *Human Psychophar-
    macology.* 2015;30(2):108–22. doi:10.1002/hup/2463

10 Canevelli, M., et al. "Effects of Gingko Biloba Supplementation in
    Alzheimer's Disease Patients Receiving Cholinesterase Inhibitors:

Data from the ICTUS Study." *Phytomedicine.* 2014;21(6):888–92. doi:10.1016/j.phymed.2014.01.003; Cieza, A., et al. "Effects of Ginkgo Biloba on Mental Functioning in Healthy Volunteers." *Archives of Medical Research.* 2003;34(5):373–81. doi:10.1016/j.arcmed.2003.05.001

11 Mancini, E., et al. "Green Tea Effects on Cognition, Mood, and Human Brain Function: A Systematic Review." *Phytomedicine.* 2017;34:26–37. doi:10.1016/j.phymed.2017.07.008

12 Kennedy, David O., et al. "Effects of High-Dose B Vitamin Complex with Vitamin C and Minerals on Subjective Mood and Performance in Healthy Males." *Psychopharmacology (Berl).* 2010;211(1):55–68. doi:10.1007/s00213-010-1870-3

13 Penckofer, S., et al. "Vitamin D and Depression: Where Is All the Sunshine?" *Issues in Mental Health Nursing.* 2010;31(6):385–93. doi:10.3109/01612840903437657

14 Knekt, P., et al. "Serum 25-Hydroxyvitamin D Concentration and Risk of Dementia." *Epidemiology.* November 25, 2014;(6):799–804. doi:10.1097/EDE.0000000000000175

15 Winblad, B. "Piracetam: A Review of Pharmacological Properties and Clinical Uses." *CNS Drug Reviews.* 2005 Summer;11(2):169–82. https://www.ncbi.nlm.nih.gov/pubmed/16007238

16 Itil, Turan M., et al. "The Effects of Oxiracetam (ISF 2522) in Patients with Organic Brain Syndrome (a Double-Blind Controlled Study with Piracetam)." *Drug Development Research.* 1982;2(5):447–61. https://doi.org/10.1002/ddr.430020506

17 Mondadori, C., et al. "Effects of Oxiracetam on Learning and Memory in Animals: Comparison with Piracetam." *Clinical Neuropharmacology.* 1986;9(Suppl 3):S27–38

18 Ostrovskaia, R. U., et al. "The Original Novel Nootropic and Neuroprotective Agent Noopept." *Eksperimental'naia i Klinicheskaia Farmakologiia.* 2002;65(5):66–72. https://www.ncbi.nlm.nih.gov/pubmed/12596521

19 Ostrovskaya, Rita U., et al. "The Nootropic and Neuroprotective Proline-Containing Dipeptide Noopept Restores Spatial Memory and Increases Immunoreactivity to Amyloid in an Alzheimer's Disease Model." *Journal of Psychopharmacology.* 2007;21(6):611–19. doi:10.1177/0269881106071335

20 Ostrovskaya, R. U., et al. "Noopept Stimulates the Expression of NGF and BDNF in Rat Hippocampus." *Bulletin of Experimental Biology and Medicine.* 2008;146(3):334–7. https://www.ncbi.nlm.nih.gov/pubmed/19240853

21 Neznamov, G. G. and E. S. Teleshova. "Comparative Studies of Noopept and Piracetam in the Treatment of Patients with Mild Cognitive Disorders in Organic Brain Diseases of Vascular and Traumatic Origin." *Neuroscience and Behavioral Physiology.* 2009;39(3):311–21. https://www.ncbi.nlm.nih.gov/pubmed/19234797

22 Interview with Geoffrey Woo, June 13, 2018

23 Li, Liaoliao, et al. "Chronic Intermittent Fasting Improves Cognitive Functions and Brain Structures in Mice." Xie, Z., ed. *Plos One.* 2013;8(6):e66069. doi:10.1371/journal.pone.0066069

24 Murray, Andrew J., et al. "Novel Ketone Diet Enhances Physical and Cognitive Performance." *The FASEB Journal.* 2016;30(12):4021–32. doi:10.1096/fj.201600773R

25 Krikorian, R., et al. "Dietary Ketosis Enhances Memory in Mild Cognitive Impairment." *Neurobiology of Aging.* 2012;33(2):425.e19–27. doi:10.1016/j.neurobiolaging.2010.10.006

26 Statista Research Department. "Number of Smartphone Users Worldwide from 2014 to 2020 (in Billions)." *Statista.* June 7, 2016. https://www.statista.com/statistics/330695/number-of-smartphone-users-worldwide/

27 PR Newswire. "Global $11.6 Billion Brain Health Supplements Market to 2024." *Markets Insider.* September 12, 2017. https://markets.businessinsider.com/news/stocks/global-11-6-billion-brain-health-supplements-market-to-2024-1001642535

28 Thielking, Megan. "Can Precision Medicine Do for Depression What It's Done for Cancer? It Won't Be Easy." *STAT,* May 9, 2018. https://www.statnews.com/2018/05/09/precision-medicine-depression-treatment/

29 World Health Organization. "World Mental Health Day 2017: Mental Health in the Workplace." Accessed July 7, 2019. http://www.who.int/mental_health/world-mental-health-day/2017/en/

30 National Institute of Mental Health. "Mental Illness." Last modified February 2019. https://www.nimh.nih.gov/health/statistics/mental-illness.shtml

31 Mental Health America. "The State of Mental Health in America." Accessed August 8, 2019. http://www.mentalhealthamerica.net/issues/ state-mental-health-america

32 World Health Organization. "World Mental Health Day 2017: Mental Health in the Workplace." Accessed August 8, 2019. http://www.who.int/ mental_health/world-mental-health-day/2017/en/

33 Chisholm, Dan, et al. "Scaling-Up Treatment of Depression and Anxiety: A Global Return on Investment Analysis." *Lancet Psychiatry.* 2016;3(5):415–24. https://doi.org/10.1016/S2215-0366(16)30024-4

34 Jain, Rachana and Megan Zweig. "2017 Year End Funding Report: The End of the Beginning of Digital Health." *Rock Health.* Accessed July 22, 2019. https://rockhealth.com/reports/2017 -year-end-funding-report-the-end-of-the-beginning-of-digital-health/

35 Interview with Thomas Insel, June 22, 2018

36 Dagum, Paul. "Digital Biomarkers of Cognitive Function." *npj Digital Medicine.* 2018;1(10). doi:10.1038/s41746-018-0018-4

37 Markey, Patrick M. and Christopher J. Ferguson. *Moral Combat.* Dallas: BenBella Books, 2017, 91

38 Przybylski, Andrew K., et al. "A Motivational Model of Video Game Engagement." *Review of General Psychology.* 2010;14(2):154–66. doi:10.1037/a0019440

39 Colder Carras, Michelle, et al. "Commercial Video Games as Therapy: A New Research Agenda to Unlock the Potential of a Global Pastime." *Frontiers in Psychiatry.* 2017;8:300. doi:10.3389/fpsyt.2017.00300

40 Interview with Adam Gazzaley, June 28, 2018

41 Just, M. A., et al. "A Decrease in Brain Activation Associated with Driving When Listening to Someone Speak." *Brain Research.* 2008;1205:70–80. doi:10.1016/j.brainres.2007.12.075

42 Ophir, Eyal, et al. "Cognitive Control in Media Multitaskers." *Proceedings of the National Academy of Sciences (PNAS).* 2009;106(37):15583–87. https://doi.org/10.1073/pnas.0903620106

43 Campbell, Karen L., et al. "Idiosyncratic Responding During Movie-Watching Predicted by Age Differences in Attentional Control." *Neurobiology of Aging.* 2015;36(11):3045–55. doi:10.1016/j. neurobiolaging.2015.07.028

44 Clapp, Wesley C., et al. "Deficit in Switching Between Functional Brain Networks Underlies the Impact of Multitasking on Working Memory in

Older Adults." *Proceedings of the National Academy of Sciences (PNAS)*. 2011;108(17):7212–17. doi:10.1073/pnas.1015297108

45   Anguera, J. A., et al. "Video Game Training Enhances Cognitive Control in Older Adults." *Nature*. 2013;501(7465):97–101. doi:10.1038/nature12486

46   Farber, Madeline. "This Video Game Could Treat Brain Disorders." *Fortune*, November 2, 2016. http://fortune.com/2016/11/02/video-games-and-cognitive-control/

47   Akili Interactive Inc. "Programs and Products." https://www.akiliinteractive.com/programs-products/

48   Davis, Naomi, et al. "Proof-of-Concept Study of an At-Home, Engaging, Digital Intervention for Pediatric ADHD." *Plos One*. 2018;13(1):e0189749. https://doi.org/10.1371/journal.pone.0189749

49   Simons, Daniel J., et al. "Do 'Brain-Training' Programs Work?" *Psychological Science in the Public Interest*. 2016;17(3):103–86. https://doi.org/10.1177/1529100616661983; Kable, Joseph W., et al. "No Effect of Commercial Cognitive Training on Brain Activity, Choice Behavior, or Cognitive Performance." *Journal of Neuroscience*. 2017;37(31):7390–7402. https://doi.org/10.1523/JNEUROSCI.2832-16.2017

Chapter 2

1   Interview with Roslyn McCoy, October 26, 2017

2   Cora videos on YouTube. Posted by Roslyn McCoy, 2010–2011. https://www.youtube.com/channel/UCyJhJw3qVGEUUfAJxxJkzJA

3   Centers for Disease Control and Prevention, National Center for Health Statistics. "Disability and Functioning (Noninstitutionalized Adults Aged 18 and Over); Summary Health Statistics Tables for U.S. Adults: National Health Interview Survey, 2017, Tables A-10b, A-10c." https://www.cdc.gov/nchs/fastats/disability.htm

4   "What Is the Function of the Various Brainwaves?" *Scientific American*. Accessed August 9, 2019. https://www.scientificamerican.com/article/what-is-the-function-of-t-1997-12-22/

5   Millett, David. "Hans Berger: From Psychic Energy to the EEG." *Perspectives in Biology and Medicine*. 2001;44(4):522–42. doi:10.1353/pbm.2001.0070

6   Bevilacqua, Dana, et al. "Brain-to-Brain Synchrony and Learn-
    ing Outcomes Vary by Student-Teacher Dynamics: Evidence from a
    Real-World Classroom EEG Study." *Journal of Cognitive Neuroscience.*
    2019;31(3):401–41. doi:10.1162/jocn_a_01274; Interview with Suzanne
    Dikker, October 17, 2017; Dikker, S., et al. "Brain-to-Brain Synchrony
    Tracks Real-World Dynamic Group Interactions in the Classroom." *Cur-
    rent Biology.* 2017;27(9):1375–80. doi:10.1016/j.cub.2017.04.002
7   Interview with Olivier Oullier, October 27, 2017
8   Interaction Metrics and 3 Innovations. "Interaction Metrics'
    Point-of-Purchase (POP) Survey Study Sparked 3 Innovations." Novem-
    ber 27, 2017. http://interactionmetrics.com/Point-of-Purchase-Survey
    -Study/Report.pdf
9   Interview with Bill Bosl, June 19, 2018
10 Centers for Disease Control and Prevention. "Epilepsy Fast Facts." Last
    modified July 31, 2018. https://www.cdc.gov/epilepsy/about/fast-facts.
    htm
11 Centers for Disease Control and Prevention. "One of the Nation's Most
    Common Neurological Conditions at a Glance 2017." Last modified
    August 9, 2017. https://www.cdc.gov/chronicdisease/resources
    /publications/aag/epilepsy.htm
12 Insel, Thomas. "Post by Former NIMH Director Thomas Insel: The
    Global Cost of Mental Illness." National Institute of Mental Health,
    September 28, 2011. https://www.nimh.nih.gov/about/directors/
    thomas-insel/blog/2011/the-global-cost-of-mental-illness.shtml
13 Interview with Phap Linh, October 20, 2017
14 Clarke, Tainya C., et al. "Trends in the Use of Complementary Health
    Approaches Among Adults: United States, 2002–2012." National Health
    Statistics Reports; no 79, February 10, 2015. Hyattsville, MD: National
    Center for Health Statistics. https://nccih.nih.gov/research/statistics/
    NHIS/2012/mind-body/meditation
15 Kazachenko, Snezhana. "Worldwide Spending on Augmented and Virtual
    Reality Expected to Double or More Every Year Through 2021, Accord-
    ing to IDC." Medium, May 4, 2018. https://medium.com/vrtoken
    /worldwide-spending-on-augmented-and-virtual-reality-expected-to
    -double-or-more-every-year-through-ff9f2901d498
16 Interview with Susan Ip-Jewell, October 23, 2017

Chapter 3

1   Interview with Mario Marzo, June 26, 2018

2   "Pianist Learns Bach in 1 Hour." (Halo Sport for Musicians: Mario Marzo.) YouTube video, 6:00. Posted by Halo Neuroscience, November 17, 2016. https://www.youtube.com/watch?time_continue=2&v=fVUvgUSX9hU

3   Interview with Brett Wingeier, June 16, 2018

4   Russell, Kane. "The Athlete's Guide to the Brain: Explosiveness." Halo Neuroscience Blog, November 29, 2018. https://www.haloneuro.com/blogs/halo/athlete-guide-brain-explosiveness

5   Halo Neuroscience. Case Study: Michael Johnson Performance. Posted March 3, 2016. https://blog.haloneuro.com/case-study-michael-johnson-performance-bd76cc6be6d2

6   Allman, Claire, et al. "Ipsilesional Anodal tDCS Enhances the Functional Benefits of Rehabilitation in Patients After Stroke." *Science Translational Medicine*. 2016;8(330):330re1. doi:10.1126/scitranslmed.aad5651

7   Meinzer, Marcus, et al. "Transcranial Direct Current Stimulation over Multiple Days Improves Learning and Maintenance of a Novel Vocabulary." *Cortex*. 2014;50:137–40. https://doi.org/10.1016/j.cortex.2013.07.013

8   Cohen Kadosh, Roi, et al. "Modulating Neuronal Activity Produces Specific and Long-Lasting Changes in Numerical Competence." *Current Biology*. 2010;20(22):2016–20. https://doi.org/10.1016/j.cub.2010.10.007

9   Knotkova, Helena, et al. "Transcranial Direct Current Stimulation (tDCS): What Pain Practitioners Need to Know." *Practical Pain Management*. 2015;15(3). https://www.practicalpainmanagement.com/treatments/interventional/stimulators/transcranial-direct-current-stimulation-tdcs-what-pain

10 Yokoi, Yuma, et al. "Transcranial Direct Current Stimulation in Depression and Psychosis: A Systematic Review." *Clinical EEG and Neuroscience*. 2018;49(2):93–102. doi:10.1177/1550059417732247

11 Kekic, Maria, et al. "Single-Session Transcranial Direct Current Stimulation Temporarily Improves Symptoms, Mood, and Self-Regulatory Control in Bulimia Nervosa: A Randomised Controlled Trial." Jiménez-Murcia S, ed. *Plos One*. 2017;12(1):e0167606. doi:10.1371/journal.pone.0167606

12 Santiesteban, I., et al. "Enhancing Social Ability by Stimulating the Right Temporoparietal Junction." *Current Biology*. 2012;22(23):2274–77. doi:10.1016/j.cub.2012.10.018

13 Clark, V. P., et al. "TDCS Guided Using fMRI Significantly Accelerates Learning to Identify Concealed Objects." *Neuroimage*. 2012;59(1):117–28. doi:10.1016/j.neuroimage.2010.11.036

14 Nelson, Justin, et al. "The Effects of Transcranial Direct Current Stimulation (tDCS) on Multitasking Throughput Capacity. *Frontiers in Human Neuroscience*. 2016;10:589. https://doi.org/10.3389/fnhum.2016.00589

15 "Brain Stimulation." YouTube video, 3:26. Posted by AirmanMagazineOnline, March 13, 2017. https://www.youtube.com/watch?time_continue=42&v=TOznTRN0KFI

16 Tsoucalas, Gregory, et al. "The 'Torpedo' Effect in Medicine." *International Maritime Health*. 2014;65(2):65–7. doi:10.5603/IMH.2014.0015. https://pdfs.semanticscholar.org/09ce/3fe232303c7273042e49b22fab27334d459c.pdf

17 Barker, Anthony T. and Ian Freeston, "Transcranial Magnetic Stimulation." *Scholarpedia*. 2007;2(10):2936. http://www.scholarpedia.org/article/Transcranial_magnetic_stimulation

18 "Dr. Anthony T. Barker Wins First International Brain Stimulation Award." Elsevier (press release), August 10, 2016. https://www.elsevier.com/about/press-releases/research-and-journals/dr.-anthony-t.-barker-wins-first-international-brain-stimulation-award

19 Goudra, B., et al. "Repetitive Transcranial Magnetic Stimulation in Chronic Pain: A Meta-analysis." *Anesthesia, Essays and Researches*. 2017;11(3):751–57. doi:10.4103/aer.AER_10_17

20 Pages, Kenneth. "TMS Can Help Patients with Depression." *Psychiatric News*, November 17, 2017. https://psychnews.psychiatryonline.org/doi/full/10.1176/appi.pn.2017.pp11b3

21 McClintock, S. M., et al. "Consensus Recommendations for the Clinical Application of Repetitive Transcranial Magnetic Stimulation (rTMS) in the Treatment of Depression." *Journal of Clinical Psychiatry*. 2018;79(1):35–48. doi:10.4088/JCP.16cs.10905

22 NNDC. "The National Network of Depression Centers (NNDC) rTMS Task Group Publish Comprehensive Recommendations on Repetitive Transcranial Magnetic Stimulation (rTMS)." June 27, 2017. https://nndc.org/the-national-network-of-depression-centers-nndc-rtms-task-group-publish-comprehensive-recommendations-on-repetitive-transcranial-magnetic-stimulation-rtms/

23 Padgett, Jason and Maureen Ann Seaberg. *Struck by Genius: How a Brain Injury Made Me a Mathematical Marvel.* New York: Houghton Mifflin Harcourt, 2014

24 Snyder, Allan. "Explaining and Inducing Savant Skills: Privileged Access to Lower Level, Less-Processed Information." *Philosophical Transactions of the Royal Society B.* 2009; 364(1522). doi:10.1098/rstb.2008.0290

25 Sacks, Oliver. *The Man Who Mistook His Wife for a Hat: And Other Clinical Tales.* New York: Touchstone, 1985

26 Snyder, A., et al. "Savant-like Numerosity Skills Revealed in Normal People by Magnetic Pulses." *Perception.* 2006;35:837–45. doi:10.1068/p5539

27 Chi, Richard P. and Allan W. Snyder. "Brain Stimulation Enables the Solution of an Inherently Difficult Problem." *Neuroscience Letters.* 2012;515(2):121–24. doi:10.1016.j.neulet.2012.03.012

28 *Automatic Brain: The Magic of the Unconscious Mind.* Directed by Francesca D'Amicis, et al., 2012. https://www.amazon.com/Automatic-Brain-Magic-Unconscious-Mind/dp/B01J2BFF8E. (Originally released as *The Magic of the Unconscious: Automatic Brain.* 2011. https://www.films.com/ecTitleDetail.aspx?TitleID=27351)

29 Grisham, John. *The Tumor.* Charlottesville, VA: Focused Ultrasound Foundation, 2016

30 American Association of Neurological Surgeons. "Glioblastoma Multiforme." Accessed July 7, 2019. https://www.aans.org/Patients/Neurosurgical-Conditions-and-Treatments/Glioblastoma-Multiforme

31 Kassell, Neal, et al. "Curing with Sound." YouTube video, 18:33. Posted by TEDx Charlottesville, December 1, 2015. https://www.youtube.com/watch?v=VbDZzBcMd5E

32 MedlinePlus. "Levodopa and Carbidopa." Accessed July 7, 2019. https://medlineplus.gov/druginfo/meds/a601068.html

33 Moore, Thomas J., et al. "Reports of Pathological Gambling, Hypersexuality, and Compulsive Shopping Associated with Dopamine Receptor Agonist Drugs." *JAMA Internal Medicine.* 2014;174(12):1930–33. doi:10.1001/jamainternmed.2014.5262

34 American Academy of Neurology. "Parkinson's Medication Linked to Gambling." *ScienceDaily,* August 12, 2003. www.sciencedaily.com/releases/2003/08/030812073612.htm

35 Kassell, Neal, et al. "Curing with Sound." YouTube video, 18:33. Posted by TEDx Charlottesville, December 1, 2015. https://www.youtube.com/watch?v=VbDZzBcMd5E

36 Elekta.com. "What Is Gamma Knife Surgery?" Accessed July 7, 2019. https://www.elekta.com/patients/gammaknife-treatment-process/

37 Interview with Dr. Neal Kassell, August 23, 2018

38 Bond, Aaron E., et al. "Safety and Efficacy of Focused Ultrasound Thalamotomy for Patients with Medication-Refractory, Tremor-Dominant Parkinson Disease: A Randomized Clinical Trial." *JAMA Neurology.* 2017;74(12):1412–18. doi:10.1001/jamaneurol.2017.3098

39 Lipsman, Nir, et al. "Blood-Brain Barrier Opening in Alzheimer's Disease Using MR-Guided Focused Ultrasound." *Nature Communications.* 2018;9(1):2336. doi:10.1038/s41467-018-04529-6

Chapter 4

1   Interview with Mark Pollock, July 17, 2018

2   Mark Pollock with Ross Whitaker. *Making It Happen.* Dublin: Mark Pollock, 2005

3   World Health Organization. "Spinal Cord Injury." November 19, 2013. http://www.who.int/news-room/fact-sheets/detail/spinal-cord-injury

4   Armour, Brian S., et al. "Prevalence and Causes of Paralysis—United States, 2013." *American Journal of Public Health.* Oct. 2016;106:1855–57. doi:10.2105/AJPH.2016.303270

5   Pollock, Mark and Simone George. "A Love Letter to Realism in a Time of Grief." YouTube video, 19:16. Posted by TEDx, April 2018. https://www.ted.com/talks/mark_pollock_and_simone_george_a_love_letter_to_realism_in_a_time_of_grief?language=en

6   Angeli, C. A., et al. "Altering Spinal Cord Excitability Enables Voluntary Movements After Chronic Complete Paralysis in Humans." *Brain.* 2014;137(Pt 5):1394–409. doi:10.1093/brain/awu038

7   Gad, Parag, et al. "Weight Bearing Over-ground Stepping in an Exoskeleton with Non-invasive Spinal Cord Neuromodulation After Motor Complete Paraplegia." *Frontiers in Neuroscience.* 2017;11:333. doi:10.3389/fnins.2017.00333

8   Christopher & Dana Reeve Foundation. "Paralysis in the U.S." Accessed July 8, 2019. http://s3.amazonaws.com/reeve-assets-production/RFParalysisintheUSBrief.pdf

9   Christopher & Dana Reeve Foundation. "Costs of Living with SCI." Accessed August 11, 2019. https://www.christopherreeve.org/living-with-paralysis/costs-and-insurance/costs-of-living-with-spinal-cord-injury

10   Christopher & Dana Reeve Foundation. "Stats About Paralysis." Accessed July 8, 2019. https://www.christopherreeve.org/living-with-paralysis/stats-about-paralysis

11   Amr, Sherif M., et al. "Bridging Defects in Chronic Spinal Cord Injury Using Peripheral Nerve Grafts Combined with a Chitosan-Laminin Scaffold and Enhancing Regeneration Through Them by Co-Transplantation with Bone-Marrow-Derived Mesenchymal Stem Cells: Case Series of 14 Patients." *The Journal of Spinal Cord Medicine*. 2014;37(1):54–71. doi:10.1179/2045772312Y.0000000069

12   Ahmad, A., et al. "Optogenetics Applications for Treating Spinal Cord Injury." *Asian Spine Journal*. 2015;9(2):299–305. doi:10.4184/asj.2015.9.2.299

13   Carnegie Mellon University. Press Release: "Renowned Neuroscientist Karl Deisseroth to Receive Carnegie Mellon's Dickson Prize in Science." January 29, 2014. https://www.cmu.edu/news/stories/archives/2014/january/jan29_dicksonprizedeisseroth.html

14   Ahmad, A., et al. "Optogenetics Applications for Treating Spinal Cord Injury." *Asian Spine Journal*. 2015;9(2):299–305. doi:10.4184/asj.2015.9.2.299

15   Interview with Geoffrey Ling, MD, August 31, 2018

16   Montgomery, Nancy. "2016 Marks First Year Without Combat Amputation Since Afghan, Iraq Wars Began." *Stars and Stripes,* March 18, 2017. https://www.stripes.com/2016-marks-first-year-without-combat-amputation-since-afghan-iraq-wars-began-1.459288

17   Brumfiel, Geoff. "The Insane and Exciting Future of the Bionic Body." Smithsonian.com, September 2013. https://www.smithsonianmag.com/innovation/the-insane-and-exciting-future-of-the-bionic-body-918868/

18   Ifft, Peter J., et al. "A Brain-Machine Interface Enables Bimanual Movements in Monkeys." *Science Translational Medicine*. 2013;5(210):210ra154. doi:10.1126/scitranslmed.3006159

19   Chase, Steven, M., et al. "Behavioral and Neural Correlates of Visuomotor Adaptation Through a Brain-Computer Interface in Primary Motor Cortex." *Journal of Neurophysiology.* 2012;108(2):624–44. https://doi.org/10.1152/jn.00371.2011

20   Neergaard, Lauran. "Paralyzed Man Uses Mind-Controlled Robot Arm to Touch." *Sydney Morning Herald,* October 10, 2011. https://www.smh.com.au/technology/paralyzed-man-uses-mindpowered-robot-arm-to-touch-20111010-1lh6u.html

21   Ling, Geoffrey. "Saying Yes to Innovation [AngelMD Alpha Conference 2018]." YouTube video, 38:08. Posted by AngelMD Inc., February 8, 2018. https://www.youtube.com/watch?v=PMsvJQO11-0

22   Gohd, Chelsea. "Florida Man Becomes First Person to Live with Advanced Mind-Controlled Robotic Arm." *Futurism,* February 3, 2018. https://futurism.com/mind-controlled-robotic-arm-johnny-matheny/

23   Karimi, M. T. "Robotic Rehabilitation of Spinal Cord Injury Individual." *Ortopedia, Tramatologia, Rehabilitacja.* 2013 Jan–Feb;15(1):1–7. doi:10.5604/15093492.1032792

24   Baldwin, Roberto. "Ford Thinks Exoskeletons Are Ready for Prime Time in Its Factories." *Engadget,* August 7, 2018. https://www.engadget.com/2018/08/07/ford-exoskeletons-eksovest/

25   Ford Media Center. "Ford Pilots New Exoskeleton Technology to Help Lessen Chance of Worker Fatigue, Injury." November 9, 2017. https://media.ford.com/content/fordmedia/fna/us/en/news/2017/11/09/ford-exoskeleton-technology-pilot.html

26   Park, Sung Hyun, et al. "3D Printed Polymer Photodetectors." *Advanced Materials,* 2018. doi:10.1002/adma.201803980

Chapter 5

1   Cyborg Foundation. Accessed July 8, 2019. https://www.cyborgfoundation.com/

2   *Human by Design.* Deus Ex, 2016. https://www.amazon.com/Human-Design-Presented-Mankind-Divided/dp/B01ISIPKB4

3   NIH Genetics Home Reference. "Achromatopsia." Accessed July 8, 2019. https://ghr.nlm.nih.gov/condition/achromatopsia#statistics

4 Harbisson, Neil. "D&AD President's Lecture." YouTube video, 3:23. Posted by D&AD, May 18, 2015. https://www.youtube.com/watch?v=2lHPpyRZujM

5 Akst, Jef. "The Sound of Color." *The Scientist*, May 1, 2012. https://www.the-scientist.com/notebook/the-sound-of-color-41058

6 Alfaro, Arantxa, et al. "Hearing Colors: An Example of Brain Plasticity." *Frontiers in Systems Neuroscience*. 2015;9:56. doi:10.3389/fnsys.2015.00056

7 Munsell Color. "Neil Harbisson Interview—Part 5: Beyond Hearing Color." Accessed July 8, 2019. https://munsell.com/color-blog/neil-harbisson-infrared-hearing/

8 Harbisson, Neil. A Collection of Essays. Cyborg Arts Limited. Accessed September 3, 2018.

9 Business Insider Tech. "This Real-life Cyborg Has an Antenna Implanted into His Skull." YouTube video, 4:27. Posted by BI Tech, March 3, 2015. https://www.youtube.com/watch?v=NivuCuwZ944

10 Interview with Kevin Warwick, October 2, 2018.

11 Nuyujukian, Paul, et al. "Cortical Control of a Tablet Computer by People with Paralysis." *Plos One*. 2018, November 21;13(11):e0204566. https://doi.org/10.1371/journal.pone.0204566

12 Pearce, J. M. S. "Henry Head (1861–1940)." *Journal of Neurology, Neurosurgery & Psychiatry*. 2000;69:578. http://dx.doi.org/10.1136/jnnp.69.5.578

13 Lenfest, Stephen M. "Dr. Henry Head and Lessons Learned from His Self-Experiment on Radial Nerve Transection." *Journal of Neurosurgery*. 2011;114(2):529–33. doi:10.3171/2010.8.JNS10400

14 Biello, David. "Albert Hofmann, Inventor of LSD, Embarks on Final Trip." *Scientific American*, April 30, 2008. https://www.scientificamerican.com/article/inventor-of-lsd-embarks-on-final-trip/

15 Marshall, Barry and Paul C. Adams. "*Helicobacter Pylori*: A Nobel Pursuit?" *Canadian Journal of Gastroenterology*. 2008;22(11):895–96. https://www.ncbi.nlm.nih.gov/pmc/articles/PMC2661189/

16 Warwick, K., et al. "Thought Communication and Control: A First Step Using Radiotelegraphy." *IEE Proceedings—Communications*. 2004;151(3). doi:10.1049/ip-com:20040409

17 Warwick, Kevin, et al. "The Application of Implant Technology for Cybernetics Systems." *Archives of Neurology.* 2003;60(10):1369–73. doi:10.1001/archneur.60.10.1369

18 Rosellini, Will. "Beyond Human." TEDxPlano. YouTube video, 20:08. Posted by TEDx Talks, May 8, 2015. https://www.youtube.com/watch?v=sTOej9IUF6I

19 Interview with Will Rosellini, June 21, 2018

20 Gardner, John. "A History of Deep Brain Stimulation: Technological Innovation and the Role of Clinical Assessment Tools." *Social Studies of Science.* 2013;43(5):707–28. doi:10.1177/0306312713483678

21 Parkinson's Foundation. "Statistics." Accessed August 10, 2019. http://parkinson.org/Understanding-Parkinsons/Causes-and-Statistics/Statistics

22 Aquilina, O. "A Brief History of Cardiac Pacing." *Images in Paediatric Cardiology.* 2006;8(2):17–81. https://www.ncbi.nlm.nih.gov/pmc/articles/PMC3232561/

23 National Institute on Deafness and Other Communication Disorders (NIDCD). "Cochlear Implants." Accessed August 10, 2019. https://www.nidcd.nih.gov/health/cochlear-implants

24 Spinks, Rosie. "Meet the French Neurosurgeon Who Accidentally Invented the 'Brain Pacemaker.'" *Quartz*, June 13, 2016. https://qz.com/704522/meet-the-french-neurosurgeon-who-accidentally-invented-the-brain-pacemaker/

25 World Health Organization. "Deafness and Hearing Loss." Accessed July 8, 2019. http://www.who.int/news-room/fact-sheets/detail/deafness-and-hearing-loss

26 Garberoglio, Carrie Lou, et al. "Deaf People and Employment in the United States: 2016." Washington, DC: U.S. Department of Education, Office of Special Education Programs, National Deaf Center on Postsecondary Outcomes. https://www.nationaldeafcenter.org/sites/default/files/Deaf%20Employment%20Report_final.pdf

27 Cornea Research Foundation of America. "Artificial Cornea." Accessed July 8, 2019. http://www.cornea.org/Learning-Center/Cornea-Transplants/Artificial-Cornea.aspx

28 CentraSight. "Implantable Telescope Technology for End-Stage Age-Related Macular Degeneration (AMD)." Accessed July 8, 2019. https://www.centrasight.com/about-centrasight/implantable-telescope-technology/

29 Issani, Rozina. "Living in the Dark." *Toronto Life*, May 19, 2016. https://torontolife.com/city/life/rozina-issani-retinitis-blindness-memoir/

30 Second Sight. Accessed August 10, 2019. http://www.secondsight.com/g-the-argus-ii-prosthesis-system-pf-en.html

31 USC Roski Eye Institute. "Mark Humayun, MD, PhD." Accessed July 8, 2019. https://eye.keckmedicine.org/doctors/dr-mark-humayun/

32 Moore, Samuel K. "Vagus Nerve Stimulation Succeeds in Long-Term Stroke Recovery Trial." *IEEE Spectrum*, May 30, 2017. https://spectrum.ieee.org/the-human-os/biomedical/devices/vagus-nerve-stimulation-succeeds-in-longterm-stroke-recovery

33 Dawson, Jesse, et al. "Safety, Feasibility, and Efficacy of Vagus Nerve Stimulation Paired with Upper-Limb Rehabilitation After Ischemic Stroke." *Stroke; a Journal of Cerebral Circulation*. 2016;47(1):143–150. doi:10.1161/STROKEAHA.115.010477

34 Anumanchipalli, Gopala, K., et al. "Speech Synthesis from Neural Decoding of Spoken Sentences." *Nature*. 2019;568:493–98. https://www.nature.com/articles/s41586-019-1119-1

35 Weiler, Nicholas. "Breakthrough Device Translates Brain Activity into Speech," University of California News, April 25, 2019. https://www.universityofcalifornia.edu/news/synthetic-speech-generated-brain-recordings

36 National Institute of Mental Health. "Post-Traumatic Stress Disorder." Accessed August 10, 2019. https://www.nimh.nih.gov/health/statistics/post-traumatic-stress-disorder-ptsd.shtml

37 Noble, L. J., et al. "Effects of Vagus Nerve Stimulation on Extinction of Conditioned Fear and Post-Traumatic Stress Disorder Symptoms in Rats." *Translational Psychiatry*. 2017;7(8):e1217. doi:10.1038/tp.2017.191

38 Metz, Rachel. "This Company Embeds Microchips in Its Employees, and They Love It." *MIT Technology Review*, August 17, 2018. https://www.technologyreview.com/s/611884/this-company-embeds-microchips-in-its-employees-and-they-love-it/

39 Holley, Peter. "This Company Microchips Employees. Could Your Ailing Relative Be Next?" *Washington Post*, August 24, 2018. http://www.latimes.com/business/technology/la-fi-tn-microchip-20180824-story.html

40 "Radio Frequency Identification (RFID) Privacy Laws." National Conference of State Legislatures. Accessed August 10, 2019. http://

www.ncsl.org/research/telecommunications-and-information-technology/
radio-frequency-identification-rfid-privacy-laws.aspx

41   Markoff, John. "Elon Musk's Neuralink Wants 'Sewing Machine-Like'
Robots to Wire Brains to the Internet." *New York Times,* July 16, 2019.
https://www.nytimes.com/2019/07/16/technology/neuralink-elon-musk.
html; Scaturro, Michael. "Elon Musk is Making Implants to Link
the Brain with a Smartphone." CNN, July 18, 2019, https://www.
cnn.com/2019/07/17/tech/elon-musk-neuralink-brain-implant/index.
html; Robbins, Rebecca. "Elon Musk Wants to Test Brain-Reading
Implants in Paralyzed Patients Next Year." Stat News, July 17, 2019.
https://www.statnews.com/2019/07/17/elon-musk-wants-to-test-brai
n-reading-implants-in-paralyzed-patients-next-year/

42   Fourtané, Susan. "Neuralink: How the Human Brain Will Download
Directly from a Computer." *Interesting Engineering,* September 2, 2018.
https://interestingengineering.com/neuralink-how-the-human-brain-will
-download-directly-from-a-computer

43   Tangermann, Victor. "Elon Musk Says an Update on His
Brain-Computing Interface Is 'Coming Soon.'" *Business Insider,* April 24,
2019. https://www.businessinsider.com/elon-musk-ab-update-on-brai
n-computing-interface-is-coming-soon-2019-4

44   Kernel. https://kernel.co/

45   "Next-Generation Non-Surgical Neurotechnology (N^3)." FedBizOpps.
gov. Accessed August 10, 2019. https://www.fbo.gov/index.php?s=oppor
tunity&mode=form&id=767054e365fc2ac4cd05a338a6d35a1d&tab=co
re&tabmode=list&=

46   Naumann, J. *Search for Paradise: A Patient's Account of the Artificial Vision
Experiment.* Bloomington, Indiana: Xlibris, 2012

Chapter 6

1   CDC. "Basic Information About Traumatic Brain Injury." Accessed July 8,
2019. https://www.cdc.gov/traumaticbraininjury/basics.html

2   CDC. "Stroke Facts." Accessed July 8, 2019. https://www.cdc.gov/stroke/
facts.htm

3   American Cancer Society. "Key Statistics for Brain and Spinal Cord Tumors." Accessed July 8, 2019. https://www.cancer.org/cancer/brain-spinal-cord -tumors-adults/about/key-statistics.html

4   Alzheimer's Association. "2019 Alzheimer's Disease Facts and Figures." http://www.alz.org/facts/overview.asp

5   Interview with Frank Tarazi, June 27, 2018

6   Kelland, Kate. "Bill Gates Makes $100 Million Personal Investment to Fight Alzheimer's." *Reuters*, November 13, 2017. https://www.reuters.com/ article/us-health-dementia-gates/bill-gates-makes-100-million-persona l-investment-to-fight-alzheimers-idUSKBN1DD0S3

7   Maurer, Konrad, et al. "Auguste D and Alzheimer's Disease." *The Lancet*. 1997;349(9064):P1546–49. https://doi.org/10.1016/ S0140-6736(96)10203-8

8   Senior Living. "1900–2000: Changes in Life Expectancy in the United States." Accessed August 10, 2019. https://www.seniorliving.org/history/1 900-2000-changes-life-expectancy-united-states/

9   Editorial. "Method of the Year 2010." *Nature Methods*. 2011;8(1):1. doi:10.1038/NMETH.F.321

10 BreakthroughPrize.org. "Life Sciences Breakthrough Prize Laureates 2016." https://breakthroughprize.org/Laureates/2/P1/Y2016

11 Gairdner.org. Canada Gairdner Awards 2018 Laureates. https://gairdner. org/winners/current-winners/

12 Interview with Ed Boyden, November 5, 2018.

13 Ryan, Tomás J, et al. "Engram Cells Retain Memory Under Retrograde Amnesia." *Science*. 2015;348(6238):1007–13. doi:10.1126/science. aaa5542; van Wyk, Michiel, et al. "Restoring the ON Switch in Blind Retinas: Opto-mGluR6, a Next-Generation, Cell-Tailored Optogenetic Tool." *Plos Biology*, May 7, 2015. doi:10.1371/journal.pbio.1002143; Ramirez, Steve, et al. "Activating Positive Memory Engrams Suppresses Depression-Like Behavior." *Nature*. 2015;522:335–39 doi:10.1038/ nature14514

14 Chen, F., et al. "Optical Imaging. Expansion Microscopy." *Science*. 2015;347(6221):543–48. doi:10.1126/science.1260088

15 Stam, C. J., et al. "Generalized Synchronization of MEG Recordings in Alzheimer's Disease: Evidence for Involvement of the Gamma Band." *Journal of Clinical Neurophysiology*. 2002;19(6):562–74. https://www. ncbi.nlm.nih.gov/pubmed/12488788

16 Cardin, Jessica A., et al. "Driving Fast-Spiking Cells Induces Gamma Rhythm and Controls Sensory Responses." *Nature.* 2009;459(7247):663–67. doi:10.1038/nature.08002

17 Iaccarino, Hannah F., et al. "Gamma Frequency Entrainment Attenuates Amyloid Load and Modifies Microglia." *Nature.* 2016;540:230–35. https://www.nature.com/articles/nature20587

18 Hampson, Robert E., et al. "Developing a Hippocampal Neural Prosthetic to Facilitate Human Memory Encoding and Recall." *Journal of Neural Engineering.* 2018;15(3). https://doi.org/10.1088/1741-2552/aaaed7

19 "Breaking News." Hampson Lab, March 28, 2018. Accessed July 8, 2019. http://hampsonlab.org/index.html

20 Squire, L. R. "The Legacy of Patient H.M. for Neuroscience. *Neuron.* 2009;61(1):6–9. doi:10.1016/j.neuron.2008.12.023

21 Milner, Brenda, et al. "Further Analysis of the Hippocampal Amnesic Syndrome: 14-Year Follow-Up Study of H.M." *Neuropsychologia.* 1968;6:215–34. https://is.muni.cz/el/1423/podzim2011/PSY221_P11/um/27733942/Milner__Corkin___Teuber__1968_.pdf

22 "Theodore Berger: Neuroengineering—The Future Is Now." YouTube video, 28:49. Posted by *MIT Technology Review,* November 8, 2013. https://www.youtube.com/watch?time_continue=7&v=bHubR09oKKE

23 Hampson, Robert E., et al. "Developing a Hippocampal Neural Prosthetic to Facilitate Human Memory Encoding and Recall" (Video abstract). *Journal of Neural Engineering.* 2018;15:3. https://doi.org/10.1088/1741-2552/aaaed7

24 Ramirez, Steve, et al. "Creating a False Memory in the Hippocampus." *Science.* 2013;341(6144):387–91. doi:10.1126/science.1239073

25 Bali, Parul, et al. "Potential for Stem Cells Therapy in Alzheimer's Disease: Do Neurotrophic Factors Play Critical Role?" *Current Alzheimer Research.* 2017;14(2):208–20. https://www.ncbi.nlm.nih.gov/pmc/articles/PMC5880623/

26 Longeveron LLC. "Longeveron Recruiting for Stem Cell Alzheimer's Trial in South Florida," May 23, 2018. https://www.prnewswire.com/news-releases/longeveron-recruiting-for-stem-cell-alzheimers-trial-in-south-florida-300653573.html

27 Snowdon, D. A. "Healthy Aging and Dementia: Findings from the Nun Study." *Annals of Internal Medicine.* 2003;139(5 pt 2):450–54. https://www.ncbi.nlm.nih.gov/pubmed/12965975

28 Vrselja, Zvonimir, et al. "Restoration of Brain Circulation and Cellular Functions Hours Post-Mortem." *Nature*. 2019;568:336–43. https://www.nature.com/articles/s41586-019-1099-1

Chapter 7

1 Grace, Katja, et al. "When Will AI Exceed Human Performance? Evidence from AI Experts." *Journal of Artificial Intelligence Research*. 2018;62:729–54. https://www.jair.org/index.php/jair/article/download/11222/26431/
2 Koene, Randal A. "Mind Uploading." Accessed July 8, 2019. http://rak.minduploading.org/
3 Interview with Gary Flake, September 6, 2018.
4 Levy, Steven. "What Deep Blue Tells Us About AI in 2017." *Wired*, May 23, 2017. https://www.wired.com/2017/05/what-deep-blue-tells-us-about-ai-in-2017/
5 Harada, C. N., et al. "Normal Cognitive Aging." *Clinics in Geriatric Medicine*. 2013;29(4):737–52. doi:10.1016/j.cger.2013.07.002
6 Terry, R. D. and R. Katzman. "Life Span and Synapses: Will There Be a Primary Senile Dementia?" *Neurobiology of Aging*. 2001;22(3):347–48; discussion 353–4. https://www.ncbi.nlm.nih.gov/pubmed/11378236
7 Meier-Ruge, W., et al. "Age-Related White Matter Atrophy in the Human Brain." *Annals of the New York Academy of Sciences*. 1992;673:260–69. https://www.ncbi.nlm.nih.gov/pubmed/1485724
8 U.S. Census Bureau. "Facts for Features: Older Americans Month: May 2017." Release Number: CB17-FF.08. https://www.census.gov/newsroom/facts-for-features/2017/cb17-ff08.html
9 Bobrov, Pavel, et al. "Brain-Computer Interface Based on Generation of Visual Images." Rogers, S., ed. *Plos One*. 2011;6(6):e20674. doi:10.1371/journal.pone.0020674
10 Interview with Alex Zhavoronkov, July 5, 2018
11 Sissons, Claire. "How Much Blood Is in the Human Body?" *Medical News Today*, March 6, 2018. https://www.medicalnewstoday.com/articles/321122.php
12 Xu, Ming, et al. "Senolytics Improve Physical Function and Increase Lifespan in Old Age." *Nature Medicine*. 2018; 24:1246–56. doi:10.1038/s41591-018-0092-9

13 Kochanek, Kenneth D., et al. "Mortality in the United States, 2016." NCHS. 2017;Data Brief No. 293. https://www.cdc.gov/nchs/data/databriefs/db293.pdf

14 PETA. "Mice and Rats in Laboratories." Accessed July 8, 2019. https://www.peta.org/issues/animals-used-for-experimentation/animals-laboratories/mice-rats-laboratories/

15 Wang, D., et al. "Deep Learning for Identifying Metastatic Breast Cancer." 2016;arXiv preprint arXiv:1606.05718. http://j.mp/2o6FejM

16 Weng, Stephen F., et al. "Can Machine-Learning Improve Cardiovascular Risk Prediction Using Routine Clinical Data?" *Plos One*. 2017;12(4): e0174944. https://doi.org/10.1371/journal.pone.0174944

17 Gulshan, Varun, et al. "Development and Validation of a Deep Learning Algorithm for Detection of Diabetic Retinopathy in Retinal Fundus Photographs." *JAMA*. 2016;316(22):2402–10. doi:10.1001/jama.2016.17216

18 Simon, Matt. "Inside the Mind of Amanda Feilding, Countess of Psychedelic Science," *Wired*, February 15, 2018. https://www.wired.com/story/inside-the-mind-of-amanda-feilding-countess-of-psychedelic-science/

19 Interview with Rachel Thomas, December 13, 2018

20 Arbel, Tali. "Researchers Say Amazon Face-Detection Technology Shows Bias." Tech Xplore, January 25, 2019. https://techxplore.com/news/2019-01-amazon-face-detection-technology-bias.html

21 "Elon Musk Answers Your Questions!/SXSW 2018." YouTube video, 1:11:37. Posted by SXSW, March 11, 2018. https://www.youtube.com/watch?time_continue=1&v=kzlUyrccbos

22 Grace, Katja., et al. "When Will AI Exceed Human Performance? Evidence from AI Experts." *Journal of Artificial Intelligence Research*. 2018;62:729–54. https://www.jair.org/index.php/jair/article/download/11222/26431/; "2016 Expert Survey on Progress in AI." *AI Impacts*, December 14, 2016. https://aiimpacts.org/2016-expert-survey-on-progress-in-ai/

23 Smith, Craig. "26 Amazing Skype Statistics and Facts (2019)." DMR, June 7, 2019. https://expandedramblings.com/index.php/skype-statistics/

24 Interview with Jaan Tallinn, October 3, 2018

25 Tallinn, J. "Beneficial AI 2017." Future of Life Institute, January 7, 2017. Accessed July 9, 2019. https://futureoflife.org/wp-content/uploads/2017/01/Jaan-Tallinn.pdf?x40372

26 Tallinn, J. "Beneficial AI 2017." Future of Life Institute, January 7, 2017. Accessed July 9, 2019. https://futureoflife.org/wp-content/uploads/2017/01/Jaan-Tallinn.pdf?x40372

27 OpenAI. "About OpenAI." Accessed August 10, 2019. https://openai.com/about/

28 Partnership on AI. Accessed August 10, 2019. https://www.partnershiponai.org/

29 Future of Life Institute. "Beneficial AI 2017." Accessed August 10, 2019. https://futureoflife.org/bai-2017/

30 Future of Life Institute. "Asilomar AI Principles." Accessed August 10, 2019. https://futureoflife.org/ai-principles/

31 Wang, D., et al. "Deep Learning for Identifying Metastatic Breast Cancer." 2016;arXiv preprint arXiv:1606.05718. http://j.mp/2o6FejM

Chapter 8

1   "Recruiting Participants in India for the Human Brain Diversity Project." YouTube video, 4:14. Posted by Sapien Labs, December 3, 2016. https://www.youtube.com/watch?v=5QeYNU_pyUE

2   Interview with Tara Thiagarajan, August 16, 2018

3   Will, Tyler R., et al. "Problems and Progress Regarding Sex Bias and Omission in Neuroscience Research." *eNeuro.* 2017;4(6)ENEURO.0278-17.2017. https://doi.org/10.1523/ENEURO.0278-17.2017

4   Ruigrok, Amber N., et al. "A Meta-Analysis of Sex Differences in Human Brain Structure." *Neuroscience & Biobehavioral Reviews.* 2014;39(100):34–50. doi:10.1016/j.neubiorev.2013.12.004

5   Amen, D. G., et al. "Gender-Based Cerebral Perfusion Differences in 46,034 Functional Neuroimaging Scans." *Journal of Alzheimer's Disease.* 2017;60(2):605–14. doi:10.3233/JAD-170432

6   Wyciszkiewicz, Aleksandra, et al. "Cerebellar Volume in Children with Attention-Deficit Hyperactivity Disorder (ADHD): Replication Study." *Journal of Child Neurology.* 2016;32(2):215–21. https://doi.org/10.1177/0883073816678550

7   Chuang, Jie-Yu, et al. "Adolescent Major Depressive Disorder: Neuroimaging Evidence of Sex Difference During an Affective Go/No-Go

Task." *Frontiers in Psychiatry*, July 11, 2017. https://doi.org/10.3389/fpsyt.2017.00119

8   Anxiety and Depression Association of America. "Women and Depression." Accessed July 9, 2019. https://adaa.org/find-help-for/women/depression

9   Liu, Katherine A. and Natalie A. Dipietro Mager. "Women's Involvement in Clinical Trials: Historical Perspective and Future Implications." *Pharmacy Practice*. 2016;14(1):708. doi:10:18549/PharmPract.2016.01.708

10   Mazure, C. M. and D. P. Jones. "Twenty Years and Still Counting: Including Women as Participants and Studying Sex and Gender in Biomedical Research." *BMC Women's Health*. 2015;15:94. doi:10.1186/s12905-015-0251-9

11   Interview with Tara Thiagarajan, August 16, 2018

12   Klimesch, Wolfgang. "Alpha-Band Oscillations, Attention, and Controlled Access to Stored Information." *Trends in Cognitive Sciences*. 2012;16(12):606–17. doi:10.1016/j.tics.2012.10.007

13   "FAQs: Global Poverty Line Update." The World Bank, September 30, 2015. http://www.worldbank.org/en/topic/poverty/brief/global-poverty-line-faq

14   Sapien Labs. "Neurolab Program." Accessed July 29, 2019. https://sapienlabs.co/neurolabs/

15   Yeatman, Jason D., et al. "A Browser-Based Tool for Visualization and Analysis of Diffusion MRI Data." *Nature Communications*. 2018;9(1):940. doi:10.1038/s41467-018-03297-7

16   Sweeney, L. "Only You, Your Doctor, and Many Others May Know." *Technology Science*, September 29, 2015. http://techscience.org/a/2015092903

17   Yoo, Ji Su, et al. "Risks to Patient Privacy: A Re-Identification of Patients in Maine and Vermont Statewide Hospital Data." *Technology Science*, October 9, 2018. https://techscience.org/a/2018100901

18   According to its homepage, this U.S. agency "invests in high-risk/high-payoff research programs that have the potential to provide our nation with an overwhelming intelligence advantage" (https://www.iarpa.gov/)

19   BRAIN Initiative. "BRAIN Investment Pays Off." Accessed July 29, 2018. http://www.braininitiative.org/achievements/brain-investment-pays-off/

20   Interview with Adam Gazzaley, June 28, 2018

21   Interview with Tom Insel, June 22, 2018

22   Interview with Neal Kassell, August 23, 2018

23 Interview with Brett Wingeier, June 14, 2018

24 Interview with Mark Pollock, July 17, 2018

Chapter 9

1   "UAE to Build First City on Mars by 2117." *Gulf News*, February 14, 2017. https://gulfnews.com/uae/uae-to-build-first-city-on-mars-by-2117 -1.1978549

2   Government of Dubai Media Office. "VP, Abu Dhabi Crown Prince Launch Mars Science City." September 26, 2017. http://mediaoffice.ae/ en/media-center/news/26/9/2017/mars.aspx

3   Salama, Samir. "Mohammad Bin Rashid Reveals Reshuffled UAE Cabinet." *Gulf News*, October 19, 2017. https://gulfnews.com/uae/government/ mohammad-bin-rashid-reveals-reshuffled-uae-cabinet-1.2108934

4   UAE 2031. "UAE Artificial Intelligence Strategy." Accessed July 29, 2019. http://www.uaeai.ae/en/

5   Yuste, Rafael, et al. "Four Ethical Priorities for Neurotechnologies and AI." *Nature*. 2017;551(7679):159–163. doi:10.1038/551159a

6   Interview with Karen Rommelfanger, November 26, 2018

7   Global Neuroethics Summit Delegates, et al. "Neuroethics Questions to Guide Ethical Research in the International Brain Initiatives." *Neuron*. 2018;100(1):19–36. doi:10.1016/j.neuron.2018.09.021

8   Heiden, Petra, et al. "Pathological Gambling in Parkinson's Disease: What Are the Risk Factors and What Is the Role of Impulsivity?" *European Journal of Neuroscience*. 2016;45(1):67–72. doi:10.1111/ejn.13396

9   Corvol, J.-C., et al. "Longitudinal Analysis of Impulse Control Disorders in Parkinson Disease." *Neurology*. 2018;91(3):e189-e201. doi:10.1212/ WNL.0000000000005816

10 Boylan, Laura S. and Vladimir S. Kostić. "Don't Ask, Don't Tell: Impulse-Control Disorders in PD." *Neurology*. 2018;91(3):107–08. doi:10.1212/WNL.0000000000005806

11 Huth, Alexander G., et al. "Decoding the Semantic Content of Natural Movies from Human Brain Activity." *Frontiers in Systems Neuroscience*. 2016;10:81. https://doi.org/10.3389/fnsys.2016.00081; Nishimoto, S., et al. "Reconstructing Visual Experiences from Brain Activity Evoked by

Natural Movies." *Current Biology.* 2011;21(19):1641–46. doi:10.1016/j.cub.2011.08.031

12 Just, Marcel Adam, et al. "A Neurosemantic Theory of Concrete Noun Representation Based on the Underlying Brain Codes." *Plos One.* 2010;5(1):e8622. doi:10.1371/journal.pone.0008622; Kassam, Karim S., et al. "Identifying Emotions on the Basis of Neural Activation." *Plos One.* 2013;8(6):e66032. doi:10.1371/journal.pone.0066032

13 World Economic Forum. "The Future of Jobs Report 2018," 2018. http://www3.weforum.org/docs/WEF_Future_of_Jobs_2018.pdf

14 McKinsey Global Institute. "Jobs Lost, Jobs Gained: Workforce Transitions in a Time of Automation." December 2017, McKinsey & Company. Accessed July 9, 2019. https://www.mckinsey.com/~/media/McKinsey/Featured%20Insights/Future%20of%20Organizations/What%20the%20future%20of%20work%20will%20mean%20for%20jobs%20skills%20and%20wages/MGI-Jobs-Lost-Jobs-Gained-Executive-summary-December-6-2017.ashx

15 Ng, Andrew. "AI Transformation Playbook: How to Lead Your Company into the AI Era." Landing AI, December 13, 2018. https://landing.ai/ai-transformation-playbook/

16 Viswanathan, Meera, et al. "Interventions to Improve Adherence to Self-administered Medications for Chronic Diseases in the United States: A Systematic Review." *Annals of Internal Medicine.* 2012;157(11):785–95. doi: 10.7326/0003-4819-157-11-201212040-00538

INDEX

ABOUT THE AUTHOR

T AN LE IS RECOGNIZED as one of the most influential pioneers in the emerging field of brain-computer interface. An inventor, explorer, and entrepreneur, she is the founder and CEO of EMO-TIV, a San Francisco–headquartered neuroinformatics company that is on a mission to improve understanding of the human brain and to develop a platform for researchers, developers, and consumers around the world to be part of a global innovation task force. Her first-of-its-kind "brainwear" reads users' brainwaves, making it possible to control virtual objects with mere thoughts. With her company's brainwear, she is leading the way to a bold new future, tapping into the power of the human brain and pushing the boundaries of our cognitive powers to open up new possibilities for improving performance and health, and, ultimately, to prevent disease.

Born in South Vietnam, Tan migrated to Australia as a refugee with her family in 1981. She began university studies at the age of sixteen and went on to complete a bachelor's degree in law and commerce in 1998 at Monash University. Inspired by her mother, Mai Ho, who became the inaugural mayor of the city of Maribyrnong in 1997, Tan Le was named Young Australian of the Year in 1998 for her outstanding community service in Melbourne's Vietnamese community. This catapulted her into a prominent role as a social activist and public speaker.

Tan's story was featured in the "Hope" section of the Eternity Exhibition of the National Museum of Australia. She was featured in *Fast Company*'s Most Influential Women in Technology in 2010 and Forbes' 50 Names You Need to Know in 2011. Among her many awards are the Advance Global Australian Award for Information and Communication Technology (2012) and the G'Day USA Innovation Award (2014). She was named a National Geographic Emerging Explorer in 2013 and has been honored by the World Economic Forum (WEF) as a Young Global Leader since 2009. Tan currently serves on the WEF's Global Future Council on the Future of Neurotechnologies.

In 2018, Tan received the Industrial Research Institute Achievement Award from the U.S. organization established in 1938 to enhance the effectiveness of technological innovation by networking the world's best practitioners and thought leaders. This award honored her "outstanding accomplishment in individual creativity and innovation that contributes broadly to the development of industry and to the benefit of society." Also in 2018, Tan received the great honor of having her portrait commissioned and added to the permanent collection of the National Portrait Gallery of Australia.

Tan has been featured in several documentaries, including *Human By Design—Redefining the Future of Mankind*, CNBC's *The Brave Ones*, and on dozens of international, national, and local television programs, including shows on Discovery Channel, CNBC, ABC, and PBS. She is a highly sought-after speaker and has delivered hundreds of keynotes at conferences for women leaders, CEO/CIOs, healthcare providers, tech innovators, and thought leaders. Her TED Talks—"A Headset That Reads Your Brainwaves" and "My Immigration Story"—have millions of views.

She lives in San Francisco with her husband, Chris, and daughter, Ai Le.